My Scotland

By Richard Callaghan
and David Simpson

MY WORLD PUBLISHING

Designed by **courage**

Text Copyright © Richard Callaghan and David Simpson
Design Copyright © **courage**

ISBN 978 0 9536984 5 5
First published 2011
Published in Great Britain by
My World Publishing
Chase House
Mandarin Road
Rainton Bridge Business Park
Tyne and Wear
DH4 5RA
Tel: 0191 3055165
Fax: 0191 3055504

*My World Publishing is an imprint of Business Education
Publishers Ltd.*

British Cataloguing-in-Publications Data.
*A catalogue record for this book is available from the British
Library.*

Printed in Great Britain by Ashford Colour Press Ltd.

· ·

Welcome to *My*Sc⊗tland

Well actually, no, welcome to *your Scotland,* because this book is just for *you.* It's all about *your* Scotland and it's for you to treasure and enjoy. Turn the pages and you're sure to find out something new about Scotland, or at least that's what we hope.

We want this book to be *fun.* We should warn you there's lots of history in here, but don't be scared, it's not dry and dusty. We don't want you coughing and sneezing.

There are *366 stories* in this book, so if you wish you can read one on every day of the year, including a leap year. In fact, just to help you, there's a calendar date on every page.

We've picked out what we consider to be the most remarkable and interesting facts and tales about *Scotland* and where possible we've linked them to the relevant date. The stories come form the whole of *Scotland,* from the *islands, highlands, lowlands, cities, towns* and *villages.*

The stories include some characters that appear here for the first time, such as the gentleman adventurer Percival Temperley, Hamish the Highland Cow, Lionel the talking letter and Mary and Mags the midge rappers. You'll also find many famous *Scots* who've made their name down the centuries including *heroes, kings, inventors, actors* and *writers* of world renown.

It's not all our work though. Twelve of the stories - that's one for every month – are the winning entries from the *My Scotland Young Writers Competition.* We received lots of fantastic stories and we'd like to thank everyone who sent their work in.

We hope you have as much *fun* reading this book as we've had writing it and hopefully you'll learn lots of new things about Scotland along the way.

Richard Callaghan and David Simpson

· ·

Your **Sc⊗tland**

Unst
Yell
Shetland
Islands
Lerwick

Westray
Sanday
Orkney
Islands
Stronsay
Kirkwall
Hoy
John O'Groats
Thurso

Lewis
Stornoway
Harris
Ullapool
North Uist
Fraserburgh
Benbecula
Nairn
Banff
Inverness
Peterhead
South Uist
Skye
Loch
Ness
Aberdeen
Canna
Rum
Mallaig
Eigg
Brechin
Fort
William
Montrose
Coll
Pitlochry
Arbroath
Tiree
Dunkeld
Dundee
Mull
Oban
Loch
Lomond
Perth
St. Andrews
Iona
Jura
Colonsay
Stirling
Dunfermline
Falkirk
Islay
Glasgow
Edinburgh
Dunbar
Paisley
Livingston
Berwick
Coldstream
Kilmarnock
Kelso
Melrose
Campbeltown
Arran
Ayr
Jedburgh

*Northern
Ireland*
Stranraer
Dumfries
England

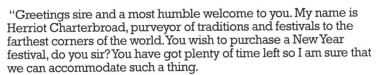

HOGMANAY

Should auld acquaintance be forgot,
And never brought to mind?
Should auld acquaintance be forgot,
And auld lang syne!

"Greetings sire and a most humble welcome to you. My name is Herriot Charterbroad, purveyor of traditions and festivals to the farthest corners of the world. You wish to purchase a New Year festival, do you sir? You have got plenty of time left so I am sure that we can accommodate such a thing.

Can I offer you the Chinese New Year? No? How about the Vietnamese Tet festival? Something more Western? I think I have the very thing, if you will just excuse me for a moment... Ah, yes, here we are, how about a traditional **Scottish Hogmanay**?

A fine festival is Hogmanay sir, one of my favourites. It comes with hundreds of years of tradition and culture, including traditions such as "first-footing"... You don't know what first footing is sir? Ah, it is the most wonderful of traditions, where the first person to cross the threshold of the house after midnight ought to be someone not resident, and they should bear gifts to bring luck to the household for the coming year.

Yes, it has many other traditions, sir, many others. There have also been large parties in the great cities of Scotland for many years to celebrate the bringing in of the New Year, people have much enjoyment from these, often singing "Auld Lang Syne", the words of which were written by the famous Scottish poet Robert Burns, although the poem is said to be much older.

It is a wonderful festival; most reasonably priced too... you'll take it? Splendid!"

For auld lang syne, my dear,
For auld lang syne.
We'll tak a cup o' kindness yet,
For auld lang syne.

THE IBROX DISASTERS

Two of the worst disasters in the history of British football took place in Scotland, both at Ibrox, almost seventy years apart.

The first Ibrox disaster came in 1902 during a Scotland vs England match. The back of the new West Tribune Stand collapsed, and the supporters who were standing there fell as much as forty feet. The stand was built out of wood, with a metal frame, and when it collapsed the people fell through. Twenty five people died and five hundred and seventeen were injured. After the disaster clubs stopped building stands this way and built them out of concrete instead.

The second Ibrox disaster was on January 2 1971, during a game between Rangers and Celtic. After 89 minutes, Celtic scored to make the game 0-1, and many Rangers fans decided to leave the ground. As thousands of fans tried to make their way out, by Stairway 13, Rangers equalised through Colin Stein. The excitement caused someone on Stairway 13 to trip, and their trip turned into a fall, and the fall into a chain reaction which led to an enormous crush.

Sixty six people died, and over two hundred others were injured in the crush on Stairway 13, the worst disaster in British football at the time. It directly led to the redevelopment of Ibrox, although it would take another disaster, the Hillsborough disaster of 1989 before British clubs were forced to adopt all seater stadiums.

PREHISTORIC SCOTLAND

Few places in Britain have a prehistory as rich as Scotland's. You can journey back over 10,000 years to the **Paleolithic** period and find evidence of people living in this land. In 2005 flints from around 12,000 BC were discovered near Biggar and are the earliest known evidence for human habitation in Scotland.

Paleolithic was the **OLD STONE AGE** but if you head forward into the **MIDDLE STONE AGE** you find evidence of Scotland's oldest known human settlement, at **Cramond** near Edinburgh, dating from 8,500 BC.

Things got busy in the **NEW STONE AGE**, the age of the first farmers. Finds from this time include the 85 foot **Balbridie Hall** in Aberdeenshire which housed about 50 people around 3,900-3,200 BC. From a similar era (3,600-2,800 BC) Scotland's oldest **Crannog** an artificial island can be found at **Eilean Domhnuill** on North Uist.

Other finds from this age include the **Callanish Stone circle** on Lewis dating from 2,900-2,600 BC and the **Tomb of the Eagles** on South Ronaldsay, Orkney dating from 3,150 BC. Here 16,000 human bones and hundreds of eagle bones were found in a tomb. Also on Orkney are the impressive standing stones of Stenness which form part of a henge and the famous **Skara Brae**, the best preserved Neolithic village in northern Europe.

BRONZE AGE finds include the **Migdale Hoard** from Skibo Castle in Sutherland. Dating from 2,250-1,950 BC it includes axes and beads. A rather more unusual Bronze Age find are the **Cladh Hallan mummies** of 1,600-1,100 BC of South Uist. They are Britain's only known discovery of prehistoric mummies.

Stepping into the **IRON AGE** Scotland's best preserved broch or ancient stone tower house is the **Broch** of **Mousa** on Shetland dating from 100 BC. It is one of around 500 ancient brochs in Scotland.

Scotland's most impressive Iron Age hill fort is **Traprain Law** in East Lothian; dating from 1,500 BC-150 AD. It was the fortress of the Votadini tribe.

	8,500 BC MIDDLE STONE AGE		2,250 BC BRONZE AGE	
12,000 BC OLD STONE AGE		3,900 BC NEW STONE AGE		100 BC IRON AGE

4

THE WIND

Whistling through the fresh green trees,
Blowing waves on navy seas,
Bustling golden autumn leaves
The wind shall blow,
Moving fast or slow.

Past castles, great and old,
Past purple hills standing bold,
Through winters crisp and cold
The wind shall blow.

Drowning sounds,
Moving debris from the ground,
The wind shall blow
Forever more, in my homeland.

My
Sc✹tland
Young Writer

Name: Jamie Cameron Watt
Age: 11
School: Knockando Primary School, Moray

THE LOCH NESS MONSTER

ᙢᕼᘿ ᒪᗝᑢᕼ ᘉᘿᔕᔕ ᗰᗝᘉᔕᙢᘿᖇ

*We are delighted to present you with a sensational opportunity to personally own the most legendary Scottish animal currently on the market, the **Loch Ness Monster.***

ᒪᗝᑢᕼ ᘉᘿᔕᔕ: 23 x 1.7 miles, surface area 21.8 sq miles

A truly unique Scottish Loch, sited just southwest of Inverness, with an average depth of 433 feet is the perfect home for your monster. Included with Loch Ness is 1.8 cubic miles of water, and a 685 square mile drainage basin, making this superb combination of water and monster storage.

ᙢᕼᘿ ᗰᗝᘉᔕᙢᘿᖇ: 4' x 25' (approx body) 10'-12' (neck)

A fantastic choice for any prospective owner, the Loch Ness Monster was first noted in Loch Ness in the time of Saint Columba (565 AD), with modern viewings beginning in 1933. The monster retains many original features, and is thought to share common ancestry with the dinosaurs. Many of the features of the monster are in the plesiosaur style, although the monster is very much a one of a kind.

Whether you are looking for an investment opportunity, a family monster, or a second monster, the **Loch Ness Monster** represents an amazing opportunity which is very rarely available. Viewings are strongly recommended.

Did you know?
So exactly who are the Scots?

- Scots were first mentioned by the Romans who called them Scotti. They were noted for raiding Roman Britain.

- Scotti is thought to derive from an old Gaelic word Scuit meaning 'man cut off'. It may be a reference to an outcast pirate or raider, but in truth no one knows.

- It is probable that Scotti was a name the Romans gave to a particularly troublesome group of Gaels who were prone to raiding.

- It may come as a surprise to learn that the Scotti actually came from Ireland.

- Dal Riata was the name of the Kingdom founded by the Scotti in the Argyll area of western Scotland. Dal is an old Irish Gaelic word meaning 'portion'. Riata was probably someone's name.

- Dal Riata came into existence in Argyll around 500 AD when it is thought it was colonised by the Scotti from Ireland.

- The Iron Age fort of Dunadd near Kilmartin in Argyll is thought to have been the Royal capital of Dal Riata.

- Based on archaeological evidence, some historians argue these Gaelic speaking Scots had already colonised Argyll at least a century earlier.

- The Dal Riata Scots or Dal Riatans were linguistically, culturally and politically connected to Ireland. It made them distinct from the rest of what we now call Scotland.

- The Kingdom of Dal Riata included Argyll and Bute along with Antrim in Ireland.

- The name Argyll may be connected with the ancient Irish Kingdom of Airgíalla situated in the Louth and Monaghan areas of that country.

- The Dal Riata and its Gaelic speech expanded east into the Kingdom of the Picts. The unified Kingdoms were called Alba and later Scotland.

Professor C. Cloggs

UNIVERSITY OF GLASGOW

What do Charles Kennedy, Stuart Murdoch, James Herriot, Ming Campbell, Fred Goodwin, Andrew Neil, Gerard Butler, Donald Dewar, John Logie Baird and one of the authors of this book have in common? ...No, not that... No, not that either... No, they all went to the University of Glasgow.

The University of Glasgow is the fourth oldest university in the English speaking world, and was founded in 1451 by a Papal Bull of Nicholas V. No, it isn't a bovine university; a Papal Bull is a letter, charter or declaration from the Pope. It was a letter to the Bishop of Glasgow, William Turnbull, which gave him permission to start a university.

It's a very well respected university, part of the Russell Group of research-led universities, which means that as well as teaching the people in the list above (and a lot more people besides), the University of Glasgow is also a place where world class research is undertaken in a whole load of different fields.

Glasgow University is the only Scottish university to have law, medicine, dentistry and veterinary medicine departments, as well as many others. There are almost 24,000 students at Glasgow University at any one time, giving it almost the same population as Alloa!

It's a great place to study, with so many people who work there being the best in their subjects, and it's all here in the heart of Scotland, what more could you ask for?

SCOTTISH BANKS

"You want me. You need me. I can be dirty; sometimes I need to be laundered. I'm the root of all evil, but I make the world go round. That's right, I'm **MONEY**!

I tend to have a pretty good time, I have to admit. I spend a lot of time in swanky restaurants, and posh shops, and nestled in the wallets of the rich and famous, but even when I'm doing all that, going out with football players and movie stars, it's always nice to feel like I've got somewhere of my own to come back to. That's why I really like banks, they're great places for me to relax and stretch out, and in Scotland you've got three that I really like.

The first is the **Bank of Scotland**, which you founded way back in 1695 - just for me. It was only the year after that the Bank of England was founded, so suddenly I went from having hardly anywhere to live to having houses in Edinburgh and London, it was great. It's the second oldest surviving bank in the UK, and the first bank in Europe that was allowed to print its own paper notes, of *me*.

Then there is the **Royal Bank of Scotland**, which came about in 1727, and that was the first bank in the world to offer an overdraft, meaning people could use more of *me* than they actually had, as long as they paid it back later. That was great for *me*, and really great for the bank, I'll tell you.

Then, in 1838 I finally got a Glasgow home, when the **Clydesdale Bank** formed. It was the first Scottish bank to open in the north of England, meaning I could get everywhere, it was fantastic. I love the banks in Scotland."

WHAT'S YOUR NAME?

ANDERSON
Developed in Scotland independently of the Scandinavian surname Andersen. Numerous in Shetland and the north east. In the Highlands they were called MacAndrew. From *Gilleandreas* meaning 'servant of Andrew', Scotland's patron saint.

Armstrong
The ancestors of the first man on the moon were Border Reivers from near Gretna Green. One theory traces them to Siward Beorn, a Viking Earl of Northumbria. Another says they descended from Fairbairn, a medieval armour-bearer of a Scottish King. When the King's horse died in a battle Fairbairn lifted the King onto his horse using one arm. Fairbairn was awarded lands in Liddesdale.

Baird
Originally De Bard, a Norman family who apparently rescued King William the Lion from a wild boar. They held land in Lanarkshire in the thirteenth century and are numerous there and in Ayrshire.

BARCLAY
From *De Berchelai* meaning 'beautiful meadow'. Barclays were Normans who settled at Berkeley, Gloucestershire. They arrived in Scotland with Margaret, Queen of Malcolm III and are numerous in Aberdeenshire.

Boyle
Originally Normans called De Baeauville. Numerous in Lanarkshire and Glasgow. Also an Irish surname.

BRUCE
Originally De Brus these Normans were landowners in Hartlepool and Yorkshire in England. In 1138 a Robert De Brus fought against the Scots at the Battle of the Standard although he owned lands in Dumfriesshire. De Brus was an ancestor of King Robert the Bruce.

Buchan
From Buchan in Aberdeenshire. Buchan means 'place of the cow'. Not to be confused with Buchanan, a family named from Buchanan nearer Loch Lomond, a Gaelic name meaning 'priest (canon) house'.

Cameron
Allegedly descended from Camchron, whose name means 'crooked nose'. Another theory says that it means 'crooked hill' and originates in Fife. Cameron territory was the Locaber region near Fort William. Numerous in the north west.

EDINBURGH NEW TOWN

"Good evening, my name is James Craig, and I am an architect. I'm here to talk to you about my vision for Edinburgh, and the way that I think we can turn Edinburgh into a city fit for the nineteenth century.

As you know, it has been a difficult few years for Scotland, but since the failure of Charles Stuart's rising in 1745 things have been much more settled. Now, it's time for Scotland to take her rightful place at the heart of the British Empire, and for her capital to be one of Europe's great cities.

You're all used to the conditions in Edinburgh, and let's just say it's not always the healthiest of cities. People living crowded into houses, streets filled with rubbish and stinking open sewers. But this cannot go on.

We are going to build a New Town, to the north side of the castle. It'll have three streets to begin with, named Queen Street, George Street and Princes Street. The Nor Loch beside the castle, which was once so beautiful but is now so dirty and smelly, will be drained and public gardens will be built there instead.

It is a bright new day for the city. We'll have streets far more in keeping with the great metropolises of London and Paris, with buildings which not only serve a purpose but are also ones of great beauty.

I'm sure this is just the first step and that mine will be a baton that will be taken up by Edinburgh people for many years to come, and that together we will make this New Town one of the great cities of the world."

EDINBURGH NEW TOWN

And the winner, here to make his speech, is 26 year old James Craig!!

THE FIRST SCOTSMAN IN AMERICA?

Not much is known about the life of Henry I Sinclair, the Earl of Orkney. We know he was born sometime around 1345. We know he died around the year 1400. The rest of his life is shrouded in mystery, but there are many tales of his exploits. Whether they're true or not...

When Henry was born, Orkney was in the possession of the King of Norway, and so it was the Norwegian King Haakon VI that made Henry the Earl of Orkney. Henry won this honour despite competition from two cousins of his, and he pledged his loyalty to the Crown of Norway.

The most famous tale about Henry is that he was actually the explorer-prince known as "Prince Zichmni". Zichmni is mentioned in letters by the Zeno brothers from Venice, which were supposedly written in 1400 and rediscovered in the sixteenth century. Zichmni is supposed to have led an expedition across the Atlantic to Greenland and then to North America.

Many people think that the Zeno letters were fakes, which weren't really written in 1400. Even if they were written then, many people also think that Henry couldn't be Zichmni.

Some people think that Henry was a member of the Knights Templar, the Christian military order which features very prominently in many of the legends of that time. Henry's grandson, William, built Rosslyn Chapel which many say is a Templar church, and is said to be the resting place of the Holy Grail.

They say that if Henry was a Templar, he might have gone to America on a Templar expedition, that the Templars knew the way to America before anyone else. Whatever the case, there are certainly some great stories about Henry!

ANGUS SPEAKS

"Hello my name's Angus, but you can call me **Beefy**. My family and I are from Aberdeenshire and Angus. That's why we're called 'Aberdeen Anguses', or should that be Aberdeen Angusi?! Oh, I don't know - why should I? I'm just a cow after all.

I can tell you we get called 'Angus Cattle' for short and for centuries we were called 'Angus Doddies'.

I guarantee I'm the tastiest piece of meat in Scotland. In fact I'd *steak* my life on it.

Unlike those *udder* famous Scottish cattle in the Highlands we don't have horns. We are normal looking cows, not at all like those wild and crazy highland hippies.

Do you know I've been using the *Anguscestry* website and have traced my family history back to the nineteenth century?

I discovered one of my oldest known ancestors was a cow called **Old Granny**, who was born in 1824. She gave birth to 29 calves. Another famous ancestor was a bull called **Old Jock** who was born in 1842.

Some members of our family migrated to America in 1873 and there are lots of us over there now. We can be solid black or red. In fact in America, Red Angus and Black Angus are regarded as separate breeds.

Our Black variety is the most popular breed of any kind of beef cattle in the United States where you'll find more that 320,000 of us. But you know we wouldn't be here at all if it wasn't for a Scottish breed of human called **Hugh Watson** who started us off.

So thanks Hugh Watson for raising our *steaks* and making us such a successful slaughter-house breed. If you were here today, I'd be very pleased to give you a huge **PAT** on the back!"

ARRAN

The Isle of Arran is situated between the Kintrye peninsula to the west and the Ayrshire coast to the east. It is the largest island in the **Firth of Clyde**, the seventh largest in Scotland and the third highest Scottish island after Skye and Mull. Its highest peak is Goat Fell in the north west at 2,866 metres.

Arran is regarded as **Scotland in Miniature** because the north part is highland and the south part lowland.

Over 5,000 people live on Arran making it the fifth most populous island in Scotland. It is thought Arran's name is Welsh meaning 'high place'. Its outline is said to resemble a sleeping warrior and it's certainly higher than the neighbouring coastlines of Ayrshire and Kintrye.

Arran has been occupied since ancient times as demonstrated by the modest stone circles on its west coast. The first language known to have been spoken on Arran was Welsh (Cymric).

Subsequent inhabitants of Arran included Gaelic-speaking Scots and Norse-speaking Vikings.

Brodick on Brodick Bay provides the main ferry link to Ayrshire. Its name derives from the Viking *Breid Vikr* meaning 'broad bay'. It is not Arran's largest village. That honour goes to **Lamlash** on Lamlash Bay three miles to the south. Here there are good views of neighbouring **Holy Island**, a retreat inhabited by Tibetan Buddhist monks.

Tourism is important to Arran with 40 per cent of its houses providing tourist accommodation. Visitors are attracted by the islands geology, its seven golf courses and **Brodick Castle**, the former seat of the Duke of Hamilton.

Sadly, the one thing for which Arran is not famed is sweaters as is sometimes mistakenly thought. Aran sweaters come from the Aran Islands in Ireland!

GREYFRIARS BOBBY

On February 8, 1858 John Gray, known as "Old Jock", a night watchman with the Edinburgh Police, passed away from tuberculosis. None was more saddened by his loss than his faithful Skye Terrier, Bobby, who had been inseparable from his master for two years.

Old Jock was buried in the graveyard of Greyfriars Kirk in Edinburgh's old town and Bobby was so keen to stay by his master's side that he was soon found sitting on Old Jock's grave.

For years to come, Bobby spent most of his days sitting on this grave, only leaving to receive regular meals from a restaurant close to the graveyard.

In 1867 poor Bobby's life came under threat when it was suggested it should be brought to an end, since he had no owner.

Fortunately, by this time Bobby's remarkable story was widely known and the Lord Provost of Edinburgh, Sir William Chambers stepped in to renew Bobby's licence. The City of Edinburgh was now Bobby's owner, but Bobby remained loyal and faithful to Old Jock's grave.

Sadly, on January 14, 1872 Greyfriars Bobby, as he had come to be known, passed away, having outlived his master by 14 years.

He was buried just inside the gate of the churchyard as near to his master as the church authorities allowed. The following year a statue of Bobby was erected near the George IV Bridge by Lady Burdett-Coutts in memory of this extraordinarily loyal little dog.

Bobby's story has certainly not been forgotten. Over the years a number of books and films have been made about his life. In 1981 a little granite stone was unveiled at Bobby's grave. It reads:

GREYFRIARS BOBBY

DIED 14 JANUARY 1872
AGED 16 YEARS
LET HIS LOYALTY AND DEVOTION
BE A LESSON TO US ALL

HECKLING

Any noted comedian, brave performer or skilled politician will at some stage have to deal with the heclers, who may shout out insults, out-compete the speaker or ask awkward or embarrassing questions that put the performer on the spot.

It's a little known fact that "heckling" is a word of Scottish origin and has some rather surprising roots. Heckling has its origins, not in parliament or in the theatre or music hall but in the Scottish weaving industry.

Heckling was originally - believe it or not - the process of combing hemp or flax. It was a process accomplished by pulling the material through a kind of comb called a Heckle. The workers who carried out this activity were Hecklers and worked in heckling sheds.

It was a laborious task, but Hecklers were well-paid in times of prosperity and employed fellow workers to keep their minds occupied by reading out newspapers or pamphlets that kept them informed. The readings often aroused hot debate and arguments amongst the workers and the heckling sheds must have been at times rather lively places to work.

Hecklers were soon noted for being well-informed and radical in their outlook. They gained a reputation for their awkward and provoking questions at public meetings and so in early nineteenth century Scotland the terms "heckler" and "heckling" took on brand-new meanings.

It is thought that the new meaning first originated in the town of Dundee. Here the Hecklers of the town's weaving trade were noted for being an especially radical and troublesome challenge for public speakers of the political kind.

Unfortunately for the Hecklers their trade became obsolete with increased mechanisation. Today the textile roots of modern hecklers are long forgotten.

SCOTTISH FOOTBALLERS X1

Scotland has had many great footballers in the past, and we've tried to put together some teams with just a few of them in. See if you agree with us...

GK: Jim Leighton
635 games for Aberdeen, Manchester United, Dundee and Hibs; 91 Scotland caps.

RB: Sandy Jardine
Over 450 games for Rangers, and almost 200 games for Hearts; 38 Scotland caps.

LB: Tom Boyd
More than 250 games for Motherwell, more than 300 games for Celtic, and 31 games for Chelsea; 72 games for Scotland.

CB: John Greig
Rangers legend who played 755 times for the club, with 44 Scotland appearances.

CB: Alex McLeish
Almost 500 games for Aberdeen, and a number as player-manager at Motherwell; 77 Scotland caps.

RW: Jimmy Johnstone
"Jinky" Johnstone, Celtic's greatest ever player; more than 500 appearances for Celtic, and games for a host of other clubs. He also won 23 Scotland caps.

LW: Jim Baxter
"Slim Jim" Baxter played 254 games for Rangers, almost 100 games for Sunderland and 50 games for Nottingham Forest, as well as 34 games for Scotland.

CM: Billy Bremner
A Leeds United icon, Bremner played more than 600 times for the Yorkshire club between 1959 and 1976, captaining them during the 1960s and 70s, before finishing his career at Hull and Doncaster. He played 54 times for Scotland.

CM: John Collins
In a career stretching between 1984 and 2003, Collins played more than 600 times for Hibernian, Celtic, Monaco, Everton and Fulham. The classy midfielder also featured 58 times for Scotland, including appearances in the 1998 World Cup in France.

ST: Ally McCoist
Rangers' record goal scorer with 355 goals for the Ibrox club; 61 games for Scotland.

ST: Kenny Dalglish
"King Kenny", Celtic and Liverpool legend with 230 goals in 560 league games for the two clubs. The only Scotland player to have **more than 100 caps** to his name.

STANDING AROUND ALL DAY DOING NOTHING

"Hi I'm Fergus, welcome to the west coast of Lewis, our Hebridean home. My friends and I have been standing here for about 5,000 years, though we've lost count of exactly how long.

It's a tiring job standing around all day but we are standing stones after all. It's in our job description. Collectively we're called the **Callanish Stones** or **Clachan Chalanais** in Gaelic.

Okay it sounds boring, but it's a job and it's all we know. It's worthwhile though because we have ancient astronomical importance, or so they say.

We're all made from Lewisian Gneiss rock, so we're a pretty solid bunch. There are thirteen big guys and girls like me called primary stones that form a circle 13 meters in diameter, but there are lots of other stones too. There are almost fifty of us in total, including two rows forming an avenue to our centre.

If I'm honest I can't remember how we got here. Humans brought us here I think, but it's a long time ago. Our purpose? Well as I said, something astronomical, to do with the movement of the sun and moon. Some say we formed an ancient calendar. The locals say that at sunrise on a midsummer morning 'the shining one' walked our avenue to herald the cuckoo's call.

Morag, my neighbour, doesn't agree, she says we used to be living giants until Saint Kieran turned us to stone for refusing to become Christian. Some locals believe this too.

Someone very important is buried in a cairn at our centre but no one remembers who it is, though I do remember they came centuries after we arrived. Donald may know, he's the tallest of us all and guards the tomb, but no one talks to Donald, we're all a little intimidated by him and are too afraid to ask."

JAMES WATT

***Watt* do you mean you don't know who James Watt was?** James Watt was born in Greenock on January 18 1736, and at the age of nineteen he was sent to Glasgow to learn how to make mathematical instruments.

***Watt* happened when James went to Glasgow?** Well, in 1757 he set up his very own mathematical instrument manufacturing business, but in 1764 he was given a Newcomen engine to repair, an event which was going to be very significant both for James and for the world.

***Watt* was a Newcomen engine?** It was an early steam engine, which harnessed the power of steam to pump water out of mines. They had been around since 1712 and were very common.

***Watt* happened when James was given it to repair?** James recognised that it wasn't as efficient as it could be, and that there were a number of different ways to improve the engine. He started to experiment.

***Watt* happened then?** His first partner was James Roebuck, but when Roebuck went bankrupt in 1773 Watt went to Birmingham's Matthew Boulton with his ideas. Boulton and Watt worked together producing steam engines.

***Watt* effect did Watt's engines have?** Watt's engines were very powerful, four times more powerful than the Newcomen engines, and they were very good at pumping water out of mines. In 1781, however, Watt produced a rotary engine which could be used for a whole host of different things. Watt's engines were one of the most important developments of the early Industrial Revolution.

***Watt* did Watt get out of it?** Watt had patented his design in 1755, and so for the next quarter of a century he and Boulton were the only ones allowed to produce such machines, and they charged people accordingly. Watt died a very wealthy man in 1819, and will always be remembered as a great Scottish inventor.

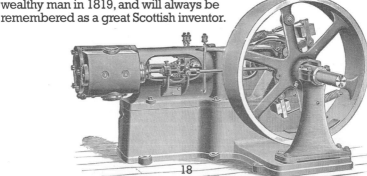

THE ABERDEEN CHILD SLAVE

In 1763, a court case concerning Peter Williamson revealed that 600 children from around Aberdeen had been kidnapped and enslaved between 1740 and 1746.

Children were seized and shipped to America and sold as slaves, never seeing their families again. Aberdeen merchants, magistrates, sea captains and a deputy town clerk were all implicated in this dreadful trade.

In 1743, Williamson, aged 13 was captured as he played near Aberdeen dock and was thrown on board a ship with others. Landing in America after 11 weeks, he was sold for $16. Peter was lucky to have survived, nearly a quarter of the children died during the journey.

Peter's new owner was a fellow Scot, Hugh Wilson who had also been kidnapped as a boy at Perth and sold into slavery. Hugh's experience meant Peter was treated humanely.

Free of slavery by his twenties, Peter married a planter's daughter, but one day while she was away Peter was captured and again enslaved, this time by American Indians.

Fortunately after some months Peter managed to escape only to find his wife had died. He then joined the army to fight the French but was captured near New York in 1756. He was released in exchange for French hostages.

Shipped to England, Peter landed at Plymouth and began walking to Aberdeen. Arriving at York in poverty, he made money selling his story and dressed and danced like an American Indian for publicity.

Peter was determined to expose the Aberdeen authorities, but on arriving there, was imprisoned, released and banished. Moving to Edinburgh, he opened a coffee house frequented by lawyers who encouraged him to sue the Aberdeen officials, which he did successfully.

In his later days Peter owned an Edinburgh pub, compiled Edinburgh's first street directory, launched a weekly newspaper and introduced a penny post.

He died in Edinburgh on January 19 1799.

THE SCOTTISH THISTLE

Scots love their national emblem, but why pick a prickly thistle to represent your nation?

Apparently it goes back to the Battle of Largs in 1263. In that year disputes arose between Haakon, King of Norway and Alexander III, King of Scotland over who controlled the Inner and Outer Hebrides.

Haakon landed on the coast of Largs on the Firth of Clyde in North Ayrshire. According to legend he intended to surprise the sleeping Scots by creeping up on them, silently, after ordering his men to remove their footwear.

It doesn't take a genius to work out what happened next. **Ouch!** In the darkness one of the Vikings stood on a thistle and his screams (the wimp) alerted the sleeping Scots.

The result of the battle was inconclusive, but the important thing is that thanks partly to the thistle, the Scots didn't lose. Haakon died later in the year and three years later, his successor Magnus V sold the islands to the Scots.

It's a good story, but the first known use of the thistle as a Royal Scottish symbol was not until 1470 when it appeared on coins issued by James III.

The thistle's place as an emblem of Scotland is thought to have been reinforced in 1540 when a chivalric order called **The Order of the Thistle** was allegedly established by King James V.

The authenticity of the order's creation in 1540 is disputed but a chivalric order of the same name was established, or perhaps revived, in 1687 by James VII (James II of England).

Knights and ladies appointed to the order can use the letters KT and LT after their name. The Latin motto of the order and indeed of Scotland itself is *Nemo me impune lacessit* which translates as, "No one provokes me with impunity".

The Order of the Thistle

Battle of Largs

THE DUNDEE JUTE TRADE

Student: Hey, you've got one of those shopping bags, the ones that cost you money. I like the material they're made out of.

History Man: Yes, I do, it's better than having a plastic one. The material it's made out of is called jute.

Student: Mmmm, I like jute. New, is it?

History Man: Far from it. In fact, people have been making things out of jute in Scotland for hundreds of years.

Student: Does it come from here?

History Man: No, it comes from India. It's the fibre that comes from jute plants, but when India was part of the British Empire Dundee was one of the most important centres for the production of jute products.

Student: Why Dundee?

History Man: Well, in order to spin jute it had to be treated with whale oil, and Dundee was a major centre for the whaling trade. This meant that there was easy access to the oil, and Dundee merchants took advantage of this.

Student: Did a lot of people work in the jute industry?

History Man: Yes, it was a major industry in Dundee. In the late nineteenth century, at the industry's height, there were 60 jute mills in Dundee and 50,000 people employed in them.

Student: So who was responsible for this? And why don't we make it any more?

History Man: The merchants and mill owners earned the name "Dundee Jute Barons", because of the great prosperity they had gained from jute production. But at the end of the nineteenth century they began to move production to India, to take advantage of the cheaper workers there.

Student: That's a shame, but at least I know what those bags are made of now...

WILLIAM PATERSON AND THE BANK OF ENGLAND

Scots have come up with many great innovations and inventions throughout history. Scottish inventions have saved lives and changed the course of history. You probably know about a lot of them, but here's one you might not know. It was a Scotsman who invented the Bank of England.

The Bank of England was thought up by William Paterson, a Scottish trader and banker who was born in Dumfriesshire in 1658. He wrote the pamphlet *A Brief Account of the Intended Bank of England* in which he set out his plan for a central bank which would raise money to lend to the government.

In 1694 the Bank of England was established. The King needed to raise money to increase the size of the Royal Navy, in order to make England more powerful and to extend its empire around the world. The Bank of England raised £1.2 million for the King in 12 days, which is the equivalent of about **£100,000,000** in today's money!

In exchange for raising all of this money, half of which went towards the Royal Navy, the subscribers were to be incorporated as the Governor and Company of the Bank of England, and were given the rights to do things like print their own banknotes. This was the first time that there'd been paper money in England, and it was all down to a Scotsman!

Paterson fell out with his colleagues in 1695 and went back to Scotland where he masterminded the failed Darien Scheme, but the bank he created is still going to this day.

SCOTLAND'S FIRST BATTLE

Student: There have been a lot of battles in Scottish history, but which was the first?

History Man: The first known battle in our history took place in the year 83 AD or possibly the year 84 AD.

Student: You mean you don't know?

History Man: Well the precise year isn't known for certain, but it was certainly one of those two.

Student: What was the name of this battle then?

History Man: The Battle of Mons Graupius.

Student: A strange name for a battle, so where was this battle?

History Man: Er...well actually, no one really knows for sure. It could have been in Perthshire or Kincardineshire or perhaps in the hills called the Grampian Mounth to the south of Aberdeen.

Student: Could have been? It all seems very vague, not very believable is it?

History Man: Well it was a battle between the Caledonians and the Romans who invaded the Highlands under the leadership of the Roman Governor of Britain, Julius Agricola. Roman historians - in this case Tacitus - recorded events far away from the places that they actually took place, sometimes with only a vague knowledge of the local geography.

Student: So what was the outcome of this battle?

History Man: Well it is claimed that there were 30,000 people in each of the two opposing armies during the battle but some sources claim the Romans were outnumbered. The Romans were victorious after blocking off access to the main granaries of the natives which forced them to fight. Rome inflicted an overwhelming defeat on the Caledonians or at least that's what the Romans said, but despite this victory they were never able to properly conquer Scotland.

Student: I think these Romans just made it up. They could have been more helpful in telling us where the battle took place.

23

24

UP HELLY AA

Up Helly Aa is the name given to Europe's largest Fire Festival, held in Shetland every year. The event takes place on the last Tuesday of January and is a spectacular sight to see.

The festival is centred in Lerwick, the principal town of the Shetlands, but other similar events take place across the Shetland Islands on a smaller scale. Essentially Up Helly Aa is a winter festival that marks the end of the Yule season and the event involves a night-time procession of as many as a thousand men dressed as Vikings and an assortment of other costumes, each carrying a flaming torch.

The men are led by a chief called the Guizer Jarl who must have been a member of the Up Helly Aa Committee for at least fifteen years. Only one new member is elected to this committee every year.

The costumed members of the procession are called the squad and begin their day early in the morning with a march through the town, but the highlight of the event is the night-time torch procession.

The event has its roots in the ancient tradition of carrying barrels of flaming tar at Christmas, New Year as well as at the end of Yule day (Up Helly Aa). It is partly a celebration of Shetland's Viking heritage but in truth the festival began in the early 1880s. Since 1889 the ceremony has included the burning of a Viking longship into which the flaming torches are thrown in the spectacular culmination of the event.

Following the procession the squads of torch bearers visit local community venues to perform comedy, dancing or singing.

ORGANISE YOURSELF A BURNS SUPPER

Keep January 25th free as the supper should be held as near to Robbie's birthday as possible.

When your guests arrive, serenade them with a piper, have them seated and give a welcoming speech.

Say Grace, but not just any grace, recite the *Selkirk Grace* well-known to Burns:

**Some hae meat and canna eat, And some wad eat that want it;
But we hae meat, and we can eat, And sae let the Lord be thankit.**

Let the supper begin, with a Cock-a-Leekie soup, then make way for the haggis, the star of the night.

Guests should stand to greet the honoured guest as it enters on a silver platter.

The appointed speaker will then recite Robert Burns' *Address to a Haggis*, with those famous opening lines:

**Fair fa' your honest, sonsie face,
Great chieftain o' the puddin'-race!**

The speaker should be poised to cut the haggis on the line of the third verse:

**An cut you up wi' ready slicht,
Trenching your gushing entrails bricht.**

At the end of the final (eighth) verse the haggis is raised in triumph to the words:

Gie her a haggis!

After the guests devour the haggis complete with neeps and tatties, it should be followed by a clootie dumpling or typsy laird dessert. Then it's time for a recital of selected Burns songs and poems followed by *The Immortal Memory,* a speech about Burns' life and achievements.

The host may now say a few words of appreciation thanking the speaker, followed by a male guest making a "toast to the lassies", praising the women of the world, to which a female guest might reply with a "toast to the laddies".

There may be more readings from Burns before closing with a recital of "Auld Lang Syne".

SCOTLAND PLACE-NAMES
WHAT DO THEY MEAN?

ABERDEEN

Means 'mouth of the River Don'. From the Pictish/Old Welsh word *Aber* meaning 'confluence' or 'river mouth'. Gave its name to **Aberdeenshire**.

ABERFELDY

In Perthshire where a burn joins the Tay. From the Welsh or Pictish *Aber* (See Aberdeen) and Gaelic *Phellaidh*. It translates as *Paldoc*, the name of a saint who lived nearby.

ALLOA

Small town of 20,000 people on the north bank of the Forth east of Stirling. Gaelic *ail-mhagh* 'rocky plain'. **Alloway** in Ayrshire (birthplace of Robbie Burns) has the same meaning.

ANGUS

One of Scotland's historic counties. South of Aberdeenshire, it is named after Angur, an eighth century Pictish King. It was also called **Forfarshire**.

ANNAN

Small town on the Solway Firth west of Gretna Green. Named from Anava, a Gaelic goddess of prosperity.

ARDROSSAN

North Ayrshire coastal town combines the Gaelic words *Ard, Rois* and *An*, meaning, 'promontory', 'cape' and 'little'.

ARGYLL

Historic region and county on the west coast north of the Clyde. The first place settled by the Scots who brought the Gaelic language from Ireland. Gaelic *Airer Gaidheal* means 'coastline of the Gaels'.

ATHELSTANEFORD

Village in East Lothian twenty miles east of Edinburgh. Reputedly named after King Athelstan of England, defeated here after invading Lothian in the tenth century.

HISTORIC TOWNS AND CITIES: ABERDEEN

STATUS: City and port.

RIVERS: The **River Don** (Old Aberdeen) and the **River Dee** (New Aberdeen).

NAMES AND NICKNAMES: The Granite City or **Grey City** from the stone of its buildings or **The Silver City with the Golden Sands**: this nickname comes from the sparkling mica in its stone and its extensive beaches. It's thought the Romans called Aberdeen **Devana**.

MOTTO AND EMBLEM: "Bon Accord" from the French meaning "Good Agreement". The city's emblem is traditionally a leopard.

POPULATION: Over 210,000

KEY FACTS AND INDUSTRIES: Scotland's third largest city. Famed as a centre for the North Sea oil industry. Its traditional industries are fishing, paper making, shipbuilding and textiles. It has three cathedrals.

KEY DATES: 1179: granted charter by William the Lion. **1264:** Aberdeen Castle built. (It has long since gone.) **1319:** Robert Bruce's great charter gives Aberdeen greater powers and independence. **1366:** English burn much of Old Aberdeen and a new town called New Aberdeen is built to the south. **1495:** Kings College founded in Old Aberdeen. **1593:** Marischal College founded in new Aberdeen. **1686:** Mercat Cross built. **1805:** Union Street opens. **1860:** Marischal College and Kings College merge as Aberdeen University. **1975:** The first North Sea Oil arrives in the city. **1992:** Robert Gordon University granted University status.

THINGS TO SEE:

- **Marischal College** of 1593.
- **St Machar's Cathedral**, a fourteenth and fifteenth century cathedral, now technically a High Kirk.
- **King's College** and chapel of 1505.
- **Brig O' Balgownie**, a thirteenth century bridge.
- **Old Aberdeen** with its pink granite shops.
- **Mercat Cross**, a substantial structure of the seventeenth century.
- **Wallace Tower**, a tower house of 1616, moved from its original site to a new location two miles away in 1963.
- **Gordon Highlanders Museum**, found on the city's western outskirts.
- **Union Terrace Gardens**, in the city centre.

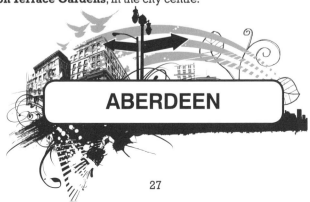

SCOTTISH INFAMY LEAGUE (SIL)

APPLICATION FORM

Name(s):
William Burke and William Hare

Occupation:
Labourers on Union Canal,
Body Snatchers and Murderers.

Date(s) of nefarious activity:
November 1827 - October 31 1828.

Reasons for nefarious activity:
Financial reward. Doctor Robert Knox required bodies for the study and teaching of anatomy at the University of Edinburgh Medical School.

Method of nefarious activity:
Beginning with bodysnatching to make money, before quickly graduating to murder of weak/sick. Murders committed by suffocation, one person blocking nose and mouth whilst the other holds person down, a practice which became known as "Burking". Bodies then sold to Doctor Robert Knox. Murders assisted by Burke's mistress Helen McDougal and Margaret Hare, William Hare's wife.

Number of victims:
Between 13 and 30, most likely to be around 17.

Cause of detection:
Murder of Maddy Doherty, body discovered by Mr and Mrs Gray and reported to police. Police discovered body at Edinburgh Medical School.

Result of detection:
William Hare and Helen McDougal turned King's Evidence, William Burke is convicted of the murder of Mrs Doherty. Hanged in Grassmarket, Edinburgh on January 28 1829. Body taken and dissected at University of Edinburgh Medical School. Skin made into pocket book.

Reason for inclusion in SIL:
Have become world famous, had books, songs and films written about them - arguably the two most famous murderers in Edinburgh's history. Their inclusion in the Scottish Infamy League ought to be guaranteed.

NOT THE NORMAN CONQUEST

1066, the year the Normans invaded Britain, changed British history forever. Well, actually no, that's not quite right. English history changed forever, yes, as the English were conquered, but Scotland. Certainly not.

It was another bunch of French speaking invaders called the Plantagenets that invaded and subdued Scotland beginning with the English King, Edward I, but that came later and here we are talking about the Normans.

Norman influence in Scotland was significant, but happened in a very subtle way and there was no Norman conquest.

King David I was key to the Norman influence in Scotland. In 1093, his father King Malcolm III was killed during his invasion of Northumberland. David went into exile.

Malcolm was succeeded by David's uncle Donald III, then by David's half brother Duncan II and then by David's brother's Edgar and Alexander I. All of these kings had genuine claims and were supported by the Norman kings of England.

David spent his exiled childhood at the Norman court of the King of England. It was here that he learned about Norman culture and became a naturalized Norman.

David came from a Gaelic background, brought feudalism and granted land to Norman noble families who had arrived with William the Conqueror and his successors. Norman families like Graham, Comyn, Baliol and of course Bruce came to play important roles in Scottish history.

The Norman influence was particularly marked in the lowland areas of the south where David introduced and encouraged and established powerful land-holding French-style monasteries at places like Jedburgh and Melrose. David encouraged Scotland's textile trade and developed Scotland's first towns, known as Royal Burghs that were based on a Norman model. They were sometimes protected by Norman castles and included Aberdeen, Edinburgh, Montrose, Perth and Stirling.

SCOTLAND IN THE MOVIES

London, 2012. Two film executives, Steve and Phil, are considering new films they could make about Scotland.

Steve: Right, let's think about this. National heroes, what about William Wallace?

Phil: *Braveheart.* They already did *Braveheart*, with Mel Gibson.

Steve: Ok, what about Rob Roy?

Phil: *Rob Roy.*

Steve: Yes, Rob Roy, what about *Rob Roy*?

Phil: I'm saying, they already did *Rob Roy*, with Liam Neeson.

Steve: Hey, I heard a great one about some servant Queen Victoria had...

Phil: *Mrs Brown.*

Steve: No, Queen Victoria.

Phil: No, *Mrs Brown.* They already did that, *Mrs Brown* with Judi Dench and Billy Connolly.

Steve: Ok, here's one. It's about this guy, a highlander, who's immortal and has to fight other...

Phil: *Highlander.* They already did that, it's called *Highlander*, with Christopher Lambert in it.

Steve: This is tough. What about one where there's a girl who starts playing football...

Phil: *Gregory's Girl.* And *Whisky Galore*, and *Kidnapped.* They've done them all mate.

Steve: Ok, what about this. A policeman goes to a remote island to investigate some weird goings on, and then maybe at the end he'll get burned alive in a big wicker man?

Phil: It's called *The Wicker Man,* it was made in 1973 and then remade in 2006 with Nicholas Cage.

Steve: Damn. How about this one then, it's about a group of heroin addicts in late 1980s Edinburgh, and the various things which happen to them, which might include having to dive into a nasty toilet or having a dead baby walk across the ceiling?

Phil: That sounds great, totally original, what are you going to call it?

Steve: I was thinking *Heroin Addicts in late 1980s Edinburgh and the various things which happen to them including a scene in a toilet and another one where there's a dead baby.* What do you reckon?

Phil: Let's do it!

Steve and Phil do a high-five.

LEGEND OF THE SALTIRE

According to legend, the inspiration for the Scottish flag and Scotland's association with St Andrew has its roots in a ninth century battle. Let us set the scene:

The year: *832 AD.* **Location:** *A place in East Lothian that will come to be called Athelstaneford. King Angus is preparing to lead an army of Picts and Scots into battle against the Angles led by Athelstan. The night before the battle, Angus prays for victory.*

"Lord, I pray to you on the eve of this battle, that you grant me wisdom and foresight, that you bless my soldiers with strength of arm and courage of heart. I promise you that if you do these things I will make sure my subjects worship you and believe in you and l will make St Andrew the Patron Saint of Scotland."

According to one story, Andrew then appeared to Angus and promised victory. The next morning, with the armies massing on the battlefield, Angus looks into the sky and is amazed by the sight of...

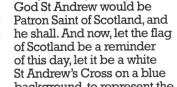

"Look, look at the sky! The clouds have formed a saltire, a diagonal cross like that on which Andrew was crucified! It is a sign from God, I prayed to him last night and he answered my prayers. Rejoice! Rejoice! I promised God St Andrew would be Patron Saint of Scotland, and he shall. And now, let the flag of Scotland be a reminder of this day, let it be a white St Andrew's Cross on a blue background, to represent the white cross of clouds on the background of the blue sky."

The Scots won of course... and from that day to this, St Andrew has been Scotland's Patron Saint, and the white saltire on a blue background has been Scotland's flag.

TARTAN

Tartan may derive from an old French word **tiretaine** a kind of 'woven cloth'. It is essentially a woven pattern of diagonal and horizontal criss-cross patterns of differing colours that intersect each other.

Such patterns have been used around the world for many centuries and were probably widespread in northern Europe during Roman times.

In 1933 a fragment of woven Tartan from the third century was uncovered at Falkirk inside a Roman earthenware pot with 2,000 coins. This is the earliest known example of Scottish tartan, as well as being Scotland's largest Roman coin hoard.

Originally the word tartan was applied to woven, usually woollen cloth, rather than the pattern, so it was possible to have tartan without any pattern at all. In the Highland zone the pattern itself was often called **breacan**.

Despite the example found at Falkirk, Tartan as we know it today does not seem to have been prevalent in Scotland until the late 1500s.

Originally varying designs of tartan were associated with different regions and islands of Scotland. It was not until the nineteenth century that particular patterns came to be associated with particular clans.

Nevertheless, tartan patterned clothing was a popular dress for the Highland clansmen and in 1746 **The Dress Act** following the Battle of Culloden forbade the wearing of tartan as a suppression of Gaelic highland culture. The act was not repealed until 1782.

In 1822 there were as many as 200 recorded patterns, but over the years more and more have been created and discovered and there are perhaps as many as 7,000 different tartan designs today.

1822 was the year in which George IV visited Scotland and Scotland became increasingly interested in its tartan heritage, largely due to the enthusiasm of Sir Walter Scott who encouraged the King and natives to adopt the highland dress for the Royal visit.

Sunday, February 2, 1919

Thistle Press

Strikers riot on Glasgow streets

Some of the fiercest rioting in Scotland's recent history took place in Glasgow on Friday (January 31), as a reported 60,000 demonstrators clashed with police in George Square. The protestors were in the square to hear speeches by the leaders of the so-called "Forty Hours" strike, which has caused much disruption to the city in recent days.

The strike was called on Monday to support a change in the law to limit the working week to 40 hours, in order to both improve conditions for workers currently employed, and to reduce the unemployment which has become such a problem following the end of the Great War.

While the initial cause of the riot remains unknown at this time, fierce fighting took place between striking workers and the Glasgow police, both in the square and in the streets surrounding it. It is also reported that the workers raised the red flag, the symbol of Bolshevism, in George Square. Attempts by Sheriff MacKenzie of Glasgow to read the Riot Act were disrupted when the act was ripped from his hands by rioters.

Fearing a Bolshevik revolution like that which recently taken place in Russia, Prime Minister David Lloyd George instructed troops to be dispatched to Glasgow. 10,000 soldiers armed with machine guns, tanks and a 4.5 inch howitzer entered the City, in order to prevent further trouble.

The soldiers came exclusively from non-Glaswegian regiments, with reports that Glaswegian troops were locked inside their barracks at Maryhill in order to prevent them siding against the government.

Although the fighting has now ceased, it is too early to predict what will happen as a result of this week's events. Whilst violent revolution now seems unlikely, the sight of troops on the streets of one of the Empire's great cities is startling evidence of the divisions which still exist in our great nation.

The Royal Aberguidtime Hotel

Starters

- Cock-a-Leekie Soup -
Dating back to the sixteenth century this traditional Scottish recipe is a winter warming favourite. The finest of Scottish cocks, lovingly boiled with leeks, prunes and a selection of vegetables.

- Scotch Broth -
A heart-warming concoction of Scotland's finest lamb or mutton boiled with root vegetables including neaps.

- Love Apple Soup -
An all-time favourite, known to the rest of the world as tomato soup.

- Cullen Skink -
A fine Finnan Haddock and Potato Soup, originating from the town of Cullen on the Moray Firth.

- Partan Bree -
A crab and rice soup named from the Gaelic 'Partan' (a crab) and the Doric 'Bree' (soup).

- Oatcake and Clapshot -
Scottish oatcake served with Clapshot – an Orkney favourite of mashed tatties and neaps.

- Forfar Bridie -
Traditional minced steak, butter and beef suet pasty made the Forfar way with short crust pastry.

- A Roll and Sausage -
A square-sliced Lorne sausage in a bun. Named from Tommy Lorne, a 1920s comedian.

WHAT'S YOUR NAME?

Campbell

Argyll based clan. One of the largest and most powerful clans. Gaelic name means 'crooked mouth'. Famed for their long running feud with the MacDonalds which reached a deadly peak at the massacre of Glencoe in 1692.

Carnegie

Originally called Balinhard from a place in Angus. They became Carnegies in the mid-fourteenth century after acquiring land at Carmylie in Angus.

Chisholm

Border surname derives from a place near Hawick in Teviotdale that means 'dry water meadow inhabited by cheese making cows'. Early family members were called Cheshelme.

Colquhoun

Clan associated with Loch Lomond's western shore where they settled around 1368. Originally from Colquhoun in Dumbartonshire.

Crawford

Lowland clan named from Crawford (crow's ford) in Lanarkshire. Numerous in the west and Fife.

Cumming

Reputedly descended from Robert Comines, an Earl of Northumberland, who came to England with William the Conqueror. He was killed in a siege at Durham Castle in 1069. His grandson was given land in Roxburghshire by David I. Numerous in Aberdeenshire.

Cunningham

Lowland clan from the Ayrshire district of Cunninghame which means 'milk-pail farm'. Numerous in Ayrshire.

Davidson

Possibly descended from David, a fourteenth century son of Donald Comyn and his wife Slane MacKintosh. It's also claimed they descend from a David Dubh.

DOUGLAS

Possibly descended from Flemish immigrants who came to Scotland in the reign of David I. Named from lands near Douglas Water near Lanark given by the Abbot of Kelso. The most powerful family in the Borders by the thirteenth century. Still numerous in the Borders today.

Drummond

Named from Drymen near Stirling, they are reputedly descended from a Hungarian who came to Scotland with the Saxon noble Edgar the Aetheling who fled William the Conqueror in 1067. Closely associated with Perthshire.

SWEETHEART ABBEY

Large red bricks standing tall,
Its shadow falls upon me.
The monks' spirits drift through the pillars.
John Balliol's heart hidden in a silver casket,
Now left with Lady Devorgilla.
In winter the snow rests upon this beautiful place,
Criffel's shadow blocks the sun.
This is where wonder lies.
Do you believe me?

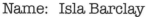

Name: Isla Barclay
Age: 10
School: New Abbey Primary School, Dumfries

VIKING SCOTLAND

Vikings were a major cultural group in Britain, but it was in the Isles of Scotland that their legacy was most lasting.

The first recorded **Viking raid** in Scotland was in 794 AD on the island monastery of **Iona** off the coast of Mull. These raiders were Norwegians who had established a base on Orkney to the north.

The Viking colonisation of **Shetland** and **Orkney** had commenced before 850 AD and would have lasting significance. Today the place-names of these islands are overwhelmingly Viking in origin and until the eighteenth century a Scandinavian language called **Norn** was spoken here.

From the mid-ninth century Viking settlements in the far north formed the heartland of the **Viking Earldom of Orkney** which included Shetland, Caithness and Sutherland. To the Orkney Vikings Sutherland was their southern land.

The Earldom (Jarldom) was part of the **kingdom of Norway**, but behaved like an independent kingdom in its own right.

Between 850 AD and 900 AD the Viking presence in the **Hebrides** became increasingly important, particularly after 875 AD when many Orkney Vikings fled there to avoid confrontation with Harald, King of Norway.

Viking settlements in this region included the Outer Hebrides, Skye, Mull, Arran, Kintyre and the Isle of Man. They formed the **Kingdom of Man and the Isles**, which the Vikings called the **Sudreys** (south islands) as opposed to Orkney and Shetland which were the **Nordreys** (north islands).

Viking power in Scotland was weakened after Alexander III fought the King of Norway at the **Battle of Largs** in Ayrshire in 1263. Three years later the Norwegians gave the Sudreys to the Scots.

Orkney and Shetland were part of Norway until 1468, when the Norwegian King gave them to King James III as part of a dowry for James's marriage to his daughter.

37

TRAQUAIR HOUSE

Traquair House near Innerleithen lies in the Tweed valley five miles south east of Peebles and claims to be the oldest continually inhabited house in Scotland.

The house began life in 1107 when it was built as a hunting lodge for the Kings and Queens of Scotland, though no part of the present building can be confidently dated earlier than the fifteenth century.

The Lairds of Traquair were historically a branch of the Stuart family who resided here from 1491. The fifth Earl to reside here was the Captain of the Bodyguard for Mary Queen of Scots and hosted the visit of that Queen to Traquair in 1566 when she brought her baby son James (the future James VI). Some of Mary's possessions and the cradle in which James was rocked can be seen at the house.

In 1628 the seventh Laird of Traquair became Earl of Traquair. He held the post of Lord High Treasurer and subsequently Commissioner for Scotland but lost the post through disloyalty to the King. He was stripped of his wealth and is said to have ended his days begging on the streets of Edinburgh.

Later residents of Traquair were noted for being staunch Catholics and supported the Jacobite rebellions in the 1700s. In 1738 the fifth Earl added the so-called Bear Gates to the house, but in 1745 following the visit of Bonnie Prince Charlie the gates were permanently closed and on the Earl's wishes will not be opened again until a Stuart sits once again on the Scottish throne.

The Earldom of Traquair died out after 1875 when there was no male heir to the Stuart family. The house passed to their nearest relatives the Maxwells, who continued to be titled Lairds of Traquair. Today the house is a popular venue for weddings and boasts its own brewery.

THE CALEDONIAN CANAL

History Man: Have you ever heard of the Caledonian Canal?

Student: We did it at school, it's somewhere in your stomach, isn't it?

History Man: No, it's actually in the Highlands, running between Corpach near Fort William to Inverness. It's 60 miles long, although most of that is actually made up of Loch Lochy, Loch Oich, Loch Ness and Loch Dochfour.

Student: Are you sure it's not in your stomach? I think it's a passage for some kind of mucus...

History Man: Positive. 38 miles of the canal are made up of those four lochs, but the rest is man-made canal. It was started in 1803 and was supposed to cost £350,000 and take seven years to build. In the end it opened in 1822, costing £840,000.

Student: Wow, that's a long way over budget. It was very useful when it opened though, right?

History Man: Well, not quite. It had been designed by Thomas Telford, and on his design the canal was 20 feet deep. But when they built it, they only built it 14 feet deep, making it too shallow for many of the bigger ships.

Student: Ah. So what did they do then? Did they just give up on the project, considering it had taken so long and cost so much?

History Man: No, they started construction again. Between 1844 and 1847 it was deepened to 20 feet. The problem was, by the time it was finished there wasn't really a need for it anymore. Steam ships had come to prominence, and they could get around the coast of the country very quickly and efficiently.

Student: So it was a big waste of time and money then?

History Man: You could say that, but it's very pretty to look at and a popular tourist attraction.

BUTE AND THE CUMBRAES

The **Isle of Bute** lies at the entrance to the Firth of Clyde just off the Cowall peninsula in the Argyll region of Scotland. Its name is thought to be Norse and may mean 'patch of land'.

It is home to over 7,000 people making it the fifth most populous island in Scotland with its population concentrated in the main town of **Rothesay** where almost 5,000 people live.

Rothesay has a Viking name meaning 'the island belonging to Rotha' and may have been an alternative name for Bute. The moated site of Rothesay Castle (a ruin) was captured by the Vikings dates from the twelfth century.

The other significant settlement is **Port Bannatyne** two miles north of Rothesay, although there are a handful of villages scattered throughout the island.

Overlooking the Firth of Clyde four miles south of Rothesay is the fantasy Gothic mansion called **Mount Stuart** which was built by the eccentric third Marquess of Bute in 1877. His descendants include Johnny Bute, the seventh Marquess of Bute, a formula one racing driver who raced under the name Johnny Dumfries in the 1980s.

Rothesay was historically the county town of Buteshire which included the islands of **Great Cumbrae** and **Little Cumbrae** in the Firth of Clyde to the east.

The Cumbraes take their name from the Cumbrians or Cymru, the Welsh speakers who once inhabited these islands. They were part of the Welsh-speaking Kingdom of Strathclyde in ancient times.

Little Cumbrae is uninhabited but Great Cumbrae is home to more than 1,400 people most of whom live in the town of **Millport**. The town is home to an Episcopalian cathedral of 1851. Known as the **Cathedral of the Isles,** it is in the Diocese of Argyll and the Isles.

KILTS

You live a twenty-first century life, and you need your clothing to measure up to the demands of the twenty-first century. You take performance seriously, but you also want something you can wear every day. You want to be comfortable, but you also want to be ready for business. You want to be casual, but you also want to be stylish.

If this is your life, there's only one piece of clothing for you. You need a **KILT**. Many people think that kilts are old-fashioned; a hangover from the end of the seventeenth century, but the kilt we're talking about is a kilt for the twenty-first century man.

Although the kilt started out in the sixteenth century as an enormous cloak, known as a "great kilt", and then developed by the end of the seventeenth century into the "short kilt", much more like the kilt we know today, the kilt is a rugged garment which can deal with the demands of the twenty-first century.

Made in the traditional way from Scottish wool with pleating at the rear, our kilts are available in a variety of different tartans. Warm enough for the long Scottish winters, but cool enough for your business meeting or a night out with friends, the kilt is the perfect alternative to trousers and suits all occasions.

So get yours today, and wow your friends, colleagues, and that special lady in your life with the effortless style of a KILT.

The word kilt comes from the Viking word kilting meaning 'a skirt'.

117 AD

Thistlus Pressus

Roman Ninth Legion disappears in mysterious circumstances

By Ricardus Callaganus

Roman authorities are today refusing to comment upon reports that the Roman Ninth Legion, Legio IX Hispana, has vanished whilst in Caledonia, beyond the northern frontier.

It is thought that the Ninth, which was made up of over five thousand battle hardened Roman warriors, had ventured into Caledonia to restore order following unrest by the native peoples of the region.

The Thistlus Pressus understands that it has now been some days since the last report from the Legio IX, and that the commanders in Londinium are beginning to fear the worst for the Legion.

Theories abound concerning the Legion's fate. Claims of curses or witchcraft have been largely discredited, the Legion having paid correct attention to all of the Gods prior to embarking on the mission. It is said that the Roman command suspects that the Ninth may have been victims of an ambush by Caledonian forces, and that this is the reason for their disappearance.

Many are now questioning the wisdom of leaving the northern frontier as open and unguarded as it currently is, and suggestions abound that a great wall may be constructed in order to prevent Caledonian retaliation.

The disappearance of the Ninth Legion is one of the great legends of Roman Britain. It has been immortalised in books such as "The Eagle of the Ninth" by Rosemary Sutcliff, T"he Shadowy Horses" by Susanna Kearsley and movies such as "Centurion" and "The Eagle of the Ninth".

The truth behind the legend is more complicated, however. There are suggestions that Legio IX Hispana did not disappear in 117 AD, that in fact it survived until at least 122 AD, and that the story of the Ninth may be just a great piece of Scottish folklore.

AUCHTERMUCHTY

Fife town with Gaelic name *Uachdar-Muc-Garadh* meaning 'upper pig enclosure'.

AYR

Town with a population of 46,000 on the west coast. Overlooks the Firth of Clyde towards the Isle of Arran. Named from the River Ayr, which has a very ancient name that may mean 'smooth flowing'. Ayr gave its name to Ayrshire.

BALMORAL

Gaelic *Bal* and *Morail* ('settlement' and 'splendid') a fitting explanation for a royal residence.

BANNOCKBURN

Famous battle site near Stirling. From the Welsh *ban* and *oc* meaning 'shining' and 'little' as well as, 'burn/stream'.

BEESWING

Dumfriesshire village named from a pub, which was named from a nineteenth century racehorse.

BERWICK

At the mouth of the Tweed. Anglo-Saxon name means 'barley farm' or 'barley trading place'. Once in Scotland, now in England, it changed hands 13 times but has been in England since 1482. The historic county of Berwickshire to the north has always been in Scotland.

BIRNAM

From the Old English *Beorn Ham* 'warrior homestead'. Birnam Wood was mentioned by Shakespeare in Macbeth as the place King Malcolm hid prior to the Battle of Dunsinane. Beatrix Potter was inspired to write *Peter Rabbit* here.

BISHOPBRIGGS

Northern suburb of Glasgow from *Bishop's riggs* meaning 'fields belonging to the bishop'.

THE MASSACRE OF GLENCOE

When William of Orange took the English and Scottish thrones, he set about attempting to guarantee the support of those people who had backed King James VII. Many Highlanders were still strong supporters of James, so William set about trying to get them on his side.

One way that he tried to do this - on the advice of his Lord Advocate John Dalrymple - was by making them swear loyalty to him. A deadline was set of January 1 1692, and the Highland chiefs were told they must swear loyalty by this date or they would be punished.

Alastair Maclain of the MacDonalds of Glencoe was late to submit, because he was waiting for permission from James. He set out on the last day of December to Fort William, but when he got there he found out he couldn't swear his oath there, that instead he must go to Inverary. This meant he didn't swear his oath until January 6.

John Dalrymple decided to make an example of the MacDonalds of Glencoe, and the King agreed and signed the orders. Captain Robert Campbell was sent with 120 men to Glencoe. When they got there they were welcomed by the MacDonalds, and stayed with them for two weeks, eating with their hosts and being cared for by them.

Then on February 12 Captain Drummond arrived with orders for Campbell. Drummond stayed and played cards with the MacDonalds and was invited for dinner the next night on February 13.

That dinner was never to come. Early the next morning 38 MacDonalds were murdered in their beds, their houses burned and their cattle run off. Many more died from exposure in the harsh winter.

It remains one of the most famous crimes in Scottish history, a betrayal of trust which reflected the government's attitude to the Highlands.

william of orange

"You are hereby ordered to fall upon the rebels, the MacDonalds of Glenco, and put all to the sword..."

GRETNA GREEN

Romance and love go with the name,
A village of enormous fame,
I know you'll know the place I mean,
I speak to you of Gretna Green,
When Hardwicke's Marriage Act came in,
English towns were in a spin,
It meant that under twenty two,
A marriage you just couldn't do,
Without your parents saying yes,
But sometimes they just didn't bless
The marriages of loving young,
So up to Scotland people sprung,
For here fourteen you had to be,
So people could be married free,
The first town once they border crossed,
Was Gretna Green and people lost
No time in saying that "they did",
And single life farewell to bid,
So Gretna Green became the place,
Where people made their happy face,
And took their vows, their promise made,
Although their parents had forbade,
So when you think of people wed,
Gretna Green sticks in your head.

SCARY SCOTTISH MYTHICAL BEASTS

THE WORM OF LINTON
Linton Hill south east of Roxburgh was the lair of a wicked wyvern called the Linton Worm. This dreadful beast liked eating cattle, sheep and people. Its activities were eventually ended by a Laird of Lariston called Somerville who fitted the end of his spear with a wheel laced with burning peat, tar and brimstone which he rammed into the worm's throat. As it writhed in agony the beast created the local hill formations known as Wormington.

WATER BEASTS
A mythical water horse lived in the River Conon at Conon Bridge near the Cromarty Firth and another lived in Loch Coruisk on Skye. In fact many such water horses are associated with Scotland. Perhaps they are relatives of the Loch Ness Monster. Dangerous water bulls can also, apparently, be found in some places, while inside waterfalls you can find horrible shaggy-haired creatures called Uruisg.

FERROCIOUS FACHANS
Fachans are mythical Gaelic beasts found in Irish and Scottish folklore. They include the Fachan of Glen Etive in Argyll, a typical example. This dwarf-like figure has one leg and one eye. He apparently has a huge gaping mouth, a mane-like tuft of unbendable black feathers on his head and strangest of all, no arms but he does have a single hand that protrudes from his chest. This beast could, it is said, destroy a whole orchard in one night.

TANGIE THE SEAHORSE
A cave at Fitful Head on mainland Shetland is said to be inhabited by a scary seahorse named Tangie. The beast was once ridden by a terrifying demon sheep-stealer called Black Eric. Black Eric was eventually defeated after falling to his death over Fitful Head when he was cornered by a local crofter called Sandy Breame. It's said that Tangie is still around and occasionally terrorises the neighbourhood.

IAIN BANKS

"It's difficult, you know, it really is. Because I'm sitting here, writing about Iain Banks, and all I really want to be is a novelist. And Iain Banks is a novelist; in fact, he's a very good novelist. He's written fourteen novels, including *The Wasp Factory, The Bridge, A Song of Stone* and *Transition*. He's even had *Espedair Street* adapted for BBC Radio, *The Crow Road* adapted for BBC TV and *Complicity* made into a film.

And that's all fine; I've no problem with that, good luck to him. Then you find out there's another novelist called Iain M. Banks, a science-fiction novelist who's had twelve novels published, nine of them including *Consider Phlebas, The Player of Games, Inversion* and *Matter* set in a universe he created known as the Culture universe. He's clearly a very successful man too, and that's great. I hope both Iain Banks and Iain M. Banks do well.

The problem is you then find out they're the same man. That's what's really annoying, that this Iain Banks, born in Dunfermline on February 16 1954 is taking the space of two novelists. If he wasn't so talented, if he didn't write so many fantastic books, then there'd be room in the world for one more novelist, and maybe I could be that novelist...

That's what's difficult, when you have to write nice things about a man who's clearly hogging the space of two people. I do like his books though..."

17

SCOTTISH BLACKMAILERS CAUGHT RED-HANDED

Two phrases forever associated with crime are amongst Scotland's less savoury gifts to the world. There would be no **BLACKMAIL** if it weren't for the Scots, or at least we wouldn't be using the word. It is generally accepted that this term originated amongst the troublesome cattle, and sheep-rustling Border Reiver clans of the Scottish and English border.

"Blackmail" was their name for a kind of protection racket in which people were protected against raids and harassment by making a payment in goods or labour. It is thought that "white rent" was an alternative where payment was made in silver.

Such practices also existed amongst the Gaelic speaking highland clans and it's been suggested the term actually comes from a combination of the Gaelic words *bl-aich* meaning 'to protect' and *mal* meaning 'tribute or payment'.

The troublesome Reivers who gave us blackmail are also thought to have introduced the term **RED-HANDED** to our vocabulary. This phrase which probably has its roots in the act of someone caught with blood on their hands certainly makes its earliest appearances in Scotland.

The phrase "red-hand" is mentioned in Scottish Acts of Parliament connected with James I in 1432 and the earliest known printed incidence of the phrase red-handed occurs in Sir Walter Scott's *Ivanhoe* in 1819.

Border Reivers who had stolen your sheep, or cattle, perhaps killing one of your clansmen in the process might be caught by you in a hot pursuit called **HOT TROD**. Since the herding of the cattle or sheep would slow the thieves down, they might be overtaken and intercepted by pursuers, and caught in the "deede doing" or at the "red-hand" as it was known. Justice in such instances was often swift. Perpetrators were killed on the spot.

Did you know?
Alba

In Scots Gaelic Alba is the name for Scotland, but the use of this term is rather more complicated than that. Let's explain:

- Alba was first mentioned in the second century AD by a rather clever chap called Ptolemy, a Roman who lived in Egypt but wrote in Greek. In Ptolemy's ancient writing Alba was called Ἀλουίων.

- In Ptolemy's time Alba was the name for the whole of Celtic Britain, in an age long before the Anglo-Saxons (English) arrived.

- Ancient Britain, including Scotland was also called Albion. Alba and Albion have the same meaning and come from an ancient word meaning 'white'. It probably refers to the White Cliffs of Dover - the first part of Britain seen from Europe.

- In later Medieval times Scotland was sometimes known in Latin as Albania, and much less occasionally as Albany in English.

- The Kingdom of Alba is the name given by historians to the Kingdom of Scotland from the beginning of the tenth century to the end of Alexander III's reign in 1286.

- The Gaelic term Rí Alban (King of Scotland) and Rì nan Albannaich (King of the Scots) was firmly established as a title for the kings of Scotland in the reign of Donald II (Domnall mac Causantín) around 900 AD.

- King Donald's predecessors back to the reign of Kenneth MacAlpin were often referred to by the Latin term "Rex Pictorum" meaning King of the Picts even though they were kings of both the Picts and the Scots.

- A twelfth century Irish chronicle called the Annals of "Tigernach" describes Domangurt, a king of the Picts who reigned around 500 AD as Ri Alban. So there were Kings of Alba long before Donald II's time.

Professor
C. Clagg

GOLF COURSES

There are around 600 golf courses across Scotland, but surprisingly for a nation that loves golf so much, there aren't any really famous golf courses in Scotland. Unless of course we include the **Old Course** at St Andrews, the oldest golf course in the world, established in 1552.

Alright we could mention **Gleneagles** near Auchterarder where the golf club at this luxury hotel was established in 1924. It has held the Ryder Cup and Johnnie Walker Championship.

Okay, we might also mention **Carnoustie** in Angus. Golf was first recorded in this area in the sixteenth century and the club itself was constituted in 1842. It's held the Open Championship seven times between 1931 and 2007.

I suppose we should mention **Royal Troon** in Ayrshire, founded in 1878 which has held the Open Championship eight times from 1923 to 2004.

Alright, since we're in Ayrshire we might as well head down the shore to Turnberry and the challenging coastal course of **Aisla-the Legend Turnberry** with its beautiful views of Ailsa Craig island out at sea. Turnberry has held the Open four times.

Since we're talking about the Open Championship I guess we might as well mention **Prestwick**, another Ayrshire golf club, established 1851. It was the birthplace of the Open back in 1859.

For the purposes of golfing history we should also mention **Muirfield** in East Lothian which was established in 1744. It is the oldest organised golf club in the world and has held the Open fifteen times.

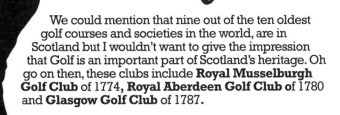

We could mention that nine out of the ten oldest golf courses and societies in the world, are in Scotland but I wouldn't want to give the impression that Golf is an important part of Scotland's heritage. Oh go on then, these clubs include **Royal Musselburgh Golf Club** of 1774, **Royal Aberdeen Golf Club** of 1780 and **Glasgow Golf Club** of 1787.

BUILDING BRIDGES

"My name is **William Arrol**, I was born in Houston in Renfrewshire 1839 and at the age of nine I entered a cotton mill, but that wasn't to be my destiny. By the time I was 13 years old, I was training as a blacksmith and went to night school to learn about engineering.

I went to work for an engineering company in Glasgow that specialised in building bridges and it was for bridge building that I would become famous. In the early 1870s I founded my own iron works and later in the decade I established the civil engineering firm of **William Arrol and Co**.

My company became famous for building bridges across the world and two of the best known are in Scotland. They are the **Tay Rail Bridge** which my company completed in 1890. It replaced the one that collapsed in 1879.

Between 1883 and 1890 we built the world famous **Forth Bridge** with up to 4,600 workers employed in its construction. Sadly it is thought that as many as 98 people were killed during its construction. Bridge building can be dangerous work.

The Forth Road Bridge is an icon of Scotland, just as the **Tower Bridge** is an icon of London and guess what? We built that too. We began construction of Tower Bridge in 1886 and we had it completed in 1894.

We have built many bridges in other parts of Britain and around the world in places such as Egypt and Australia.

In 1890 I was knighted for my services to industry and between 1895 and 1897 I was the President of the Institution of Engineers and Shipbuilders in Scotland. I passed away on February 20 1913 at my home near Ayr, but my company continued to operate until 1969 when it was taken over by Clarke Chapman."

THE ABERDEEN TYPHOID OUTBREAK OF 1964

"Hola! I am Carlos, and I am, how you say, a bacterium. I bring the disease Typhoid from my native Argentina, and I bring it to Aberdeen in 1964.

I come to Aberdeen in some Argentinean corned beef, as you Scots love the corned beef, and I am brought into Scotland by the supermarket of William Low & Co. I go from strength to strength, and in the end I infect more than 500 people.

'But Carlos', I hear you say, 'how do you infect over 500 people, when you are only in the corned beef. Surely not everyone in Scotland eats the corned beef?' And you would be right, not everyone in Scotland does eat the corned beef. I become so successful in Aberdeen because I am kept in the store, and I am cut in a slicer which is used for many other meats.

So people eat the corned beef, and I get in. People eat other food which was cut with the slicer used for the corned beef, and I get in. I make most excellent progress across Aberdeen, and in the end 309 people are in the hospital because of me.

This make me very happy, for I am a bacterium and all I want is to get into people's bodies and make more of myself, which makes the people sick. It makes the people of Aberdeen very sad though, and the supermarket never recovers, closing three years later.

It is my last big hit in Britain, since then I hardly make a dent no more, but I always think fondly of those days in Aberdeen, and wish I might be back one day soon..."

HISTORIC TOWNS AND CITIES: AYR

STATUS: Coastal town in South Ayrshire. Ayr narrowly missed out in its bid for city status in 2002.

RIVER: The **River Ayr** is a small river that enters the sea here and gave its name to Ayr. The River Doon, enters the sea near Alloway in the southern outskirts of Ayr. A thirteenth century bridge over the river called the Brig O'Doon was immortalised in the Burns poem "Tam O'Shanter".

NAMES AND NICKNAMES: Robert Burns described Ayr as "Auld Ayr, wham ne'er a town surpasses, for honest men and bonnie lasses".

MOTTO AND EMBLEM: "God Schaw The Richt" is the motto of the historic county of Ayrshire. Ayr's emblem was traditionally a three-towered castle.

POPULATION: About 46,000.

KEY FACTS AND INDUSTRIES: Overlooks the sea (the Firth of Clyde) looking out towards the Isle of Arran. **Alloway** on Ayr's southern outskirts was the **birthplace of Robbie Burns. Prestwick** which merges with Ayr to the north is noted for its airport and aviation industry and for golf at **Troon**. Ayr was once noted for textiles and shipbuilding.

KEY DATES: 1197: Castle is built here. **1315**: (April 26) Robert Bruce held the first Parliament of Scotland here. **1534**: Loudon hall first mentioned in a deed. **1652**: Cromwell's army builds a fort here. **1823**: Monument to Robert Burns built. **1936**: Macadam's monument built.

THINGS TO SEE:

- **Burns Birthplace Museum**, at Alloway south of Ayr.
- **Auld Kirk** of 1654, financed by Oliver Cromwell after he demolished the original to build a fort.
- **Tam O' Shanter Inn**, features in the poem of that name.
- **The Auld Brig O' Doon**, mentioned in the "Tam O' Shanter" poem.
- **The Auld Brig of Ayr**, mentioned in the Burns poem "The Brigs of Ayr".
- **Monument to John MacAdam**, inventor of Tarmac.

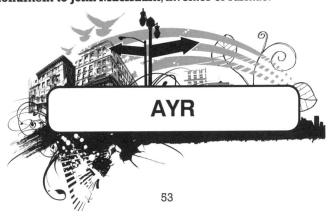

AYR

REMEMBER THE ALAMO?

Texas certainly does. One of the iconic battles in American history, where a tiny force of Texian volunteers held out against a far larger Mexican army for twelve days before it was finally beaten. The Alamo proved a very important turning point in the Texas Revolution.

The Alamo is a former mission in what is now San Antonio, Texas. It was attacked on February 23 1836 by a Mexican army thought to have numbered anywhere between 1,500 and 3,000. Reports of the numbers of Texian defenders vary, but it's generally agreed that there were somewhere between 180 and 260, four of whom were actually Scottish.

The men, Richard W. Ballentine, Isaac Robinson, David L. Wilson and John MacGregor were all Scots who'd gone to live in Texas, and then taken up arms to defend their adopted country and fight for independence from Mexico. You've got to remember that at this time Texas wasn't part of the USA, and Mexico was a very powerful country, meaning that these Scots had chosen to side with the underdogs.

One thing that the Scots at the Alamo are remembered for is John McGregor and Davy Crockett's bagpipe and fiddle duels which they performed to keep up the spirits of the soldiers there.

Although the Mexicans took the Alamo on March 6, the actions of the defenders, as well as the great cruelty of the Mexican forces, meant that many new volunteers joined the army, and Texas won the war, becoming a republic. It's a very important day in Texan history, but it should be a day that all Scottish people remember too, because it tied two great nations together forever.

THE SCOTTISH SCARLET PIMPERNEL

Ethel MacDonald was a Scottish anarchist who became very famous because of her actions during the Spanish Civil War. Born February 24 1909, she became involved in politics at a young age, joining the Bellshill branch of the Independent Labour Party (ILP) aged 16.

She left the ILP in 1931 to join the Anti-Parliamentary Communist Federation (APCF) to work for a man called Guy Aldred. The APCF split in 1934 and Aldred led a new group, called the United Socialist Movement (USM), which MacDonald joined and was to stay an active member until her death.

Her fame, and her nickname, came from her actions in Spain. She went to Spain in 1936 to show support for the Republican side in the Spanish Civil War, which included anarchist groups. She lived in Barcelona, which was the heartland of the Republican side, and began to broadcast in English on Barcelona's anarchist radio station. Her reports were heard all over the world, as far away as America, and were important factors in motivating people to support the Republican cause.

Then, in May 1937, the different factions within the Republican side began to fight amongst themselves in Barcelona, with the Communists, supported by the Soviet Union, trying to seize power from the other groups, including the anarchists.

Ethel MacDonald became known as the "Scottish Scarlet Pimpernel" because of her actions in helping a number of anarchists escape from Spain. She was arrested herself, but was eventually released and returned to Scotland. She remained an influential and important member of the USM, and wrote many articles supporting her political ideals. Sadly she developed multiple sclerosis in 1958 and died in Glasgow in 1960.

THIRTY SCOTTISH CASTLES

Scotland was once the home to perhaps as many as 2,000 castles. Today there are around 600 castles in Scotland not including prehistoric forts of ancient times. Here is a selection of some of Scotland's most notable castles:

BLAIR CASTLE

Located in Blair Atholl in Perthshire this is the home of the Clan Murray family who are the Dukes of Atholl. The castle can trace its origins back to 1269 when it was commenced by John Comyn. Today this impressive castle is an important stately home.

BOTHWELL CASTLE

Near Bothwell overlooking the Clyde in South Lanarkshire this is one of the most impressive ruins in the Scottish lowlands. It was begun in the thirteenth century by Walter of Moray an ancestor of the Clan Murray. It became the home of the Douglas family in the fourteenth century.

BRAEMAR CASTLE

This beautiful castle of pink stone and round towers in Aberdeenshire was an ancestral home of the Farquharson. It was previously a stronghold of the Earls of Mar. The present castle was built as a hunting lodge by John Erskine, the eighteenth Earl of Mar, commencing in 1628. The castle has several ghosts including that of a lady on her honeymoon who took her life when she mistakenly thought her husband had abandoned her.

CAERLAVEROCK CASTLE

Caerlaverock is a curious triangular-shaped thirteenth century castle. Situated south of Dumfries, this part-ruined castle is surrounded by a moat which gives it an island-like appearance. It was historically a home to the Maxwell family and is now occasionally used as a wedding venue because of its proximity to Gretna Green

CASTLE CAMPBELL

Castle Campbell dates from the fifteenth century and is a fortified tower house that was the seat of the Earls and Dukes of Argyll, the chiefs of the Clan Campbell. It is located to the north of the town of Dollar in Clackmannanshire about ten miles east of Stirling. It was originally known as "Castle of Gloom" and had once belonged to the Clan Stuart. After passing to the Campbell family by marriage the name was changed in 1489.

THE CURSE OF SCOTLAND

When you're playing cards, if you get the nine of diamonds people will tell you that you're holding "The Curse of Scotland". Why is it called the Curse of Scotland? Well, there are a lot of different stories, and nobody quite knows which is true.

One story is that the Earl of Stair, John Dalrymple, the man responsible for the Glencoe Massacre, used the nine of diamonds as a signal that the massacre should go ahead. Another variation on this is that he signed the back of a nine of diamonds to authorise the massacre. It's possible that the name comes from the massacre, but it's unlikely either of these stories is true. Interestingly, though, the Earl of Stair's coat of arms features nine diamonds!

Another story goes that the battle at Culloden, after the Duke of Cumberland gave the infamous "no quarter" order, the order to show no mercy to the Scots. The officer given the task of carrying it out was nervous, and asked for the order to be written down. It's said that the Duke wrote the order on the back of a nine of diamonds. This is thought to be very unlikely though, since there are records of the phrase being used in 1710, 36 years before the order was given.

A final explanation is that it comes from the sixteenth century card game of "Pope Joan", in which the nine of diamonds was called "the Pope". The Pope, not a popular figure amongst Scottish religious reformers at the time, may well have been known as the "Curse of Scotland".

Whether any of these stories or none of these stories are true, what's for certain is that the nine of diamonds has a unique name with many very interesting stories behind it, even if we may never know what the real story is.

27

February

CURLING

A dark night in a dimly lit bar. A broom sits at the bar, drowning its sorrows. You pull up the stool beside it and sit down, as it turns its head towards you and says:

"I could have been big, you know. I could have been a contender. I had the whole world in front of me. You listen to me, and listen good because you shouldn't make the mistakes I made.

When I was a young broom, barely more than a brush, all I wanted to do was curl. I was a master, I was a young prodigy. They'd never seen anybody like me, the way I could control the stones down the sheet...You know curling's been here in Scotland since the sixteenth century, with curling stones dating from 1511 being found! Well, they said I was right up there with the best.

I had so many opportunities, but I let it go to my head. They said I could go to Canada, that's the place everyone wants to go to be a curling broom, there's a million people in the world playing curling and 90% of them are in Canada. They even broadcast us on the TV there.

It's big in Canada, but that's only because so many Scottish people moved there, and took their traditional Scottish culture and pastimes with them. It's first mentioned in print in Perth in 1620, the World Curling Federation's based here, and it was a very popular outdoor Scottish sport in the past.

I was ready to be a star, but I got in over my head. All the lady-brooms, the polish, I could get anything I wanted any time of the day, I just couldn't cope. I burned out, I lost my head, I just couldn't take it. You know what I do now? I sweep the floors in here, just thinking of what could have been."

HAMMER OF THE SCOTS

On the tomb of the English King, Edward I at Westminster is the Latin inscription *Scottorum Malleus*, "Hammer of the Scots". Here's why:

Edward had defeated Wales and joined it to England and wanted to do the same to Scotland. When Alexander III of Scotland (married to Edward's sister) fell from his horse and died in 1286, Edward seized the opportunity.

Alexander had no male heir. Edward tried to have Alexander's granddaughter Margaret married to his son. It would bring England and Scotland together and give Edward power in Scotland but then Margaret died. It was then that Edward dealt several heavy **hammer blows** against the Scots:

- Twelve Scottish nobles stepped forward to claim the Scottish crown but couldn't agree, so in a humiliating move they let Edward decide.
- Edward chose John Baliol, and rejected Robert the Bruce, but before the new King was appointed he had to accept Edward as overlord.
- Edward consistently interfered in Scottish affairs. When Baliol tried to resist, Edward invaded Scotland, defeated the Scots at the Battle of Dunbar in 1296 and seized Edinburgh Castle.
- Baliol then abdicated leaving Scotland without a king, giving Edward more power in Scotland.
- To add to the humiliation Edward stole the "Stone of Destiny" on which the Scottish kings sat when they were crowned. He placed it below the throne in Westminster Abbey where English kings are crowned.
- Edward destroyed lots of Scottish records verifying Scotland's independence and freedom.
- The Scots under William Wallace rebelled against Edward but Edward defeated the Scots at the Battle of Falkirk in 1298.
- William Wallace, the Scottish rebel was captured in 1305, but this was to be Edward's final **hammer blow**. In July 1307 Edward died at Burgh on Sands as he was about to mount yet another invasion on Scotland.

Arbroath Abbey: Founded in 1178 by William the Lion. The monks were Tironensian Benedictines who came from Kelso Abbey. The Declaration of Arbroath was written here in 1320.

Ardchattan Priory: Located in Ardchattan Garden on the shore of Loch Etive in Strathclyde it was founded in 1230 by Duncan MacDougal, Lord of Argyll. The church and some parts of the monastery remain. It started life as a Valliscaulian monastery but later became Cistercian.

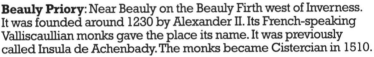

Balmerino Abbey: In Fife on the south bank of the Tay. A Cistercian monastery was founded between 1227 and 1229 by monks from Melrose at the bequest of Ermengrade the widowed queen of William the Lion.

Beauly Priory: Near Beauly on the Beauly Firth west of Inverness. It was founded around 1230 by Alexander II. Its French-speaking Valliscaullian monks gave the place its name. It was previously called Insula de Achenbady. The monks became Cistercian in 1510.

Cambuskenneth Abbey: The twelfth century ruins of this Augustinian abbey, a mile east of Stirling, were sometimes called Stirling Abbey. It was founded around 1140 by King David I. James III was buried here in 1488 following the Battle of Sauchieburn. His Queen, Margaret of Denmark was buried here in 1486. Robert the Bruce held a parliament at the abbey in 1326.

Crossraguel Abbey: Ruins of a Cluniac Benedictine monastery near Maybole village in Strathclyde. It was founded by the Earl of Carrick in 1244 and named from a cross of St. Regulus that stood on the site.

Culross Abbey: The ruins of this Cistercian monastery of 1217 are at Culross in south Fife near the Firth of Forth. The abbey's church is still used. Culross was chosen as an abbey site because it was the birthplace of St Mungo. It was founded by Malcolm I, the Mormaer of Fife.

WHUPPITY SCOORIE

Whuppity Scoorie is the name given to a famous spring time festival held in the town of Lanark from March 1 to March 7 every year.

The event begins on the first day with local children running around the Kirk of St Nicholas in an anti-clockwise direction at 6pm. They swing paper balls and make as much noise as they wish as they do so. After three circumnavigations of the church, coins are thrown that the children will scramble for. Other events of the week include a Whuppity Scoorie story-telling.

It is said that Whuppity Scoorie has pagan origins and was designed to scare away the demons of winter, though it may also be a celebration of the end of winter curfews when children were allowed to play out for longer.

The significance of running around the church may be linked to an ancient custom in which prisoners were whipped three times around the church. This would account for the "whuppity" (whipping) part of the name. "Scoorie" is thought to refer to the subsequent scouring or washing of the offenders in the nearby River Clyde.

The first known record of the event was in the middle of the nineteenth century, though in 1893 a local newspaper claimed in that year that the custom was already 120 years old.

Another variation on the name is "Whuppity Stoorie", which was allegedly the name of a fairy who took the baby boy of a Lanark farmer's wife as payment for curing her pig. The baby would only be returned if the wife learned the fairy's name. One day while out walking, the farmer's wife overheard the fairy reveal her name as she sang, "Little kens our guid dame at hame that Whuppity Stoorie is my name". On shouting out "Whuppity Stoorie" the fairy fled and the wife reclaimed her son.

2
March

THE TOP 10 THINGS TO SEE IN EDINBRUGH

Edinburgh Castle
One of Scotland's greatest fortresses, and the most visited attraction in the country, it's the only thing that could go at the top of this list.

The Royal Mile
From the Castle, walk down "the most beautiful street in the world", lined with shops, bars and restaurants. There's something for everybody here.

Arthur's Seat
If you're feeling adventurous, why not climb to the top of Arthur's Seat, the extinct volcano which forms one of Edinburgh's most recognisable landmarks.

Royal Yacht Britannia
Now moored at Ocean Terminal, Leith, the Royal Yacht Britannia was launched from Clydebank in 1953 and served as the Queen's official yacht for over 40 years. It is now a fascinating exhibition ship; why not give it a visit?

National Galleries of Scotland
Including the National Gallery of Scotland, the Scottish National Gallery of Modern Art and the Scottish National Portrait Gallery, Edinburgh's the perfect place to get your art fix.

The Camera Obscura
Marvel at the mysteries of optics as an image of the city is projected on the table in front of you. Great fun to be had.

St Giles' Cathedral
One of the great churches of Scotland, dating from the fourteenth century.

The Scott Monument
Impossible to miss, in Princes Street Gardens this monument to Sir Walter Scott has some of the best views in the city, if you can take the climb to the top.

The Old Town
Take a walk around Edinburgh's Old Town, and get a feel for the city that was here before making your way to...

The New Town
The perfect way to end a day, in one of the bars or restaurants in the New Town.

ALEXANDER GRAHAM BELL AND THE TELEPHONE

"My name is Lionel, and I'm a letter. And I'm annoyed.

You know why I'm annoyed? Because I used to be the only way that long distance communication worked. If you wanted to talk to your mother, you used me. If you wanted to buy something, you used me. If you wanted to declare your undying love for someone a long way away, you used me. I was everywhere, I was the king. But I'm not the king any more, and you know who I hold responsible? Alexander Graham Bell.

He was born in Edinburgh on March 3 1847, born into a world where I reigned supreme, but he couldn't just leave it like that, could he? He had to start researching speech when he was 16, and then emigrate to Canada and then the US, and start a school for teachers of the deaf.

Now obviously, I've no problem with this but it's his next move that has me holding a grudge. He started researching machines to turn speech into electricity, and back again. Then he goes and gets himself a patent granted for his 'telephone' on March 7 1876.

That was the beginning of the end for me, he started the Bell Telephone Company in 1877 and it got massive. I couldn't believe it, watching all these people, my people, suddenly using telephones instead! Now the only people who use me are people asking for money, and nobody wants that. I used to be a favourite, now I'm an inconvenience. And it's all down to Alexander Graham Bell."

Alexander Graham Be

4

FLORA MACDONALD'S JACOBITE GETAWAY

We're so delighted about the great deal we've got to offer you, but this is a **ONE-TIME ONLY** offer and tickets are going fast, so don't miss out!

That's right - get your **Escape Scotland** package today!

Have you come to Scotland to claim the throne you believe to be rightfully yours, but seen your campaign fail and your armies crushed at the battle of Culloden?

Are you fleeing for your life through the Highlands of Scotland, on the run from the British government forces?

Do you need a getaway right now?

Then we've got the deal for you here at

FLORA MACDONALD'S JACOBITE GETAWAYS.

Just take a look at our adventure-packed itinerary and see what we have in store for you.

ITINERARY

DAY 1
On arrival, our experienced guide will meet you on the island of Benbecula, where you will be in hiding from government forces with your companion Captain O'Neill.

You will then be disguised as Flora MacDonald's Irish maid, Betty Burke, and rowed with her, her manservant, and six men to Skye. You will land at Kilbride in Skye, where you will be concealed in rocks whilst our experienced guide brings you help from the local community.

Finally, you will be taken to Portree on Skye and from there to Raasay.

Your magical trip will end with you being spirited away from Scotland on a ship back to France.

DAY 2
Your guide, Flora MacDonald, will be arrested for her part in your escape, and imprisoned in Orkney and the Tower of London, before her release in 1747.

This really is the trip of a lifetime, the chance to experience the thrills, spills, highs and lows of a real-life fugitive on the run from the British government of the mid-eighteenth century, all ably assisted by your delightful host, Miss Flora MacDonald.

Did you know?
Ghosts of Scotland

Scotland's a famous place for ghosts and ghouls. Here are just a few scary stories:

- The 15 mile stretch of the A75 from Annan to Gretna Green is said to be the most haunted road in Scotland, with reports of spectral men who stand in front of cars, an old lady who appears in a cloud of mist and allows cars to pass straight through her, as well as an old man who has no eyes, simply deep black holes where his eyes ought to be. Scary!

- It's said that one of the buildings on Gray Street in Glasgow is haunted by the ghostly form of a man, thought to be an English soldier whose sweetheart left him for another. He was so upset by this that he took his own life, and now his ghost is cursed to walk the rooms where he spent his last moments, weeping.

- Mary King's Close in Edinburgh is believed to be one of the most haunted parts of Edinburgh. It lies below the Royal Exchange building, which was built on top of the close in the eighteenth century. The close had been badly hit by the outbreaks of the plague during the seventeenth century, and the victims of the plague still haunt it today. You can even go and visit it, deep underground. Spooky!

- A ghostly cyclist is said to travel the streets of Dundee, but can only be seen as a reflection in mirrors. He is said to have died in a traffic accident, and since that point he appears in the mirrors of cars, yet when the drivers turn around there's nobody there!

Professor C. Claggs

SCOTLAND'S TWO BIGGEST TOWNS

For two hundred years **Paisley** claimed the distinction of being Scotland's biggest town. Glasgow, Edinburgh, Aberdeen and Dundee are all bigger but are of course cities, rather than towns.

Paisley lies just south west of Glasgow forming part of the Glasgow conurbation and is the largest town in the historic county of Renfrewshire. It is home to about 74,000 people.

In the sixth or seventh century it was the site of a chapel that was home to an Irish monk called St Mirin, or St Mirren as he is remembered in the name of Paisley's football team. In 1163 a priory was established on the site by monks from Wenlock in Shropshire, England. The priory became an abbey in 1245.

Paisley Abbey can be seen on the banks of the White Cart Water close to the waterfalls called the Hammils. The abbey was a burial place for Scottish kings from the thirteenth to the fifteenth century. By the nineteenth century Paisley was a major centre for weaving famed for its Paisley shawls and Paisley patterns.

The White Adder Water begins its course near **East Kilbride**, Paisley's up and coming rival in the population stakes.

In 2009 it was revealed that this South Lanarkshire town south east of Glasgow had overtaken Paisley by 27 people, but populations fluctuate, so perhaps we should consider it a close tie.

East Kilbride is named after an Irish saint called St Bride (Brigit) and as late as 1930 was still a village that was home to no more than 900 people. In 1947 it was designated a New Town for housing population overspill from neighbouring Glasgow.

Paisley and East Kilbride's next nearest rival in terms of population is the town of **Livingston** (another new town) in West Lothian where around 55,000 people live.

THE LEGENDARY ROB ROY

"And finally, congratulations to Rob Roy MacGregor, the winner of this year's Scottish Folklore Idol. Rob, you've been a fantastic competitor, since your birth on March 7 1671, you've really livened up this competition.

From your participation in the **Battle of Killiecrankie** at the age of just 18, through to your many exploits as an outlaw, you've proved yourself a fantastic addition to Scottish legend, but before we award the winning prize of 'outstanding place in history', let's go back to the start of your journey.

You were a respected businessman, a valued member of the local community, until one fateful day in 1711 when you borrowed £1,000 from the Duke of Montrose. Early the next spring you sent your chief drover to spend that £1,000 on cattle, but he sold those cows and ran off with the Duke's money, bankrupting you in the process.

Under the warrant the Duke issued for your arrest, you became an outlaw, and one of the most memorable stories in Scottish history had begun. You conducted a private war against the Duke, kidnapping people who worked for him, stealing his money and his property, and generally making his life very difficult.

It was at this point that you took up with the Duke of Argyll, Montrose's enemy, and he protected you whilst you attacked Montrose. Although you didn't fight in the 1715 rising, you were one of the men charged with High Treason afterwards and spent the next ten years on the run from the law, until your capture by General Wade in 1725.

There was one last twist though.

As you were in Newgate Prison in London awaiting transportation to Barbados you were given a pardon by King George I.

You died in December 1734 aged 63, but you did so with your place in Scottish history secure.

ROB ROY MCGREGOR you are a worthy winner of this year's Scottish Folklore Idol."

ROB ROY MCGREGOR

SCOTTISH INVENTORS

Scotland has a rich and diverse history of inventors, and the inventions they come up with which in many cases have changed the world. Here are just three of them:

DR HENRY FAULDS
The invention of fingerprinting

Born in Beith on June 1 1843, Henry Faulds went to Glasgow as a boy to work as a clerk. He studied Medicine at Glasgow University, before becoming a missionary and moving to Japan. He founded Tuskiji Hospital in Tokyo, and it was in 1880 while there that he discovered the differences in human fingerprints, and that they could be used to identify criminals. Another man named Sir William Herschel claimed to have thought of the idea before him, and it wasn't until 1917 that Faulds got the recognition he deserved.

KIRKPATRICK MACMILLAN
The rear wheel powered bicycle

The son of a blacksmith, Kirkpatrick Macmillan was born in Coathill, Dumfriesshire on April 1 1812. He came up with the idea of a pedal driven, rear wheel powered bicycle, with metal rods connecting he pedals to the rear wheel. Unfortunately for Kirkpatrick he didn't patent his invention, and it was copied by Gavin Dalzell of Lesmahagow, who himself became regarded as the inventor of the bicycle, even though it was actually Macmillan!

CHARLES MACINTOSH
The waterproof raincoat

Glaswegian Charles Macintosh, born December 29 1766, was a chemist who invented waterproof fabrics. His waterproofing techniques allowed for the creation and marketing in 1824 of the Mackintosh raincoat, following a patent for the waterproof material the previous year. So when you stay dry in the rain, just remember it's a Scotsman you've got to thank!

GAELIC (Gàidhlig)

Gaelic (pronounced Gallick) is a Celtic language spoken by just under 60,000 people in Scotland. That's less than 2% of the population. Most speakers live in the Outer Hebrides, where more than 50% of the population speak the language. Other significant areas of Gaelic speech are the Inner Hebridean islands of Tiree, Skye, Raasay and Lismore. On the Scottish mainland, Gaelic is less common, with the biggest concentration of speakers in the western coastal areas.

Scottish Gaelic is closely related to **Manx**, spoken on the Isle of Man and even closer to the **Irish Gaelic** (pronounced Gaylic) of Ireland. Most similar of all is the Gaelic dialect of County Donegal in Ulster.

Gaelic was brought to Caledonia by an invading Irish tribe called the Scotti from perhaps as early as the fourth century. It was the Scotti who gave their name to Scotland. Gradually their language and place-names spread east, replacing the Pictish language of the Highland region.

Gaelic was not so influential in the lowlands where a form of English called **Inglis** predominated, except in Galloway where a Gaelic dialect called **Galwegian** developed.

Confusingly, in the fifteenth and sixteenth century Inglis came to be called Scots, while Scottish Gaelic was increasingly called Erse, meaning 'Irish'.

Gaelic was already declining on the Scottish mainland by this time and this decline continued following the suppression of the Highland clan system after the Battle of Culloden in 1746. By 1800, 297,823 Gaelic-only speakers lived in Scotland accounting for about 18% of Scotland's population.

Throughout the twentieth century there has been an increasing decline in the number of Gaelic speakers but an organisation called **Bòrd na Gàidhlig** helps protect and develop the language to ensure its future longevity.

PUBLIC NOTICE

Today in Portsmouth the villain known as

JOHN THE PAINTER

born JOHN OR JAMES AITKEN of Edinburgh in the year of our Lord 1752, will be hanged as punishment for his many and various crimes against the Crown.

Aitken, suspected of crimes which include highway robbery, burglary, shoplifting and other nefarious deeds, will hang today for his part in the incendiary attacks against the navies of King George present in the dockyards of Bristol and Portsmouth over these last two years. These actions have been taken against the King, it is said, in support of the rebellion in the American colonies.

It is suspected that during a time in the colonies, the villain became crazed with radical ideas and that upon his return to these shores he felt compelled to carry out attacks against His Majesty's forces and properties, causing much fear and disquiet in the populous of Britain during this most turbulent of times.

For these crimes

AITKEN WILL BE HANGED

from the mizzenmast of a ship in PORTSMOUTH HARBOUR today.

THE OUTER HEBRIDES

The Outer Hebrides, also called the **Western Isles**, consist of a group of around 100 islands of greatly varying sizes off the western coast of Scotland. They are separated from the Scottish mainland by an arm of the sea called The Minch and from the Isle of Skye in the Inner Hebrides by the Little Minch.

Fifteen of the islands are permanently inhabited. The largest island is Lewis which with Harris hosts a population of just under 20,000 people. The next four largest islands are South Uist, North Uist, Benbecula and Barra each of which has a population of more than a thousand people. In total there are over 26,000 people inhabiting the Outer Hebrides.

The islands are noted for their freshwater lochs of which there are some 7,500 making up almost a quarter of Scotland's total.

Lewis and Harris are in reality one island, though South Harris forms a distinct peninsula. Together they make up the third largest island in the British Isles. Only Great Britain and Ireland are larger.

The islands have been inhabited since Stone Age times and the Callanish Stone Circle on Lewis is a fine remnant of this enigmatic past.

The Picts were probably amongst the later ancient inhabitants as were the Scots who brought the Gaelic language from Ireland. They were followed by the Viking Norsemen who ruled these islands for almost four centuries.

Fishing, tourism, crafting and weaving, particularly of the famous Harris Tweed are amongst the industries of the island.

The Outer Hebrides have the most significant Scots Gaelic speaking population in the British Isles. Each of the islands is more than 50% Gaelic speaking with more than 70% speaking Gaelic on South Uist.

The largest settlement in the Outer Hebrides is the fishing port of Stornoway, home to around 12,000 people.

ANDREW WATSON
SCOTLAND'S FIRST BLACK FOOTBALLER

There are a lot of famous football heroes in Scottish history, but there are also some that are less well known. One such man is Andrew Watson, Scotland's first black footballer.

Born in Guyana in 1857 to Scot Peter Miller and a Guyanese woman, Rose Watson, Andrew came to Scotland in 1875 to study at the University of Glasgow. As well as studying, he also played football for a local side called Parkgrove.

He signed for Queens Park in 1880. At the time, Queens Park was the best team in Britain, and Andrew became a very important part of their side. He became the club secretary and led them to several Scottish Cup wins.

As if that wasn't enough, Andrew holds the honour of being Scotland's first black international player, captaining Scotland to a 6-1 win against England at Hampden Park on March 12 1881. He then moved to England to become the first black player to play in the FA Cup when he was playing for London Swifts. He also played for Corinthian FC, one of the best English sides at the time.

He might not be someone that you've heard of before, but Andrew Watson really is a football pioneer, Scotland's first black football captain 112 years before Paul Ince captained England and, in fact, the world's first black international football captain!

Andrew Watson played for Queens Park for seventeen years, before emigrating. He sadly died in 1902, but should be remembered as a Scottish football legend.

SCOTTISH FOOTBALL

Football has been Scotland's favourite game for many years, with the Scottish Football Association the second oldest football association in the world, and the Scottish Cup the world's oldest sporting trophy.

Queens Park was the first ever Scottish football club, forming in Glasgow in 1867. They are the oldest football club in the world outside of England, and even competed in the English FA Cup, reaching the FA Cup final twice. Queens Park were one of the best teams in Britain during these early years, and were instrumental in forming the Scottish Football Association, putting an advertisement in a Glasgow newspaper in 1873.

This advert led to a meeting on March 13 1873, and at that meeting it was agreed to form a Scottish Football Association. Since then, Scotland has had a lot of success in football. Some world class football players have been produced in Scotland, including Ally McCoist, Alan Hansen, Jim Baxter, Denis Law and of course Kenny Dalglish.

That's not even the half of it though. Scotland continues to be a breeding ground for top class football players and managers, and has some fantastic football clubs. The country itself has a very good record, qualifying for eight World Cup and two European Championship finals. Let's hope that the team qualifies for another one really soon!

SCOTLAND'S SAHARA

Culbin Forest in Moray is an area of Scotland with a varied and fascinating history. Until the seventeenth century this was a fertile area of land, with farming crofts, a church and manor house on the estate. The estate itself was owned by the Kinnaird family.

There were beaches along the edge of the estate. The sand dunes on the beaches were stabilised by plants and grasses, which stopped them from blowing away. However the people who lived in the area took these plants and used them in different ways, for example many of them may have used the grasses to thatch the roofs of their houses.

This meant that the sand dunes became unstable, and led to a number of great sandstorms. In 1676 the harvest had to be abandoned when a storm covered all of the fields with sand, killing all of the plants and meaning that nothing could grow there.

That wasn't the end of it though - in fact it only got worse. Every time there was a storm, the sands would cover more and more of the area, until in 1694 a great storm came which spelled the end of the estate. It covered everything, the house, the farms, and the church. The people were all forced to leave the land, and Culbin Sands became known as **Scotland's Sahara**.

There have been a number of attempts to reclaim the land over the years, including several in the eighteenth and nineteenth centuries, but it wasn't until the 1920s that the Forestry Commission planted the area with trees to stabilise the sands and tame them.

Culbin Forest, as it is now, is a beautiful place to visit, and a testament to man's continuing battle with nature.

CLYDEBANK
THE MOST BOMBED TOWN IN SCOTLAND

Mrs Agnes Gordon,
14 Queen Mary Road,
Clydebank,
West Dunbartonshire.

March 15, 1941.

My Dearest Billy,

I'm writing to let you know how proud I am of you, and I hope that the African sun isn't too harsh for you. What you and the boys are doing there is more important than ever now.

Things here seem bleak at times, especially after nights like the last two nights. Last night was the worst night of bombing I've ever experienced, and I heard from your uncle Joseph (yes, he's still working at the War Office) that it was the worst bombing anywhere in Scotland has ever had. According to Joe there were 236 bombers in the sky over Clydebank on the 13th and perhaps around the same last night. It certainly gave us a taste of what it must be like in London.

They came in two waves, the first wave dropping incendiary bombs on the town, to light it up for the bombers which came in the second wave. The incendiaries did a lot of damage, starting fires at Singer's Timber Yards, Yoker Distillery and Old Kilpatrick's oil depot. There was such a lot of damage done, more by the incendiaries than the other bombs I reckon.

Joe was saying that of the 12,000 houses in the town, 4,000 were completely destroyed. Only seven managed to escape completely undamaged. Our house didn't end up too bad, broken windows and battered by shrapnel, but old Mrs Grant's house was completely demolished, the poor dear.

My love to you, make sure you give the Germans hell, and come home safely.

Your loving sister

HISTORIC TOWNS AND CITIES: DUMFRIES

STATUS: A town in Dumfries and Galloway.

RIVER: Located on the **River Nith** which enters the Solway Firth just south of the town.

NAMES AND NICKNAMES: Dumfries is known as **Queen of the South**, which is also the name of the town's football team. **Doonhamers** (down homers) is a nickname for Dumfries residents.

MOTTO AND EMBLEM: "A Loreburn" was the motto of Dumfries, being a rallying cry used when the town was under attack. St Michael is the patron saint and emblem of Dumfries. He appears slaying a dragon on the town's coat of arms.

POPULATION: About 43,000.

KEY FACTS AND INDUSTRIES: The largest town in South West Scotland. Historically a market centre for the region. Its traditional industries are the manufacture of hosiery and knitwear. Robert Burns was resident here from 1791 until his death in 1796.

KEY DATES: circa **1160:** Lincluden Abbey built near the Nith. **1186:** Dumfries is created a Royal Burgh by King William the Lion. **1306:** Robert the Bruce murdered his rival the Red Comyn at Greyfriars church. **1393:** Dumfries receives its first known charter from King Robert III. **1744:** Parish church of St Michael built. **1796:** Robert Burns passed away here.

THINGS TO SEE:

• **Burns House**, where Robert Burns resided from 1791 to 1796.
• **St Michael's Church**, where Burns is buried.
• **Dumfries Windmill Museum**.
• **Dumfries Camera Obscura**, for an unusual view of the town.
• **Sweetheart Abbey**, six miles outside Dumfries.
• **Devorgilla Bridge (Old Bridge)**, a six-arched stone bridge across the Nith, c1430. It is named after the mother of King John Baliol. Her husband's heart was embalmed and buried at Sweetheart Abbey in 1269.
• **Midsteeple**, Dumfries' most prominent building, built as a courthouse and prison in 1707.

DUMFRIES

JOHN DUNS SCOTUS

Born in 1265 or 1266, possibly at Duns in Berwickshire, John Duns Scotus is one of the most important medieval philosophers and religious thinkers. His name was John Duns. "Scotus" was a nickname, thought to have been given to him because he was Scottish. He was ordained into the priesthood on March 17 1291 at Northampton, and is thought to have studied at Oxford, Cambridge and Paris; although it is at Paris that he gave his first lectures.

As with pretty much all of the philosophers of the time, the work of John Duns Scotus is about gaining a greater understanding of God and our relation to God. He wanted to show that we can come to know God through our knowledge of the world, and not just through God being shown to us in the form of a revelation.

His work is far too complicated and clever for us to fit it in here, and even to try and boil it down would be to do him a great disservice. He is one of the most important thinkers in the medieval period, right up there with Thomas Aquinas, and his contribution to the development of modern philosophy was enormous.

John Duns Scotus died in Cologne, Germany on November 8 1308, but left with his place in history assured, along with some absolutely fascinating arguments. Why don't you go and read some of his work?

John Duns Scotus
Philosopher

WHAT'S YOUR NAME?

DUNCAN
The forename Duncan is one of the oldest in Scotland and gave rise to the surname. The Duncan Clan came into being in the fourteenth century. Associated with Forfarshire and numerous in Aberdeenshire.

Dunlop
Surname from a place in Ayrshire, means 'fort on the bend'.

Elliot
Border surname from an Anglo-Saxon forename Elewald 'elf-ruler' or perhaps from the name Elias. Spellings include Eliot, Eliott and Elliott. According to a rhyme: "*Double L and single T descend from Minto and Wolflee. Double T and single L mark the race that in Stobs do dwell. Single L and single T, the Eliots of St Germains be, but the double T and double L, who they are nobody can tell*". Numerous in the Borders.

Erskine
From Erskine in Renfrewshire south of the Clyde.

Farquharson
Possibly descended from Farquhar, the fourth son of Alexander Shaw who held the Braes of Mar near the mouth of the Dee in Aberdeenshire. Numerous in north and east Scotland.

FERGUSON
From the Gaelic Mac Fhaerghuis 'son of the angry'. Probably derives from more than one family group. Fergusons in Argyll may descend from Fergus Mor Mac Erc, a king of the Dal Riata Scots. Fergusons of Ayrshire and Dumfriesshire may descend from Fergus, a Prince of Galloway. Fergusson with the double 's' is prevalent in Dumfriesshire.

FORBES
Clan of Banffshire, Buchan and Aberdeenshire. Descended from the thirteenth century John of Forbes. From the Gaelic forb-ais 'at the land'.

Fraser
Originating in France, the family came to Scotland in the late twelfth century and held lands at Keith in East Lothian. Associated with Inverness and the Great Glen. In earliest times the surname was Frysel or Fresle and may derive from a hamlet called Fresle in Normandy.

DAVID LIVINGSTONE

"Good afternoon, ladies and gentlemen. I am the continent of Africa, and I'd like to talk to you today about one of the finest Scotsmen I've ever had the pleasure of dealing with.

Often when white Europeans have come to visit me they haven't behaved awfully well. But I did like David Livingstone. Born in Blantyre in Lanarkshire on March 19 1813, he came to Africa in 1840 as a missionary. He's best known as an explorer, and as the first white European to see much of me.

He was the first white man to see the Victoria Falls on the Zambezi river between what's now Zambia and Zimbabwe, and he actually named them after your Queen Victoria. He was also the first white man to cross the entire width of southern Africa.

He travelled for a long time with his wife Mary, who he'd met in London, and their children, but she sadly died of malaria in 1862. He came home between 1864 and 1866 and told people all about the horrors of the slave trade, and raised enough money to come back in 1866.

His trip in 1866 was his last. His party was lost in 1871, but then an American called Stanley set out to find him. When he found him, he famously said, 'Dr Livingstone, I presume?' Livingstone died in 1873, and he was buried in Westminster Abbey, but I like to think his heart stayed here."

auritania

Guinea

Djibouti

Ethiopia

Togo
Ben   eria
Ghana

Somal

Central African Republic

Côte d'Ivoire   Cameroon

Equatorial Guinea   Uganda   Kenya

Democratic Republic of the Congo

Gabon   Rwanda

Congo   Burundi

Tanzania

Angola

Zambia   Malawi

Namibia   Zimbabwe   Mozambique

Botswana

79

Swaziland

MERMAID MEMORIES AND THE BENBECULA BLOBSTER

You never know what you might find washed up on the shore of Benbecula, an island in the Outer Hebrides.

In the early 1990s a carcass some 12 feet long was discovered on a beach in Benbecula by a 16 year old girl. Dubbed the Benbecula Blobster, it was a Loch Ness monster-type of creature with a curved body and much eaten away flesh. According to the girl, who found and photographed the creature, it had an absolutely disgusting smell.

But Benbecula's association with mysterious sea creatures all started back in the 1830s when a group of local women were collecting seaweed while their children played on the shore. As they played, the surprised children caught sight of a mysterious creature swimming in the water.

It resembled a tiny woman with the tail of a fish. In an attempt to catch its attention the children threw stones, one of which hit the creature's back before it disappeared under water.

A few days later, it is said the body of a tiny mermaid, the size of a child of about three or four was washed ashore. A folklorist called Alexander Carmichael heard the story and in 1900 he made note of a description from people who witnessed the discovery.

Its hair was described as long, dark and glossy and the creature had white, soft and tender skin. The lower part of the body was described as resembling a salmon without scales. A coffin was made for the creature by the local sheriff and was buried on the shore in one of the most well-attended funerals the island had ever seen. As late as the 1960s a folklorist had reported seeing the grave at a place called Nunton on the Benbecula shoreline.

TAY
- Length: 117 miles. Longest in Scotland. Seventh longest in the UK.
- Starts: Ben Lui.
- Ends: Firth of Tay, Dundee.
- Notable fact: Called the River Connonish, River Fillan and River Dochart before entering Loch Tay. It exits the loch as the River Tay.

SPEY
- Length: 107 miles.
- Starts: Loch Spey, a small loch in the Badenoch region.
- Ends: Spey Bay, eight miles east of Elgin.
- Notable fact: Scotland's fastest flowing river. Famed for whisky distilleries.

CLYDE
- Length: 106 miles.
- Starts: Lanarkshire.
- Ends: Firth of Clyde.
- Notable fact: Historically famed for its shipbuilding.

TWEED
- Length: 97 miles.
- Starts: Southern uplands.
- Ends: Berwick-upon-Tweed (England).
- Notable fact: Forms the border with England for 12 miles.

DEE
- Length: 87 miles.
- Starts: Cairngorms.
- Ends: Aberdeen.
- Notable fact: Royal Deesside is home to Balmoral Castle.

DON
- Length: 82 miles.
- Starts: Ladder Hills, Aberdeenshire.
- Ends: Aberdeen.
- Notable fact: One of two rivers ending their journey at Aberdeen.

Professor
C. Claggs

MONS MEG

"Yeah, that's right, I'm big and I'm bad, and you better not mess with me. I'm Mons Meg, the biggest cannon in Scotland. I'm 6 tons heavy, and I can fire a 150 kilogram cannonball more than 2 miles.

I was made in Belgium, like the best, and I was first tested in Mons in 1449. Philip the Good, the Duke of Burgundy gave me to King James II in 1457. I used to have a partner, but he didn't make it, I did though.

I could only be fired 10 times a day, because of the massive heat it took to get the cannonball to fly, but I'm still a pretty mighty weapon. I was difficult to use though, and because I was so heavy I could only move about 3 miles a day.

I saw some battles, but in the middle of the sixteenth century I was withdrawn from active duty and just fired to mark special occasions. One of these was in 1681 as a salute to the future King, James VII but that day I burst my barrel when I was fired. It was an English cannoneer working me then, and many Scottish people thought he did it on purpose.

For many years I lay unused in Edinburgh Castle, hidden away, and then I was moved to London in 1754. People campaigned to have me back in Scotland, particularly the famous novelist Sir Walter Scott, and so in 1829 I came back to Edinburgh, where I can still be seen today.

I'm pretty dangerous, even if I am getting on a bit, so everybody better stay out of my way. One day, you never know, I might fire again..."

WHEN WE WERE WELSH

The impressive, fortified rock of Dumbarton overlooks the Clyde estuary. It's an ancient site that played an important part in **Welsh** history. Yes you heard right – **Welsh** history, because this was the capital of the northern **Welsh**.

You see it was the capital of **Strathclyde**, a kingdom that spoke **Cumbric** or Old Welsh. This kingdom was known in Welsh as **Ystrad Clud** and its capital, Dumbarton was called **Allt Clud**, 'cliff of the Clyde'.

Strathclyde was the last surviving **Welsh** kingdom outside Wales.

At one time the lowlands below the Forth and Clyde spoke **Welsh**. Its people were **Y Gwyr y Gogledd**, meaning 'men of the north'.

These **Welsh** were here speaking their Celtic language in what we now call Scotland, long before the Gaelic Scots arrived from Ireland around 500 AD.

Welsh had been spoken throughout what is now England too. It was after all the language of the **Britons**. That's why **Allt Clud** was renamed **Dumbarton**. It means 'fort of the Britons'.

It was around 500 AD that Angles, along with Saxons from Germany and Denmark settled in what would become England - Angle Land. They also settled in what later became south east Scotland. Around 600 AD they defeated the northern Welsh Kingdom of Goddodin and seized its capital at **Din Eidyn** (Edinburgh).

Northumbrian English became the language of south east Scotland, but Welsh survived over in Strathclyde.

Strathclyde expanded south into Cumberland (**Cumbric land**) and possibly as far east as the dales of County Durham where the town of Bishop Auckland was anciently called **Allt Clud**.

From 600 AD to the time of the Norman Conquest, Strathclyde was under constant attack from Picts, Scots, Northumbrians and later Vikings and Normans. Successive conquering of the Kingdom eventually caused its **Welsh** language to disappear.

TWO OLD MEN WITH STACKS TO TALK ABOUT

OLD MAN OF STOER: (Shouting) HOY! (no reply) HOY! ARE YOU DEAF?

OLD MAN OF HOY: What...er...oh... (yawns)...sorry, I was asleep, and you are 83 miles away after all.

OLD MAN OF STOER: How is my fellow sandstone sea stack? What's the weather like up there in Orkney?

OLD MAN OF HOY: A bit windy here today and I'm feeling a wee bit tired. I'm not too well to be honest. It's hard work standing around all day at my age, especially when you're 449 feet tall. How's the weather there?

OLD MAN OF STOER: No need to rub it in about your height, you know how sensitive I am about being only 197 feet tall. It's raining down here on the Sutherland coast. Sorry you're not feeling good, what's up?

OLD MAN OF HOY: I'm feeling my age. Experts say I'm up to 400 years old and they think I might collapse at any moment. It's a wee bit depressing and it doesn't help with these rock climbers ascending me all the time.

OLD MAN OF STOER: It must be hard for you being so famous. You were brilliant in that Eurythmics video and Monty Python sketch.

OLD MAN OF HOY: Fame's not all it's cracked up to be.

OLD MAN OF STOER: Most people haven't heard of me. They keep confusing me with the Old Man of Storr, that rocky pinnacle near a mountain on Skye and he doesn't even live by the sea.

OLD MAN OF HOY: Any climbers ascended you recently?

OLD MAN OF STOER: Aye, one of my Fulmar friends squirted one the other day with stinking fish oil. Anyway I'll let you get some sleep. Shall we talk the same time tomorrow?

OLD MAN OF HOY: Aye, if I'm still standing.

ROBERT THE BRUCE

If you're looking for a high quality, low maintenance, fully functional Scottish national hero and king, why not consider choosing our brand new Robert the Bruce?

Bruce comes with a whole host of fantastic features including:

- Noble birth and title of Earl of Carrick.
- Military history stretching through many campaigns against the English.
- Iconic place in Scottish history.

But that's not all. Bruce held the title *Guardian of the Scottish people*, previously owned by William Wallace, though he did hold this title jointly with John Comyn who he killed at Dumfries in 1306.

Robert The Bruce

GUARDIAN OF THE SCOTTISH PEOPLE!!!

Crowned at Scone on March 25 1306, Bruce is a genuine authentic Scottish monarch, *a limited edition, one of a kind King of the Scots*. Bruce comes complete with his own legend too; yes it's that one about the persevering spider in that island-cave hiding place that inspired our man to defeat the English.

Bruce is a great military leader, with many significant victories under his regal belt. He is responsible for the victory at Bannockburn, along with the eventual driving of Edward II's forces from Scotland, making him a fantastic addition to any collection.

He defended Scotland from English attacks, and dispatched forces to Ireland to fight the English on Irish soil, at which point he was crowned High King of Ireland in 1316.

This means that for one low, low price you can acquire the crowns of two medieval European nations for the price of one.

Included with his reign are such advances as the Declaration of Arbroath in 1320 and the Treaty of Edinburgh-Northampton in 1328 which recognised the Bruce as King.

Finally, a death on the July 7 1329 is the perfect end to a fantastic reign that united Scotland. *This makes Robert a fantastic addition to any collection of European monarchs.*

THE COVENANTERS

Student: Hey, people keep talking to me about these Covenanters, but who were they?

History Man: They were Scottish Presbyterians who signed the National Covenant of 1638.

Student: So what was this National Covenant then?

History Man: Simply put, it was a contract between the Scottish people and God. It set out the things that Scottish Presbyterians would and wouldn't accept in the government of the Church and State.

Student: What kind of things did they want?

History Man: They wanted a Scottish Parliament and General Assembly of the Church of Scotland which were outside of the King's control, and they wanted to abolish bishops. They wanted a king governed by the law and responsible to the people.

Student: Abolish bishops? Why?

History Man: They thought that the bishops just did what the King wanted, and they wanted the King's control to be reduced. They also didn't like the prayer book which had been introduced in 1637.

Student: Why not? What was wrong with it?

History Man: It was an Anglican prayer book, and the Anglicans had the King as the head of the church. To Presbyterians this was too much like the Catholic Church they'd rejected. They thought that no man, not even a king, could be head of the church, only Jesus could.

Student: What happened then?

History Man: There were riots, and then in 1638 at the Glasgow Assembly the Covenanters abolished episcopacy, which is the government of the church by bishops.

Student: I bet the King didn't like that. What did he do in response?

History Man: No, he didn't like it, and he raised an army to invade Scotland, in what was known as the Bishops' Wars.

RUGBY IN SCOTLAND

Rugby has long been one of Scotland's favourite sports, one which is watched by thousands of people every week, whether they're watching the national team, one of the two professional teams, or one of more than 200 other teams who currently play rugby in this country.

Scottish rugby stretches back more than 150 years, with a game being played between Merchiston Castle School and the former pupils of Edinburgh Academy. The world's first rugby international was also played right here in Scotland, with the game in 1871 between Scotland and England on March 27 that year.

The Scottish Football Union, which would later become the **Scottish Rugby Union (SRU)**, was founded in March 1873. Scotland has a long and proud history of playing rugby, with the nation competing in every single rugby world cup, being a founding member of what has now become the Six Nations competition, not to mention feisty battles with the English, many of which have been won by Scotland.

When Scotland and England play one another in the Six Nations, the winning side is awarded the Calcutta Cup, a trophy which was made in India and first played for in the 1870s. It's not just about the internationals though, Scotland also has two professional teams, Glasgow Warriors and Edinburgh, who play in a league with Irish and Welsh sides. They also play in European competition with the best rugby teams from England, France, Ireland, Italy and Wales.

Apart from that, there are tons of other teams that play, and it's always a great day out for the spectators.

SCOTLAND PLACE-NAMES
WHAT DO THEY MEAN?

BONNYBRIDGE

Near Falkirk. Named from a bridge, but not for the bridge's beauty! Here the Gaelic word *Buan*, meaning 'swift', gave its name to the local stream.

BRECHIN

From a Celtic hero of Welsh origin, related to the name of Brecon in Wales.

CADZOW

Old name for Hamilton in the Clyde valley. Cadzow castle was the site of a hunting lodge belonging to the Kings of Stratchlyde, the last surviving Welsh speaking Kingdom in Scotland. Gaelic name means 'battle hollow'.

CAIRNGORMS

Named from a hill *Cairn Gorm*, Gaelic words meaning 'humped-hill' and 'blue'.

CAITHNESS

Far north eastern tip of Scotland was an ancient region of Pictland. *Cat* or *Cait* refers in some way to a 'cat'. *Ness* meaning 'headland' was added by the Vikings. Caithness was one of Scotland's historic counties.

CAMPBELTOWN

On the Kintrye peninsula. Named after Archibald Campbell, a seventeenth century Earl of Argyll.

CARNOUSTIE

Small town with a famous golf course on the coast of Angus. Gaelic *Carraig na ghiuthais* meaning 'rock of the fir tree'.

CASTLE DOUGLAS

Town in Dumfries and Galloway. Built in the eighteenth century on the site of a castle of the Douglas family.

CLACKMANNAN

Near Alloa where the Forth broadens before becoming the Firth of Forth. From the Gaelic *Clach* meaning stone, a large glacial rock. *Manan* was the ancient name for the surrounding district. Clackmannanshire was Scotland's smallest county.

O FLOWER OF SCOTLAND

O flower of Scotland,
When will we see your like again,
That fought and died for,
Your wee bit hill and glen,
And stood against him,
Proud Edward's army,
And sent him homeward,
Tae think again,

The hills are bare now,
And autumn leaves lie thick and still,
O'er land that is lost now,
Which those so dearly held,
And stood against him,
Proud Edward's army,
And sent him homeward,
Tae think again,

Those days are passed now,
And in the past they must remain,
But we can still rise now,
And be the nation again,
That stood against him,
Proud Edward's army,
And sent him homeward,
Tae think again,

Flower of Scotland, the unofficial Scottish national anthem, was written by Roy Williamson of the Corries and presented in 1967. It has been sung by the Scottish national rugby union team since 1974, and was adopted as Scotland's pre-game anthem for the Five Nations in 1990. In 2006 it won a national poll to choose a Scottish National Anthem with 41% of the vote.

WILLIAM WALLACE

William Wallace is a brave man,
Braver than he can be,
He fought the mean English,
And that's how he became history.

People from the English side
Bullied Wallace's poor family,
William's poor family
Never lived happily.

An English sheriff
Killed his wife
With one shot of his gun
Or stab from his knife.

An English king killed Wallace
And Wallace got hung, drawn and quartered.
The English won, the war all done
And the Scottish got slaughtered.

In 1297 is when the war started
And 1305 is when Wallace got captured.
But in the end, guess what happened –
Scotland was enraptured.

So you think England really won?
Naa, it was just a joke!
Scotland actually won
Without the old bloke.

Wallace is our hero
Like Robert Bruce and Mary Queen of Scots.
I can't name all of them
Because there are lots.

My Scotland
Young Writer

Name: Elizabeth Mackenzie
Age: 10
School: Lionel School, Isle of Lewis

GENERAL PATRICK GORDON

There have been many Scottish military heroes, but here's one you might not know, a Scottish hero of the Russian military, General Patrick Gordon.

Born March 31 1635 in Auchleuchries near Ellon, in Aberdeenshire, Patrick Gordon went on to be tutor, advisor and friend to one of Russia's most significant leaders, Peter the Great. Raised a Catholic, Gordon left Scotland in 1651 because he wanted to be able to practice his religion freely and he was afraid he wouldn't be able to do that in Scotland.

He entered a Jesuit College in Poland, but on leaving the college to return to Scotland he couldn't find passage home, so instead he stayed and entered military service in Poland. He served in the Swedish army of Charles X Gustav, capturing parts of Poland and Lithuania for Sweden. After serving for Sweden for some time he switched sides and joined the Polish army. He was captured by both sides whilst fighting for the other.

Then in 1661 he joined the Russian army under Tsar Alexis I, and served with distinction. In 1662, at the age of 27, he was given the rank of Lieutenant Colonel in the Russian army. He became a valuable asset for the Tsar as a confidential agent, and was sent to England on several occasions as an ambassador. He had a long and successful military career, rising to General-in-Chief, the second highest military rank in the Russian army.

He was a trusted advisor, teacher and friend to Peter the Great, assisting him in his development of Russia from a medieval nation to a modern European power, one whose will would shape the world for the next three centuries at least.

1

THE FLYING SCOTSMAN

Did you know there were actually three **Flying Scotsmen**.

1 **Flying Scotsman** is the name given to an express passenger rail service from London Kings Cross Station to Edinburgh Waverley and is a service that is still going strong today.

It has been in operation since 1862, though the steam locomotive service has now been replaced by electric powered trains.

In the early days the service was known as The Special Scotch **Express,** but was renamed The Flying Scotsman by the London North Eastern Railway (LNER) in 1924 though in truth it had been commonly known by this name since the 1870s.

2 **Flying Scotsman** is also the name given to an LNER Class A3 Pacific Steam locomotive.

This locomotive was built in Doncaster in 1923 and regularly served on the 10am London to Edinburgh service known as The Flying Scotsman. This beautiful steam locomotive represented the LNER at the British Empire Exhibition at Wembley, London in 1924 and 1925.

The engine ended service in 1963 but was restored at a locomotive works in Darlington as a show piece engine. It toured the United States in 1968-69 before returning home. It is currently owned by the National Railway Museum in York.

3 The third **Flying Scotsman** has nothing whatsoever to do with railways, but is of course the nickname for the famed experimental Scottish aviator, Ewan Noah I.M. MacKinitup.

On April 1, 1879, MacKinitup single-handedly flew from the island of Ailsa Craig off the coast of Ayrshire to the village of Glendoune on the mainland south of Girvan. This remarkable flight of 10 miles (16km) was achieved using a specially constructed pair of 12 feet long tarpaulin gannet wings that caused great consternation to the island's indigenous gannet colony. Very few witnessed this event however and there may actually be no truth in the story.

SCOTTISH STARS OF STAGE AND SCREEN
PART ONE

SIR SEAN CONNERY
One of the most famous Scotsmen on the planet, Connery is to many the definitive James Bond. Born in Edinburgh on August 25 1930 Sir Sean (who was actually born Thomas Sean Connery) worked as a bricklayer, a sailor in the Royal navy, and once had Matt Busby offer him a contract to play for Manchester United. He has starred in some of the biggest movies ever made, including seven James Bond films, *Highlander, Indiana Jones and the Last Crusade* and *The Hunt for Red October.* In 1987 Connery won an Oscar (Academy Award) for his supporting role in *The Untouchables* and has won two BAFTA Awards and three Golden Globes.

ALAN CUMMING
Born in Aberfeldy in 1965, Alan Cumming is among the most recognisable actors working today, but he's not just an actor. He's a film director, film producer, a writer, a singer and comedian. A pretty impressive list, I think you'll agree. He's been in big movies like *X-Men 2* and *Goldeneye*, as well as smaller independent films. His range and versatility mark him out as a really talented actor, and certainly one we enjoy watching!

KELLY MACDONALD
Kelly Macdonald has been gracing our screens since her appearance in *Trainspotting*, and her career shows no signs of slowing down. Born in Glasgow on February 23 1976, she has had a fruitful career on this side of the Atlantic, starring in films such as the Robert Altman directed *Gosford Park*, and the highly acclaimed TV drama *State of Play*. Since then she has become incredibly successful in America, appearing in *No Country For Old Men, Boardwalk Empire* and the final Harry Potter film to name just a few.

Sean Connery

Alan Cumming

elly MacDonald

THE RADICAL WAR OF 1820

One of the most remarkable events in Scottish history has to be the Radical War of 1820. There had been growing unrest in Britain, and in Scotland in particular, for many years, but it all came to a head in one week which could have turned the whole country upside down.

On April 1 1820, signs appeared in the streets of Glasgow, signs written by the Committee of Organisation for Forming a Provisional Government. The signs asked people to go out on strike in order to support their demands for reform. They had signed a proclamation stating their plan to split Scotland from England and take control of the country.

On Monday April 3, work stopped across central Scotland. In Stirlingshire, Dumbartonshire, Renfrewshire, Lanarkshire and Ayrshire people laid down their tools. More than 60,000 people went out on strike.

At the same time, a group of 30 radicals led by John Craig set out to march on the Carron Company ironworks in Falkirk, in the hope of getting weapons to fight with. They were, however, intercepted by the police and arrested.

The next day, Duncan Turner assembled 60 men to march on the ironworks, led by Andrew Hardie. Hardie was given the torn half of a piece of card to identify himself. Unfortunately for them the same day a group of soldiers was sent to protect the ironworks.

The two groups met early on April 5 and there was a battle. Nineteen of the radicals were captured, and four wounded. At the same time 25 men were marching from Strathaven to meet an army at Cathkin, but they turned back fearing an ambush, 25 were captured.

In the end, 88 men were convicted of treason for their involvement in the failed revolution. The strangest thing about the whole thing is that apparently the rising was a set up by government agents, trying to root out the radicals!

WHAT'S YOUR NAME?

Gordon

Anglo-Norman clan associated with Strathbogie. Appeared in the Borders in the twelfth century and named from Gordon in the Merse region of Berwickshire. Robert the Bruce granted them land at Strathbogie in Aberdeenshire.

Graham

Border surname of Dumfriesshire. Arch enemies of the Northumberland Robsons, Grahams are descended from Normans who settled at Grantham in Lincolnshire. De Grantham was shortened to De Graham when they settled in Scotland in the twelfth century. In the seventeenth century many Grahams were transported to Ireland along with many Elliots, Kerrs and Armstrongs.

Grant

Originally called Le Grant and named from the Norman-French Le Grand, the family claim descent from Kenneth MacAlpin the ninth century King of the Picts and Hakon Siggurdsson a tenth century ruler of Norway. Grants have lived in Strathspey since the early 1300s and are still numerous in north east Scotland.

Gray

Norman in origin, the Grays (also *Grey*) were present in Northumberland by the end of the eleventh century. A Gray was a mayor of Berwick in 1250. The surname spread to Scotland and particularly Lanarkshire.

Gunn

Clan of Viking origin descended from Norse chieftain Gunni who settled in Caithness in the twelfth century. Numerous in Caithness and Orkney.

Haig

Border family of Norman origin originally called De Haga. Petrus De Haga, owner of Bemersyde near Melrose was mentioned in 1162. A fortified house there still belongs to this family.

Hamilton

Clan of Norman origin descended from Walter Fitz Gilbert of Hambledon. Mentioned in the Paisley Abbey charter of 1294. Probably named from Hamilton in Leicestershire. By the fifteenth century their lands included Cadzow in Lanarkshire which they renamed Hamilton.

Hay

Clan of Norman origin associated with Aberdeenshire, Banffshire and Moray. Thought to be named from a place in Normandy called La Haye.

TRADITIONAL SCOTTISH SWEETS

"Hello there boys and girls, and welcome to my sweet shop. It's a traditional Scottish sweet shop, and I've got lots of traditional Scottish sweets for wee lads and lassies to feast on.

Would you like some Edinburgh rock? Made in the nineteenth century by Alexander Ferguson, it was a great success and ended up making him very rich indeed, this really is the taste of Edinburgh.

What about you there? How would you like some traditional Scottish tablet? No, it's supposed to be hard, a bit like a hard fudge, and it's made from sugar, condensed milk and butter. It's a very traditional sweet for little Scottish boys and girls to enjoy, I'm sure you'd love some, wouldn't you?

What about some fudge for you? They say that Scottish fudge comes from someone who made their tablet too soft. I think it's delicious though, the way it melts in your mouth.

How about some traditional Scottish macaroons? They used to be made from cold leftover mashed potato and sugar loaf but now they're made with sugar, water and egg whites to make that lovely tasty centre, and then covered in coconut. Try one, they're really lovely.

I'm sure you'd like some star rock or "starry" as they call it in Kirriemuir. It's a lovely rock, not as hard as other kinds of rock you'll have tried, and it usually comes in bags of four inch sticks.

Or some shortbread? Try it, it's such a simple food but they say that the recipe for it was actually refined by Mary Queen of Scots. In fact, petticoat tails are named for Queen Mary herself.

So eat your fill, children, everybody loves it in my sweet shop..."

DECLARATION OF ARBROATH

It's been compared to the American Declaration of Independence which it partly inspired, this famous document is an emotive statement of Scotland's right to independence.

Dated April 6 1320 and composed in Latin at Arbroath Abbey, it was drafted for the King, Earls and Barons of Scotland.

It is essentially a letter to the Pope, because in those days if the Pope recognised your independence it was sanctioned by God.

But there were two problems. Firstly the Pope had acknowledged the English overlordship of Edward I in Scotland in 1305. Secondly the Pope excommunicated Scotland's King, Robert the Bruce, for murder in 1306.

The declaration asserts Scotland's ancient and unbroken status as a Kingdom and argued that Scotland had special protection from St Andrew.

It said that Scotland had lived in peace until the reign of Edward and remarked upon Edward's deeds of:

cruelty, massacre, violence, pillage, arson, imprisoning prelates, burning down monasteries, robbing and killing monks and nuns,

It fiercely declared its loyalty to Robert but introduced the concept that the relationship between a king and his people must be by mutual consent, a revolutionary idea in an age where kings ruled by divine right:

If he should give up what he has begun, and agree to make us or our kingdom subject to the King of England... we should exert ourselves at once to drive him out as our enemy and a subverter of his own rights and ours, and make some other man who was well able to defend us our King,

As a tactic the declaration tried to convince the Pope that recognizing Scotland's independence would free up the armies of both England and Scotland to fight for the Pope in the Holy Land.

It didn't work.

The pope was unmoved, but the declaration still remains a defining moment in the history of Scotland.

HEART OF MIDLOTHIAN

What is the **Heart of Midlothian**?

Midlothian is a historic county of Scotland encompassing Edinburgh.

Historically the **Heart of Midlothian** was the site of a fifteenth century tollbooth that stood at the administrative heart of Edinburgh. It also served as a prison and was a place for public executions.

In 1818 this prison was made famous by the Sir Walter Scott novel *Heart of Midlothian* which is regarded as one of the best of his Waverley Novels.

The novel features a riot in which a Captain Porteous is captured and lynched by a mob after they storm the **Heart of Midlothian** prison, following the captain's brutal treatment of a prisoner who had helped a fellow captive escape.

Today the **Heart of Midlothian** is the name given to the heart-shaped mosaic in the pavement of the Royal Mile near the west door of St Giles Cathedral. It is thought to mark the site of the prison doorway where executions took place.

You may occasionally see people spitting on the heart. This is an old tradition that is now thought to bring good luck and guarantee your return to Edinburgh one day. Historically, spitting on the site was a public show - particularly by criminals - of derision for the old prison and the executions that took place there.

Heart of Midlothian is of course also noted as the name of one of Edinburgh's famous football clubs, known as **Hearts** for short. The football club crest is based on the mosaic in the Royal Mile.

Today Edinburgh's association with Midlothian is largely historic, since the city was officially detached from the Lothians following local government boundary reorganisations in 1974.

TERRIERS OF SCOTLAND

Prepare to be *terrier*fied! This is one of the most terrierfying stories in this whole book, because it's all about terriers, terriers from Scotland.

One of the most *terrier*fying types of terrier is the **Scottish Terrier**, sometimes called the Aberdeen Terrier. This *terrier*fying terrier has become famous as the dog in the board game Monopoly. Franklin Delano Roosevelt, the 32nd President of America had one too!

If that's not *terrier*fying enough, how about the **Cairn Terrier**? It was a Cairn Terrier who played Toto in *The Wizard of Oz*. If that's not enough, they're thought to be the oldest type of British terrier, having been around for more than 500 years.

Ok, ok, I can see you're not *terrier*fied yet. But what about this? The **Dandie Dinmont Terrier** is the only breed of dog named after a fictional character; it got its name from Dandie Dinmont in the Sir Walter Scott novel *Guy Mannering*. It's a *terrier*fyingly shaped terrier too, with a very long body, but very short legs.

No, you're still not *terrier*fied. Well, what about the **Skye Terrier**? Some people say they come from a cross-breeding of Maltese dogs and local dogs after a Spanish shipwreck on Skye in the seventeenth century. The famous Greyfriars Bobby was a Skye Terrier.

Right, this is my last chance to truly *terrier*fy you. The **West Highland White Terrier** is a *terrier*fying terrier, having been picked by many companies to advertise their products, including dog food, whisky, and featuring in many different TV shows and movies.

Ok, I give up, you can't be *terrier*fied by the *terrier*fying terriers and anyway, they're just too cute for that!

SPEAKING BRAID SCOTS

Scots is the language spoken throughout most of Scotland. Some regard it as a language in its own right. Others consider it a dialect of English, but either way there is no doubting its close relationship to English.

Scots has been spoken in lowland Scotland for more than ten centuries and in most of the Highlands and some of the islands it has now largely replaced Scots Gaelic as the native tongue.

The language (or dialect) of the lowland Scots can also be called Lallans and until the fifteenth century it was called Ynglis or Inglis.

By the fifteenth century it was simply called Scottish, with the Gaelic language of the Highlands then known as Erse.

It was Angle (English) settlers from the Kingdom of Northumbria who first brought the form of English we now call Scots to what is now Scotland. These Northumbrians settled as far north as the Firth of Forth.

From around the thirteenth century, Scots came to be increasingly spoken beyond the lowlands. Its spread northwards was encouraged by the development of new urban centres called "burghs" where Scots, rather than Gaelic was spoken.

As with the English spoken in England, many Viking and later Norman-French words were introduced to the Scots language overtime. Nevertheless Scots retained many old links to the Angle speech of the Northumbrians but in time developed or retained distinctive features of its own.

In the 1600s many lowland Scots settled in Northern Ireland where a new variation of the Scots language called Ulster Scots developed.

Scots is recognised as a regional language by the UK government under the European Charter for Regional or Minority Languages, but it is the habitual speakers of **Braid Scots** and historic literary works such as those of Burns and Walter Scott that do so much to keep the Scots language alive and well.

IONA

Iona lies a mile off the coast of Mull and has long been a centre of Scottish spirituality and Christianity. Measuring 3.4 miles by 1.5 miles, few places of comparative size can have played such a major role in Scotland's history.

It was here in 563 AD that the Irish Abbot, **Saint Columba** established a monastery that played a major part in the conversion of Britain to Christianity.

At that time Iona was situated in the Dal Riata, a region inhabited by Gaelic speakers with close ties to Ireland. It became the centre of Christian Scotland from where Columba and his followers set off to covert the Picts to Christianity.

Iona's influence went further. The Iona monk, St Aidan went on to establish the monastery of **Lindisfarne** in Northumbria from which the northern English were converted.

Iona was a centre of learning and Christian art. The wheeled circular Celtic cross may have developed here and the scriptorium at Iona may have been involved in making the eighth century **Book of Kells** for which Ireland is renowned.

Iona suffered at the hands of Viking raiders between 794 AD and 825 AD but survived and its mystique and influence lived on. In the ninth century, as the Kingdom of Scotland emerged as Alba, the Scottish Kings claimed to have their roots on the island.

It soon became a centre for Royal burials. It is known that Kings Kenneth MacAlpin, Donald II, Malcolm I, Duncan I, Macbeth and Donald III all have their final resting place here. A document of 1549 even claims that 48 Scottish Kings, 8 Norwegian Kings and 4 Irish Kings are buried on Iona.

A nunnery and new abbey was built here in the early 1200s and the abbey survives. It was re-glazed and re-roofed between 1938 and 1965 and is still used for daily services and Christian teaching.

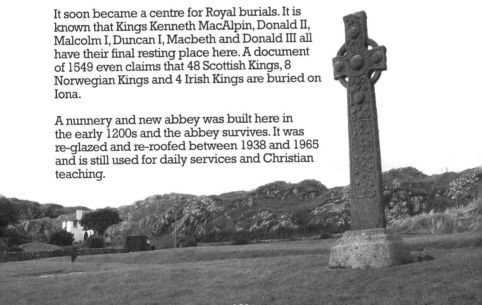

11

THE BENNIE RAILPLANE

"Ladies and gentlemen, my name is George Bennie, and I'm here today to talk to you about my invention, one which will revolutionise public transportation not just in Scotland, but all across the world. It is called the Bennie Railplane, and in my opinion it represents the greatest development in transportation since the birth of the railway.

The Railplane is carried on two elevated tracks, one above and one below the cigar-shaped carriage. The carriage itself is driven at each end by a four bladed propeller, powered with an electric motor. This allows the Railplane to glide seamlessly to its destination, passing above the heads of passengers on old-fashioned trains.

The system will allow the Railplane to travel at amazing speeds of up to 150 miles an hour, meaning that the journey between Glasgow and Edinburgh could be achieved in less than 20 minutes. On top of this, each Railplane carriage will be fitted out for the comfort of our passengers, and will allow them to reach their destination in speed and in style.

I have constructed an experimental test track for the Railplane at Milngavie, and I invite any members of the public or press to come and try it. You will be amazed, I assure you, by the speed, safety and comfort of the Railplane, the form of transport which I am absolutely convinced is going to change the world in which we live."

George Bennie's Railplane test track opened in 1930, largely funded by George himself. He spent the next 7 years trying to get funding to build a fully working Railplane system, but could find no financial backers, and was declared bankrupt in 1937. The train from Glasgow to Edinburgh takes 50 minutes.

SCOTLAND PLACE-NAMES
WHAT DO THEY MEAN?

COLDSTREAM

On the Scottish side of the Tweed. Refers to the 'chilly river crossed by a ford'. There is a bridge here today.

COMRIE

Perthshire village. Gaelic *Comar* meaning 'confluence'. The River Earn and River Lednock meet here. Situated on a highland fault line, it is called 'shaky village' because it's the most active place for earthquakes in Britain.

COWDENBEATH

Town in Fife north of Dunfermeline, means 'birch lands' (Gaelic *Beith*) 'belonging to someone called Cowden'.

CROMARTY

On the Black Isle peninsula near Inverness. Gaelic name means 'place by the bend'. Partly gave its name to the historic county of Ross and Cromarty.

CULLODEN

Town and battle site east of Inverness. From *Cul* and *Iodair* 'ridge' and 'small pool'.

CUMBERNAULD

Scottish new town of some 50,000 inhabitants. The Gaelic name of the original village, *comar na allt* means 'meeting of the streams'.

DALKEITH

Town south east of Edinburgh. A Welsh name *Dol Coed* meaning 'field wood'.

DINGWALL

Situated on the Cromarty Firth. Viking name means 'assembly field', the site of a Viking parliament called a Thing. Has the same root as the Tynwald, the parliament of Viking origin on the Isle of Man.

DOLLAR

Clackmannanshire town with Welsh name *dol ar* meaning 'ploughed field'.

STRONTIUM

"Awright you toilets, I'm Strontium, and you'd better not mess with me. That's right, I'm a metal, and I might not be very hard (in fact, I'm softer than Calcium) but I'm very reactive. I'll react to anything, so you'd just better be careful you don't upset me. I react to air, I react to water, you look at me funny and I'll react, I'm so reactive!

There's a lot of me about too, I make up 0.04% of the Earth's crust, so you'd better watch out, that's all I'm saying. What am I doing in a Scotland book? Well, I'll have you know, I am actually Scottish. The reason I'm called Strontium? I was discovered in the lead mines near Strontian, in Sunart, Lochaber way back in 1790.

So yeah, I'm a Scottish metal, the most Scottish of all the metals. I was named by Thomas Charles Hope who was professor of chemistry at the University of Glasgow in 1793, that's how tough I am. I'm everywhere too; you need me, because I'm used in cathode ray tubes to stop loads of X-rays escaping.

Ok, so cathode ray tubes are on the decline, all you people with your fancy plasma screen TVs don't need old Strontium any more, or that's what you think. But I'm not just in TVs, I'm all over, I'm used in neuroscience experiments and in distress flares. I'm everywhere; I'm even in your bones.

That's right, I'm in your bones, and what's more I can be used as a medicine to make your bones stronger. Even more than that, one isotope of me, Strontium-90, is radioactive, so you'd definitely better beware.

I'm going now, but you'd better remember not to mess with me. I'm the Scottish metal!"

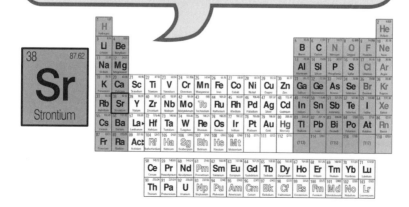

ABERDEEN FC

1967 WASHINGTON WHIPS
(Aberdeen Dist., Scotland)

One of Scottish football's most successful clubs, Aberdeen FC has been around since April 14 1903, when it was formed by a merger of three other football teams, Aberdeen, Victoria United and Orion. The club played its first match on August 15 1903, a 1-1 draw against Stenhousemuir.

Elected to the Scottish Second Division in 1904, playing first in black and gold stripes (which they would keep until the Second World War) they finished seventh in their first season, but were elected to join the Scottish First Division for 1905-06. It is a league they've been members of ever since, an honour they share with Celtic and Rangers.

First team coach Donald Colman came up with one of the great innovations of football whilst at Aberdeen. He decided that it would be good if he could see the feet of the players, so he invented the dugout, which was then copied by Everton and took off around the world. Aberdeen won its first league title in 1954-55 under the management of ex-Sunderland striker Dave Halliday.

In 1967 the club sent its players to America to play as the Washington Whips in the summer United Soccer Association league, a league in which European and South American teams played for American sides.

Aberdeen's golden age was undoubtedly during the late 1970s and 1980s, when Alex Ferguson was the manager. Ferguson led the club to three league titles, four Scottish Cups, one Scottish league cup, one Cup Winners Cup and one European Super Cup, before leaving to manage Manchester United.

Aberdeen are undoubtedly one of the great sides in Scottish football, one with a massive history and influence on the game, and although their last major silverware was the Scottish League Cup in 1996 we certainly hope there'll be more just around the corner.

ENGLAND 2-3 SCOTLAND

"This is the BBC in London. The news today, April 15 1967. Today at Wembley Stadium England, the World Champions were beaten 3-2 by Scotland, in an unexpected display of footballing skill by the visitors.

In front of a capacity crowd of almost 100,000 people, including almost 30,000 from north of the border, the ability of the Scots was there for all to see. Although Denis Law scored Scotland's first goal in the twenty-seventh minute, the real praise for Scotland's performance must go to the inventive and playful performance of Scotland's midfielder, Mr Jim Baxter.

'Slim Jim' showed his character at one point by playing 'keepy-uppy' by the corner flag, yet Scotland's control of the game is not fully reflected in their goals. Bobby Lennox put Scotland 2-0 up with 12 minutes to go, but Bobby Charlton kept the game alive for the World Champions by pulling one back in the eighty-fourth minute.

Scotland again went two goals ahead through McCalliog before being pegged back by England's World Cup Final hero Geoff Hurst, but the gentlemen in blue were not to be denied, and the match finished in an historic victory for Scotland.

The Scottish fans could not contain their emotion, and many invaded the Wembley pitch. It has been an exceptional performance of the Scottish team today, in a result which will certainly be remembered for many years to come."

ENGLAND
2-3
SCOTLAND

ENGLAND
2-3
SCOTLAND

THE BATTLE OF CULLODEN

1746

BonnyCharlie Making nite attack on @DukeOfCumberland's forces at Nairn on @GeorgeMurray's advice - Hope it goes well

BonnyCharlie Nite attack failed @GeorgeMurray took his troops home, got to w8 till the morning to fight @DukeOfCumberland now

DukeOfCumberland Set off for battle at Culloden against @BonnyCharlie and @GeorgeMurray – looking forward to it #battleculloden

BonnyCharlie Set up for #battleculloden between walls of Culloden enclosures in nrth and Culloden Park in sth. Last stand for #jacobiterebellion45

GeorgeMurray @BonnyCharlie fighting battle in wrong place – too easy for @DukeOfCumberland's artillery

DukeOfCumberland Can't believe luck @BonnyCharlie set up perfect for my cannons #battleculloden

BonnyCharlie @DukeOfCumberland firing on us. I blame @GeorgeMurray

GeorgeMurray said @BonnyCharlie was wrong – #battleculloden going badly

DukeOfCumberland @BonnyCharlie + @GeorgeMurray's Jacobites charging now. 2 ltl 2 late I'm afraid

BonnyCharlie #battleculloden lost – am fleeing Culloden now

DukeOfCumberland Instructing commanders no mercy to @BonnyCharlie and @GeorgeMurray forces - #battleculloden big victory for @GeorgeTheSecond

GeorgeTheSecond Victory at #battleculloden good. @DukeOfCumberland crushing @BonnyCharlie. Scotland's mine Charles

BonnyCharlie Going to flee Scotland dressed as woman – End of #jacobiterebellion45.

17
KELPIES OR WATER HORSES

If you see a lone figure or solitary creature standing by a Scottish loch, river or stream, please be wary, it may be a Kelpie. That was advice Highlanders took very seriously in times gone by. Kelpies, perhaps deriving their name from the Gaelic *Colpach* meaning 'colt', are mythical water horses and are very dangerous.

These shape-shifting creatures may transform into beautiful young ladies on the waterside, enticing young men to death by drowning. They may appear as innocent-looking ponies offering children rides on their back. Once mounted, children are stuck fast as the horse takes them to the depths of the water to eat them alive, leaving only their livers to float to the surface.

Said to have seal-like skin, which once touched would lead to a drowning-death. One story retells how a Kelpie drowned nine young children in one go whilst the tenth escaped by cutting his finger off with a knife after touching the creature's nose.

Related to Kelpies and also found in Scotland were the mythical water bulls and Boobries, which are diving water birds the size of 17 eagles. Boobries love eating cows, sheep and otters.

Another form of Water Horse with a similar appetite to the Kelpies, were the deadly Each Uisge (pronounced 'ech-ooshkya') found in sea lochs and fresh water lochs. These creatures usually transformed into the shape of human males. Water weeds in their hair are the often only indication the person is not quite who he seems.

The legendary Kelpie of Raasay, an island off Skye was most likely an Each Uisge. It took the life of a blacksmith's daughter who got revenge by enticing the creature with the smell of a roasted sow. He took the creature's life by piercing it with two freshly cast red-hot hooks which turned the beast to jelly.

SCOTTISH BARONIAL

Scottish Baronial is a kind of architectural style. Developing in Scotland in the nineteenth century it was part of the architectural movement known as Gothic revival, but had a distinctly Scottish flavour.

Scottish Tower houses of Medieval times provided inspiration for the Scottish Baronial style beginning with Sir Walter Scott's house of 1816 at Abbotsford near Melrose in the Scottish Borders. Scott and his successors made a conscious effort to enhance Scotland's distinct identity through its architecture.

The French Chateaux of the Loire region also seem to have played their part in inspiring the Scottish baronial style, but while Scottish Baronial buildings are often elegant, they retain a more rugged castle-like appearance than their continental counterparts.

Scottish Baronial buildings can be public buildings or private homes and are usually built with massive solid local stone. They can range from relatively modest houses to massive castles such as Balmoral which had been reconstructed in the Scottish Baronial style by the 1840s.

Notable architects who worked in the style were William Burn, Robert Adam and Gillespie Graham, but the leader of the movement was undoubtedly the Edinburgh-born architect David Bryce (1803-1876) who is said to have firmly established the style in Scotland. Bryce designed more than 230 buildings during his career.

Features of the Scottish Baronial style include uneven roof lines broken by tall rounded towers and rounded projecting turrets called bartisans.

Rounded towers are often topped by pointed roofs that resemble witches' hats and draw comparisons to the chateaux and castle architecture of France and Germany.

Other features might include triangular gable ends with jagged edges called crow-steps or corbie steps from the Scots word for crow, but perhaps it is the solid stone nature of these buildings in their distinctively Scottish settings that make the Scottish Baronial Style so unique and individual.

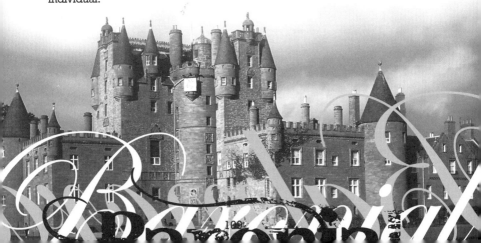

19
April

A SCOTTISH YEAR

In the winter ye hiv
Grey skies, rain and snow,
The highlands are freezing,
The city is cold, the snow is falling.
In the summer ye hiv
A wee bit a sunshine and they're
Away tae the beach.
Ye still get mer rain,
Ye still get thunder, but
The landmarks and castles
Are great,
The fitball stadiums
Are amazing.
Scotland is a great place tae stae,
But
The English are rite next door.

My Scotland
Young Writer

Name: Jordan James McMeekin
Age: 11
School: Camstradden Primary School, Glasgow

STATUS: City.

RIVER: Located on the north bank of the **Firth of Tay**. It is linked to Fife on the south bank by the Tay Road Bridge and Tay Rail Bridge.

NAMES AND NICKNAMES: Known as the "city of jam, jute and journalism" from some of its most notable industries. It was sometimes called "Juteopolis".

MOTTO AND EMBLEM: Dundee has two Latin mottos *Dei Donum* (Gift of God) and *Prudentia et Candore* (with thought and purity). The city's arms feature two dragons and white Madonna Lillies. The Madonna is a patron saint of the city.

POPULATION: Around 152,000, Scotland's fourth largest city.

KEY FACTS AND INDUSTRIES: Dundee was famed as a textile town, particularly as a processor of the vegetable fibre called Jute. The publishing firm of D.C. Thomson is one of Dundee's most famous institutions publishing the *Dundee Courier, Evening Telegraph, Sunday Post* and the children's comics the *Beano* and *Dandy*. The city is also famous for marmalade and Dundee Cakes.

KEY DATES: DATE: 1191: King William the Lion makes Dundee a Royal Burgh. **1291**: The forces of Edward I of England seize Dundee. **1327**: Robert Bruce grants Dundee a charter. **1545**: A defensive wall is built around Dundee. **1797**: Marmalade is allegedly invented in Dundee in this year. **1853**: St Paul's Cathedral is built in Dundee. **1879**: The Tay Rail Bridge Disaster. **1881**: Dundee University founded. **1966**: Tay Road Bridge opens.

THINGS TO SEE:

• **RRS *Discovery***, Captain Scott's Antarctic explorer ship beneath the Tay Bridge.
• **Verdant Works**, recreated Jute Works visitor attraction.
• **Statues of Desperate Dan and Minnie the Minx**, from *The Dandy* children's comic.
• **McManus Art Gallery and Museum**, a magnificent Gothic revival building that originally opened in 1867.
• **Statue of Admiral Duncan**, hero of the Battle of Camperdown.

DUNDEE

JOHN MUIR
AMERICA'S FIRST
ENVIRONMENTALIST

"I hate the environment, me. Hate it. Birds and bees, little bugs getting in the way, animals carrying diseases all over the place, foxes ripping open the bins when you put them out on a night. It's a nightmare.

It'd be better if someone just took it in hand and decided to concrete over everything. Bulldoze all the trees, poison all the rivers, and turn the whole place into a car park. Then we could use all of the natural resources for ourselves, rather than worrying about the fate of some rare type of squirrel or rat.

Sadly, not everybody agrees with me on this. One person in particular who would have said I was talking nonsense was John Muir, the Scot who became a leading environmentalist in America.

He was born in Dunbar on April 21 1838, but he moved to America when he was just 11 years old. His family bought a farm in Wisconsin. He went to university, and then to Canada to avoid being drafted into the union army, and returned a changed man. He became interested in nature, and writing, and took this as his career.

He also began to be a political activist, and was crucial in establishing Yosemite as a national park, and founded the Sierra Club, which has gone on to be one of the most influential environmental pressure groups in American politics.

I suppose he did some good stuff, and I can see the point of Yosemite, so maybe Muir was right on this one. Just don't tell him I said that…"

SIERRA CLUB
FOUNDED 1892

John Muir

BORDER REIVERS

Student: Okay Mr History Man, what's today's lesson?

History Man: Well I thought I'd talk about the Border Reivers.

Student: What were they then?

History Man: They were a bit like the Highland clans, but lived in the border region of Scotland. They were most active in the 1500s, and could be found on the English side of the border as well.

Student: I guess the English and Scottish clans fought each other?

History Man: Sometimes, but it was more complex than that. Some English clans fought one another; some Scottish clans fought one another. It was not unknown for clans on opposite sides of the border to unite against a common enemy.

Student: It sounds rather lawless to me.

History Man: It was. At the Battle of Flodden in 1513, Border Reivers from both nations banded together and stripped the slain of both armies of their possessions.

Student: Not very nice. No sense of loyalty.

History Man: Loyalty to the family came first. The English historian Trevelyan said they were cruel, coarse savages, slaying each other like beasts but he remarked that many were poets of the highest order. Interestingly Sir Walter Scott was descended from a Border Reiver family.

Student: So Scott was a Border Reiver surname, what other names did they have?

History Man: Douglas, Johnston, Armstrong, Eliott, Carlyle, Maxwell, Hepburn, Pringle, Kerr, Hume and Graham were among the prominent Scottish names while names in England included Charlton, Robson, Milburn and more Armstrongs.

Student: No MacDonalds, MacKenzies or MacLeods then?

History Man: No, those are Gaelic names. The Borders was an English speaking region.

Student: So what happened to these Reivers in the end?

History Man: Their way of life ended when James VI of Scotland became James I of England in 1603. He transported some of the worst offending Reivers to Ireland.

NORTH BERWICK WITCHES

In the winter of 1590 a group of supposed witches from North Berwick are said to have gathered at Leith near Edinburgh. One was armed with a terrified cat with pieces of human flesh from the body of a hanged man tied to its paws. The cat was tossed into the icy waters of the Firth of Forth casting a spell, causing a sudden storm that wrecked a vessel in the ensuing winds.

It was not the vessel the witches had in mind. The target of their dark art was the Royal ship which returned safely to Scotland from Norway with James VI and his new bride, Anne of Denmark on board.

The alleged activities of the North Berwick witches were uncovered by David Seton, Deputy Bailiff of Tranent near Edinburgh. He noticed that one of his maid servants, Gilly Duncan had been behaving strangely and was regularly leaving his house at night without permission.

He tortured her with thumbscrews and although she kept her silence, he discovered she had a mole on her neck. He considered this proof that she was witch. Eventually she is said to have confessed to being a member of a witches' coven and revealed the identity of five members.

The plot to murder King James was uncovered, or so it is said, and the coven's leader was revealed to be Francis Hepburn, the Earl of Boswell. The other witches were revealed to be Euphemia MacLean, (a daughter of Lord Cliftonhall), a schoolmaster called John Fian, a woman called Barbara Napier and a midwife called Agnes Simpson.

All the witches, except Boswell, who fled to Naples, were tortured and executed in Edinburgh. Before her death Agnes Simpson revealed that on Halloween 1590 up to 200 witches had gathered at North Berwick church with the Devil in attendance.

SCOTTISH SNOOKER WORLD CHAMPIONS

Scotland has produced a whole host of great sportsmen, a number of whom have gone on to become World Champions in their particular sports. One sport in which Scots have had a lot of success is snooker, with Scotland producing four world champions.

Walter Donaldson

Walter Donaldson was born in Coatbridge on January 4 1907, and became the first Scottish World Champion when he beat Fred Davis at Leicester Square Hall, London in the 1947. Amazingly he was only the second man to ever win the World Championship, his predecessor Joe Davis (Fred's brother) having won the previous 15. He won the World Championship once more in 1950, and appeared in eight finals between 1947 and 1954.

Stephen Hendry

A true legend, Hendry became the youngest ever World Champion in 1990, and went on to win seven World Championships, including four famous finals against Jimmy White in the early 1990s. Born in South Queensferry January 13 1969, he was world number one for eight consecutive years during the 1990s. He holds world records for ranking titles (36), competitive century breaks (756), and jointly with Ronnie O'Sullivan, the most competitive 147 breaks (10).

John Higgins

Born May 18 1975 in Wishaw, John Higgins has been World Champion four times in 1998, 2007, 2009 and 2011. Up to the end of the 2010-2011 season, he is fourth overall in the modern era (since the tournament went back to being a knockout in 1969) behind Stephen Hendry (7 wins), Steve Davis (6) and Ray Reardon (6).

Graeme Dott

Born May 12 1977 in Larkhall, Graeme Dott won the World Championship in 2006. He has also featured in two other World Championship finals up to the end of the 2010-2011 season, losing against Ronnie O'Sullivan in 2001 and Neil Robertson in 2010.

THIRTY SCOTTISH CASTLES

CAWDOR CASTLE

This castle, 10 miles east of Inverness, is an impressive tower house noted for its spectacular gardens. Parts of the castle are thought to date back to 1380, but the earliest documentation states that it was commenced in 1454. The castle is built around a Holly Tree that has been dated to 1372. The castle currently belongs to a member of the Campbell family.

COMLONGON CASTLE

Situated about six miles south east of Dumfries this red sandstone tower house castle of the fifteenth century was extended in the nineteenth century to include a mansion of Scottish baronial style. The building is now used as a hotel. The castle was built by Cuthbert of Cockpool who died in 1493. The walls of the castle are four metres thick in places.

CRAIGEVAR CASTLE

This is a tower house castle of pink-stone near Alford in Aberdeenshire built by William Forbes alias "Danzig Willie" in 1626. It is claimed to be a source of inspiration for the Walt Disney fairytale castle.

CULZEAN CASTLE

Starting life as a small tower house in the 1400s this historic home of the Scottish Kennedy Clan was transformed into a magnificent stately castle overlooking the Ayrshire coast by the architect Robert Adam from 1777.

DIRLETON CASTLE

The impressive ruins of this medieval castle are located on a rocky outcrop near North Berwick in East Lothian. The castle was commenced by John De Vaux in 1240 but was acquired by the Ruthven family in the early 1500s. The castle is noted for its gardens which date back to the sixteenth century and a notable doocot (dovecot) of the same period in the castle grounds.

THOMAS REID

Thomas Reid was born in Strachan, Kincardineshire on April 26 1710, and went on to be one of the most important Scottish philosophers to have ever lived. Reid's philosophy was in a lot of ways a reaction to the philosophy of Locke and Descartes, and that of his friend David Hume, born the following year.

One of the things Reid is famous for arguing in favour of is common sense philosophy. This means something very specific in philosophical terms. Reid's common sense philosophy is basically an argument that there are some things, some beliefs about the world, that we just can't help believing simply because of the way that we're built.

So Descartes argues that we shouldn't believe in anything apart from our own existence, because it could all be an illusion put into our heads by an evil demon. Hume follows this down the line by saying that actually we shouldn't even believe in the existence of a self because we can't point to an idea we have that is "the self".

Reid is trying to argue against these viewpoints. Reid says that we have no more reason to believe in Descartes' evil demon than we do in the existence of the world as it appears to be, and he says that the "common sense" beliefs that humans have, such as beliefs that there is an external world, or that there is a self, support this argument.

He says that since everybody thinks there's an external world, a claim which is supported by the way our language is structured, you'd need an awful lot of evidence to prove that it isn't true. He says that Cartesians can't provide that, and until they can we should stick to our "common sense" beliefs.

SCOTTISH DESCENDANTS AROUND THE WORLD

Everywhere in the world you will find people claiming Scottish descent. In fact it is estimated that there could be as many as 80 million people claiming Scottish identity. That's not bad for a nation that's only home to about 5.25 million people.

In the **United States** census of 2000 about 4.8 million people claimed Scottish ancestry and a further 4.3 million described themselves as being Scots-Irish also sometimes called "Scotch-Irish". The Scots-Irish are descendants of Lowland Scots who originally settled in Ulster in the north of Ireland.

The figures for both cultural groups are regarded as significant underestimates. Some studies have suggested that the actual number may be between 30 and 40 million people. **California** has the highest total number of Scots (over 620,000) and also the highest number of Scots-Irish (around 410,000). The highest proportion of Scottish-Americans live in the New England state of **Maine** where they account for 4.8% of the population.

In **Canada** about 4.8 million people claim to be of Scottish descent with a staggering 2.1 million living in **Ontario** alone. The provinces in Canada with the highest proportion of Scots are **Prince Edward Island** (41%) and **Nova Scotia** (32%). Nova Scotia is of course a Latin name meaning New Scotland. In some parts of Nova Scotia, particularly **Cape Breton Island** a Canadian form of Scots Gaelic is spoken.

In **Australia** the 2006 census identified 1.5 million as having Scottish ancestry with a further 130,204 people who were actually Scottish born. In **New Zealand** the number of people with Scottish industry is also very high as indicated by the dominance of the Scottish Presbyterian church on the **South Island** where one of the principal cities, **Dunedin** takes its name from an old name for Edinburgh.

IAN RANKIN

I've got to tell you, I'm having a bit of trouble with this one. You see, I'm trying to write something to tell you about Ian Rankin, the bestselling Scottish novelist and creator of the character of John Rebus. I'm trying to think of a way to tell you that he was born in Cardenden, Fife on April 28 1960, and that he went to the University of Edinburgh.

I'm trying to think of a way to tell you that he graduated from Edinburgh in 1982, and spent the next three years writing while he tried to do a PhD in Scottish Literature. I'm trying to think of a way to tell you that he published his first novel, *The Flood* in 1986, and his first John Rebus novel *Knots and Crosses* the following year.

I'm trying to think of a way to tell you that he's written sixteen Rebus novels since then, and that his characters and stories have been turned into television shows which have seen his lead character played by John Hannah and Ken Stott.

I'm trying to think of a way to tell you that he continues to publish novels, even though they're no longer Rebus novels, with his most recent one, *The Impossible Dead* released in October 2011. I'm trying to think of a way to tell you that he's written a graphic novel, *Dark Entries*, and that he now lives in Edinburgh with his partner and two children.

I've been trying to think of a way to tell you all that, but I'm afraid I've got what you might call a case of "writer's block". Sorry Ian, I'm sure you'll understand.

THE EARL AND COUNTESS OF STRATHEARN

In historic times the Earls of Strathearn were called the "Mormaers of Strathearn". They have been around from at least the 1100s and take their title from the valley of the Earn in Perthshire. One such Earl is known to have fought for the Scots against the English at the Battle of Standard in Yorkshire in 1138 but the title died out in the thirteenth century.

The title **Duke** or **Earl of Strathearn** has been revived on a number of occasions and was often used for members of the Royal family for short-lived periods in the past.

As a title for members of the Royal family it is often combined with other titles. Thus we had the titles: **Duke of Cumberland and Strathearn** which lasted from 1766 to 1790; **Duke of Kent and Strathearn** (1799-1820) and **Duke of Connaught and Strathearn** (1874-1942). The last of these titles was held by Prince Arthur William Patrick Albert, the third son of Queen Victoria who died in 1942.

In its most recent revival, the title **Earl of Strathearn** was bestowed in its own right by Her Majesty the Queen upon Prince William of Wales on April 29 2011. His wife Catherine is the **Countess of Strathearn**. These are the official titles by which these two prominent and internationally famous members of the Royal family are known in Scotland.

William's father, Charles the Prince of Wales is known as the **Duke of Rothesay** in Scotland. His wife, Camilla otherwise known as the Duchess of Cornwall is known as the **Duchess of Rothesay** in Scotland. The Queen is of course the Queen in Scotland and her husband holds the distinctly Scottish title of the **Duke of Edinburgh** wherever he may be in the world.

TREASURE CHESS

"We were an elite band of Viking warriors, on board a ship from Norway 800 years ago. There were 8 kings including me, 8 queens, 15 knights, 16 bishops and 12 foot soldiers. There may have been more lost at sea, I don't recall.

We're a scary lot, with fearsome expressions. Some say we're comical, but we're not meant to be, especially those frenzied berserker-soldier rooks biting their shields with their teeth.

We were heading for Ireland I believe, but I don't really remember. Then disaster struck. I don't know what happened. Somehow we found ourselves buried in a sandbank on the Lewis, an island then ruled by Norway, so it was home from home.

There we slept in a chamber beneath the sand for hundreds of years until 1831, when in early April, I think, we were found, they say, by a cow.

'Finders keepers' they say, but credit went not to the cow but to Malcolm "Sprot" MacLeod who exhibited us in his byre before selling us to a collector. Undignified to say the least, but I suppose we should be grateful that we were found at all.

There were 78 of us, or at least that's how many survived, including 19 grave-like slabs called pawns. Most of us are made from walrus ivory, though some are whale tooth. Collectively we formed at least five separate chess sets and we are one of Scotland's most remarkable treasures.

It's thought we'd been lost by a twelfth century chess-piece salesman. Sadly our merry band was broken up. I ended up in the Royal Museum in Edinburgh with 10 of my friends, but most of my colleagues went to London and are in the British Museum. I know we're well-cared for, but it's a shame we're separated. You should come and visit us - we're well worth a *check, mate*."

RANGERS FC

Rangers are one of the great Scottish football clubs. The most successful domestic team on the planet, with 54 league titles to the end of the 2010-2011 season, they have been a force in Scottish football more or less since they were founded in 1873. They had played two games in 1872, the first being in May but 1873 is the year that's usually associated with the foundation of the club because it was the year of the first Annual General Meeting and the first time that the club elected staff.

One of the 10 original members when the Scottish League was formed for the 1890-91 season, Rangers has never been out of the top flight since. They even won the league that first season, although it was shared with Dumbarton when a title-deciding play-off game finished in a 2-2 draw.

One of the most influential managers in Rangers' history is Bill Struth, who managed the club for 34 years and won 18 league titles, 10 Scottish Cups and 2 League Cups, including winning the treble in 1949 for the first time. The club won its first European competition in 1972, winning the Cup Winner's Cup with a 3-2 victory over Dynamo Moscow.

The club has been consistently successful over the course of its entire history, but during the 1980s when English clubs were banned from playing in European competition Rangers became even more important in the United Kingdom as a whole, and had some very prominent players. Graeme Souness took the club to three league titles during the late 1980s, before being replaced by Walter Smith who famously won seven league titles in a row during the 1990s, meaning that the club won nine in a row from 1989-1997. Smith returned in the period 2007-2011 guiding the club to three more league titles.

HISTORIC TOWNS AND CITIES: DUNFERMLINE

STATUS: Town in Fife.

RIVER: Dunfermline is located in Fife just to the north of the **Firth of Forth**. The town has easy access to the Forth Road Bridge.

NAMES AND NICKNAMES: Called the "The Auld Grey Toun" because of the stonework of its buildings.

MOTTO AND EMBLEM: Variations of the Dunfermline coat of arms include the motto *Semper* meaning 'always' and *Esto Rupes Inaccessa* meaning 'may the rock be inaccessible'.

POPULATION: About 46,000.

KEY FACTS AND INDUSTRIES: Dunfermline was the capital of Scotland for six centuries. Seven Scottish Kings are buried here, namely Malcolm III, Edgar, Alexander I, David I, Malcolm IV, Alexander III and Robert the Bruce. Dunfermline was traditionally noted for its textile industries.

KEY DATES: 1070: Dunfermline Palace built by King Malcolm III. **1128:** Dunfermline Abbey founded. **1315:** Palace rebuilt after destruction by English King Edward I. **1329:** Robert the Bruce buried at Dunfermline Abbey. **1394:** James I born in Dunfermline Palace. **1600:** James I born in Dunfermline Palace. **1624:** Great Fire of Dunfermline. **1835:** Philanthropist Andrew Carnegie born in Dunfermline.

THINGS TO SEE:

- **Dunfermline Abbey**, beautiful abbey dating back to the twelfth century.
- **Shrine of St Margaret**, Queen to Malcolm III at Dunfermline Abbey.
- **Dunfermline Palace**, ruins of Royal palace dating from the fourteenth century.
- **Dunfermline Abbots House**, sixteenth century house that survived the fire of 1624.
- **Birthplace of Andrew Carnegie**, Dundee born philanthropist, who made his fortune from iron and steel after emigrating to America in 1848.
- **Pittencrief Park**, a gift from Andre Carnegie
- **Pittencrief House**, small museum in the grounds of the park.
- **Guildhall**, in the High Street dates from 1807.
- **Pitreavie Castle**, eighteenth century house between Dunfermline and Rosyth connected with the Bruce family.

THE ELECTRIC BRAE

"Come in, my boy, come in. I am Perce Ception, but you can call me Percy for short. I am the king of all optical illusions. I created illusions like this:

This is the Muller-Lyer Illusion, it looks like the top line is shorter, but both of the lines are actually the same length! Ha ha! Perce Ception strikes. Or what about this one?

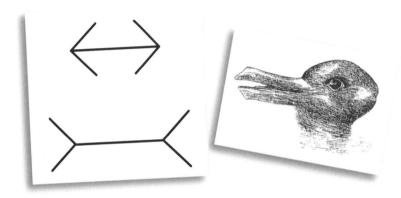

Is it a duck? Or is it a rabbit? Aha! I have got you! But my finest, my favourite illusion must be the Electric Brae in Ayrshire. You see, it is a road which, if you park on it, will do amazing things! It slopes towards the sea, but I have arranged the land around it so that it looks as if it slopes inland. So when you stop on it, and let your handbrake off, you will seem to roll uphill! Ha ha! I am Perce Ception, the finest trickster in all of the land!"

Uphill

Downhill

Uphill

Downhill

ISLAY, COLONSAY, ORONSAY AND JURA

Islay (Norse: Ile's island) is called the **Queen of the Hebrides**.
It's one of the Inner Hebrides and the fifth largest island by area in
Scotland and has a population of over 3,400. It is located 13 miles
west of the Kintrye peninsula.

Islay's capital is the coastal settlement of **Bowmore**, but other
notable villages include Port Ellen, Bridgend, Portnahaven and Port
Charlotte.

Historically Islay was the seat of the MacDonalds, **Lords of the
Isles,** who were virtual rulers of Islay and neighbouring islands
in medieval times. Tracing their origins to a twelfth century Viking
leader **Somerled**, they were crowned as kings on the shores of
Loch Finlaggan in the north of the island. The ritual probably dated
back to the crowning of earlier Celtic chieftains.

Today Islay is famed for malt **whiskys** produced at eight different
distilleries on the island.

At **Port Askaig** on the east of the island a ferry across the **Sound of
Islay** links Islay to neighbouring Jura.

Jura has a Norse name meaning 'Doriad's island' or 'deer island'
and is home to less than 200 people even though it is Scotland's
eighth largest island. Its main settlement is the coastal village of
Craighouse in the south east and its main geographical features is
the **Paps of Jura hills**.

The writer **George Orwell** lived the last three years of his life on
Jura and completed his novel *1984* on the remote house of Barnhill
in the north of the island.

Eight or nine miles west of Jura are the islands of Colonsay and
Oronsay.

Colonsay has been inhabited since Mesolithic times and is
currently home to around 100 people. **Oronsay**, its smaller
neighbour to the south is home to about five people and is the site
of a ruined fourteenth century Augustinian monastery.

THE ONLY SANE MAN IN GLASGOW

Alexander Wylie Petrie or the "Glasgow Clincher" as he became known (a name he took from the newspaper he published) was a thorn in the side of Glasgow Council, or Glasgow Corporation as it was then called. However, he was a thorn with a highly entertaining story.

Petrie started to publish the *Glasgow Clincher* in 1897, and distributed it himself around the streets of Glasgow. He was constantly questioning and criticising the local council when they did things which he didn't like, and expressed himself in such a way that he became rather famous in Glasgow.

His fame became so much of a problem for the Corporation, that they had him arrested for disorderly conduct many times whilst he was producing the *Clincher*. Eventually they decided that they'd had enough of him and actually had him arrested and sectioned.

This means that they put him, against his will, into a sanitorium for the mentally insane. The hospital he was put into was called Woodilee Hospital, which was a mental hospital in Lenzie. The actions of the Corporation annoyed an awful lot of people, and a public campaign was started to get him released.

Eventually he was released, and given a certificate of sanity signed by a doctor, to prove that he wasn't insane. After this he'd proudly tell people that he was "the only sane man in Glasgow", and that he had the piece of paper to prove it!

WOODILEE HOSPITAL

Alexander Wylie Petrie
Glasgow Clincher

Did you know?
Scottish Northumbria

- From 600 AD most of south east Scotland was in the Kingdom of Northumbria.

- Northumbria was Anglo-Saxon. Its people were Angles from Germany and Denmark. They expanded north into what is now Scotland from their fortified capital at Bamburgh on the Northumberland coast.

- By 600 AD they captured land up to Edinburgh that was previously Welsh speaking territory. Northumbrian English became the predominant language of the region.

- Even today, English spoken in Scotland retains similarities with the dialect of England's north using Anglo-Saxon words like "gan" meaning 'to go'.

- By 1018 Northumbria was absorbed by England and ceased to exist as a Kingdom but survived as an Earldom stretching north to the Lothians.

- That changed after the Battle of Carham on Tweed in 1018. The Scots seized the Northumbrian territory from the Lothians to the Tweed. With the exception of Berwick this land has remained Scottish ever since.

- The English Bishop of Durham died of a broken heart when he learned of this lost land because it had been the birthplace of St Cuthbert Northumbria's revered saint.

- Over time, the English spoken in Scotland's south east took on distinct features of its own but lowland Scotland retained linguistic, cultural and religious links to Northumberland. The ties were made stronger by the fact that Gaelic was spoken in the Highlands.

- Cumberland was in Scotland at this time and Carlisle occasionally served as a Scottish capital.

- When David I became King of Scotland he recognised the ties with Northumberland and in 1138 through invasion and political manoeuvring annexed Northumberland and Durham so they were under virtual Scottish rule. This situation lasted for 18 years.

Professor
C. Cloggs

DAVID HUME

David Hume, born in Edinburgh on May 7 1711, was arguably the greatest philosopher to write in English, a pillar of the Scottish Enlightenment, and one of the best minds Scotland has ever produced. The best way to talk about the genius of David Hume is to tell you just a little bit about one of his ideas. This is only one idea, and it's so much more complicated than could ever fit onto this page, but here goes.

Hume was an empiricist, which means that he thought that knowledge of the world comes through our senses, and only through our senses. We get all our ideas about the world from the sense impressions we have of it.

Hume says that this means that if we perceive a shoe, we get an idea of the size of it, the shape of it, the way it smells, how it feels in our hands and so on. But he said that those properties are the only things you perceive. You can't perceive a shoe without the properties, because if you imagine a shoe the only things you can imagine are its colour, shape, size and weight. Our senses give us no evidence for a shoe apart from those properties.

Hume extends this to us. You perceive yourself, he says, but what happens when you do? You get ideas of your size, shape, colour, smell, and so on. But do you perceive a "self" which is more than those things? How could you describe such a thing?

Hume says that you can't, that the "self" is an illusion which can't be supported by evidence. Hume says that all you are is a "bundle" of perceptions, and nothing more. Effectively, he says that a special, non-sensational "you" doesn't exist.

This has barely touched the wonder of what Hume says - you should really go and read his books.

Looking to get away from Nazi-occupied Norway this summer? If so, why not try the Shetland Isles? Shetland is the perfect place for that Third Reich getaway, so why don't you start yours today?

"But the Nazis control all traffic in and out of Norway," I hear you cry, "So how am I supposed to get to the Shetland Islands?" That's where the Norwegian Naval Independent Unit (NNIU) comes in.

The NNIU has been running secret boats from Shetland to Norway and back since 1940, and will continue to do so until Nazi occupation of Norway ceases. Nicknamed ***The Shetland Bus***, this combination of Norwegian and British sailors and ships transports agents from the British SOE (Special Operations Executive) to Norway to assist Norwegian resistance fighters.

In addition to the British agents, the Shetland Bus carries weapons, equipment and supplies for the Norwegian resistance. Then, once the boats have deposited their cargoes safely onto Norwegian soil, they return to Shetland carrying Norwegian agents and refugees from the Nazis.

It is estimated that, should the occupation of Norway end on May 8 1945, the Shetland Bus will have carried 192 agents and 383 tons of weapons to Norway, and brought 73 agents and 373 refugees back.

Should you choose to join us, your journey on the Shetland Bus will be under the control of one our experienced captains, including "Shetland Larsen", Leif Andreas Larsen from Bergen, who will have made the round trip 52 times by 1945 and become the most decorated naval officer of the Second World War.

SCOTS LAW

History Man: So, have you thought about what you want to be when you grow up?

Student: Well, I think either an astronaut, or a lawyer. Probably a lawyer though, I don't like heights.

History Man: What kind of lawyer, a Scots Lawyer?

Student: What do you mean? I'm Scottish.

History Man: But will you be a Scots Lawyer? Will you practice Scots Law?

Student: What's the difference?

History Man: Well, Scotland has a unique legal system, which is very different from the rest of the United Kingdom. There are some really big differences, for instance, juries in Scotland are made up of 15 people unlike English juries which consist of 12 people. Also, the age when you're considered an adult is 16 in Scotland, and in Scotland the accused in a trial can't choose whether they want to be tried by judge or jury.

Student: Really? That's interesting. So why does Scotland have a different system? Why didn't it just become part of the British system after the Acts of Union?

History Man: Scots Law was protected in the Acts. Many Scottish people opposed union with England, and one group that the unionists needed to get to support the move was the legal community in Edinburgh. So they promised to protect Scots Law, and so protect the jobs of Scottish lawyers, in order to get their support.

Student: So it's totally separate then?

History Man: Well, not quite. It's still distinct from English law, but the introduction of things like the European Court of Human Rights has meant that there's more in common across Europe now, and that includes in Scotland. It's still a unique system though, and well worth protecting.

RUDOLF HESS AND THE FLIGHT TO SCOTLAND

There have been many strange and fascinating events in Scottish history, but few more so than the one which happened on May 10 1941. That night Rudolf Hess, Germany's Deputy Fuhrer and one of the most powerful men in Europe at the time, climbed into a Messerschmitt Bf 110 fighter and took off. His destination? Scotland.

Germany's war in Europe was about to take a new and difficult turn. The previous year had been dominated by the Battle of Britain, the attempts of the Germans to use air power to dominate Britain in the way that they had the rest of Western Europe. It had been a failure, Britain's air defences had held. Now Germany looked east, to the Soviet Union. Hess knew that the attack on Russia was about to begin, and desperately wanted to make peace with Britain to avoid a war on two fronts.

Hitler ordered the Luftwaffe to shoot Hess down, but he managed to avoid them, and parachuted out of his plane over Scotland, landing at Floors Farm near Eaglesham, breaking his ankle in the process. He came to speak to the Duke of Hamilton, Douglas Douglas-Hamilton, a Scottish noble and RAF officer he believed to be opposed to Winston Churchill's government.

It did not end well for Hess. He was arrested, and when he revealed his identity to the Duke he was immediately imprisoned. Winston Churchill had him put in the Tower of London, and then in other prisons, before he was returned to Germany for the Nuremberg Trials in 1946. His flight to Scotland failed, but it remains a very interesting piece of Scottish history.

Did you know?
Shipping and Shipbuilding on the Clyde

- When Scotland united with England in 1707 it opened up new trading opportunities with the colonies, this encouraged trade on the Clyde. Shipbuilding was one of the many shipping-related industries that developed.

- In 1668 Glasgow was not yet a suitable location for a major port as the river was too shallow, so Glasgow businessmen developed the port of "Port Glasgow" near the deeper coastal waters of the Clyde to the west.

- In the late 1700s the Clyde was so shallow to the west of Dumbarton that you could easily wade across it a low tide. The river bed had to be scoured to deepen the Clyde and this opened up the possibility for developing shipping and shipbuilding at Glasgow.

- In 1812 Europe's first ocean-going steamship, the Comet, was launched at Port Glasgow.

- The town of Clydebank did not exist at the beginning of the 1860s but by the end of the nineteenth century it was home to around 30,000 people. Its growth was based on shipbuilding.

- Between 1860 and 1870 iron ships totalling 800,000 tons had been built on the Clyde.

- In the 1870s steel ships were increasingly built on the Clyde, almost all Clyde ships were built of steel by the end of the 1880s.

- The RMS Queen Mary Ocean Liner launched at John Brown's shipyard at Clydebank on September 26 1934 held the Blue Riband (fastest crossing of the Atlantic by an ocean liner) from 1938 to 1952. The liner is now a hotel, restaurant and museum at Long Beach, California.

- Other liners launched at John Brown's yard included RMS Queen Elizabeth (September 27 1938) and RMS Queen Elizabeth II (September 20 1968).

- During World War Two the Clyde shipyards were a major target of the German Luftwaffe.

- At one time there were around 70 shipyards on the Clyde. In 2011 there are only three.

Professor C. Claggs

THE BISHOPS' WAR

History Man: Hey, do you remember what I told you about the Bishops' Wars?

Student: You started to tell me they were something to do with the National Covenant, and abolishing bishops, but what happened next?

History Man: Well, you remember the King had raised an army to invade Scotland? Well the Covenanters raised an army too, to defend the National Covenant. The problem for King Charles was that he didn't really have the money to raise a proper army.

Student: What about the Covenanters? Did they have a decent army?

History Man: They had two things on their side, religious conviction and a commitment to defend something that they believed in, the Covenant, and a whole number of experienced soldiers who'd been serving overseas who came back to help, and so moulded them all into a proper army.

Student: So Charles didn't have much of an army, and the Covenanters did, what happened then?

History Man: Charles' army got to the border and realised they couldn't win, so they signed a peace treaty at Berwick. This allowed for a new General Assembly in Scotland, with the King agreeing that all questions should be referred to it or the Parliament of Scotland.

Student: OK, what did the King do then? Surely he didn't like having to do a deal?

History Man: No he didn't, but he needed money. When the King needed money at that time, he had to call a Parliament to get them to give him more. The problem was that to get them to give him it, he needed to give them something in return because many English people were angry with the King too. But that'll have to wait for another day...

WHISKY GALORE AND OTHER SCOTTISH WORDS

Whisky Galore was a novel of 1947 by Scots author Compton Mackenzie which gave rise to the 1949 movie of the same name.

The story was based on real life events in 1941 when the islanders of Todday in the Outer Hebrides helped themselves to a cargo of whisky from the shipwrecked *S.S. Politician*.

WHISKY is a Gaelic word. It could be Irish or Scots Gaelic in origin, but did you know **GALORE** is also Gaelic and may likewise have originated in either nation.

Scots have given many great things to the World, including it must be said, gallons *galore* of whisky over the centuries, but let's not forget its contribution of words to everyday English.

You know the song **Donald Where's Yer Troosers**? It was a 1961 hit about a Scotsman who wears a kilt rather than trousers. Did you spot the Gaelic word? Yes trouser is a Gaelic word, but not the word kilt which is Norse.

If you want to get away from the **HUBBUB** (Scots or Irish Gaelic) head off for a dance with your **CLAN** (Gaelic) at the **CEILIDH** (Gaelic) and wear your **TROOSERS**! If it's raining put on your **MACKINTOSH** (named from a Scotsman), and stick to the **TARMAC** road (another Scotsman). Head through the **WEE GLEN**, and pass the **CAIRN** down near the **LOCH**.

Once inside you'll find it very **COSY**. Yes cosy, popularised by the Americans has its roots in Scots.

Be proud of this knowledge, don't be a **DUNCE** (from the Scotsman John Duns Scotus) though there's a **SMIDGEN** (Scots or Irish Gaelic) of doubt about this one.

So there we have just a small selection of words that the Scots have given to the world. All we need to do now is come up with a **SLOGAN** (Scots Gaelic: a war cry) to advertise the fact.

SCOTLAND PLACE-NAMES
WHAT DO THEY MEAN?

DUFFTOWN

Town in Moray in the north east established in 1817 by James Duff, Earl of Fife.

DUMBARTON

On the Clyde estuary. From the Gaelic *Dun Breatainn* meaning, 'stronghold of the Britons'. Britons were Welsh speakers, whose kingdom of Strathclyde had its capital on a rock here overlooking the Clyde. Britons called Dumbarton *Allt Clud*. Dumbarton gave its name to Dunbartonshire which is spelled with an 'n' instead of an 'm'.

DUMFRIES

Town on the Nith with a population of 31,000. Gaelic *Dùn Phris* meaning, 'a woodland' (*phris*) 'fortress' (*dun*). Gave its name to Dumfriesshire.

DUNCANSBY HEAD

Combines Gaelic forename *Dungal*, with Viking word *byr* meaning 'village' and English word *head*. Near John O' Groats.

DUNBLANE

Means the Fort of Saint Blane. It was the site of the saint's principal monastery.

DUNDEE

City of 142,000 people on the Tay. Gaelic *Dun Daig* meaning 'the fort of someone called Daig', though it's tempting to guess it means 'fort on the Tay'.

DUNKELD

From the Gaelic Dun *Chailleainn* meaning 'fort' (*dun*) of the Pictish tribe called the Caledonians. They had a royal fort here.

EDINBURGH

First mentioned in a Welsh poem as *Din Eidyn* around 600 AD when it was associated with a Welsh tribe called the Gododdin. It was seized by the Northumbrians, who renamed it Edinburgh perhaps in honour of their King, Edwin. Burgh and Din both mean 'fortified stronghold', but the meaning of *Eidyn* is not known.

MARY QUEEN OF SCOTS CROWNBOOK™ WALL

Mary Stuart

Wall | Info | Photos | Events

> What's on your mind?   **Share**

Mary Stuart is excited to be Queen of Scotland – and I'm not even one!
Comment - Like - 09/09/1543 at 3:30pm

Mary Stuart is moving to France – things kicking off between England and Scotland.   Comment - Like - 18/08/1548 at 11:54pm

Mary Stuart has married **Dauphin Francis** of France
♥ Comment - Like - 24/04/1558 at 9:54am

Mary Stuart Mary I of England's dead- According to father in law **Henry II** I'm now Queen of England!!! :)   Comment - Like - 17/10/1558 at 2:13pm

Mary Stuart My father in law's dead :(Still, I'm now Queen Consort of France :)   Comment - Like - 10/07/1559 at 3:15am

Mary Stuart My people signed Treaty of Edinburgh recognising Elizabeth I as Queen of England and Scotland. I'm not having any of that though, I'm the Queen!   Comment - Like - 06/07/1580 at 5:52pm

Mary Stuart Hubby Francis has died :(
Comment - Like - 05/12/1560 at 7:23am

Mary Stuart is now single
♥ Comment - Like - 05/12/1560 at 7:25am

Mary Stuart Back in Scotland - gonna reclaim my throne.
Comment - Like - 19/08/1561 at 7:34pm

Mary Stuart wants to make up with **Elizabeth I** - No need for us to fight.
Comment - Like - 20/12/1561 at 5:24pm

Mary Stuart Ruling Scotland is ace - few battles and that but all going good.   Comment - Like - 08/10/1562 at 8:27pm

Mary Stuart has married **Henry Stuart**, Lord Darnley.
♥ Comment - Like - 29/07/1565 at 1:15pm

Mary Stuart is upset with Lord Darnley for betraying her and murdering **David Rizzio**   Comment - Like

Mary Stuart has a baby - James - tired but dead pleased!! :)
Comment - Like - 19/06/1566 at 2:15am

Mary Stuart has heard that Lord Darnley killed by explosion 2nite, probably be Earl of Bothwell   Comment - Like - 09/02/1567 at 11:52pm

Mary Stuart is now single
♥ Comment - Like - 09/02/1567 at 11:58pm

Mary Stuart has married **Earl of Bothwell**.
♥ Comment - Like - 15/05/1567 at 4:47pm

MUSICAL EDNAM

**From the Office of the Prime Minister,
10 Downing Street,
London.**

August 18, 1893,

My dear Temperley,

I come to you once more with a mission of the utmost importance to the Crown, safe in the knowledge that you will treat it with the discretion with which you have always carried out such missions. You are certainly to be applauded on your recent exploits, the speed with which you returned the Great Moravian Pearl in particular has been appreciated at the highest level.

However, the question I must ask you now to address is much more domestic than foreign. It concerns a village in the Scottish county of Roxburghshire, the village of Ednam. Ednam sits on the River Eden, and is by and large a peaceful place, but it has been brought to our attention for two reasons.

James Thompson, the renowned Scottish poet and writer of *The Seasons* was born in Ednam. Thompson was also, you may be interested to learn, the man who wrote the words to that great patriotic air and favourite of Her Majesty's, *Rule Britannia*. Now I understand that you may say that this is no great surprise, that many of our greatest writers and artists have been produced by the smallest of villages, that is the thing which makes Britain great.

Indeed, Temperley, I would agree were it not for one thing. Henry Francis Lyte was also from Ednam, and Henry Francis Lyte is the author of the words to the well known hymn *Abide With Me*, also one of Her Majesty's favourites. Now you begin to see our question? For what are the chances that two great songs could have been penned by people from the same small village?

You and Thornton must go and investigate this, I await the result of your investigations.

W Gladstone

William Gladstone.
Prime Minister.

DUNDEE MARMALADE

"Brothers, comrades, I come before you today to tell you a tale of woe. I am Sergio Naranja, the leader of the Seville Oranges Protection Front (SOPF). I come before you, most importantly, to warn you. A great crime has been perpetrated against us, against our kind, against our people for more than two hundred years. I speak to you of Dundee Marmalade.

Dundee Marmalade was invented in Dundee by James Keiller and his mother Janet. They had run a shop selling sweets and jams, and had never given the SOPF any cause to fear them. Then in 1797 they established a factory to make marmalade, and that was where their crimes against Orangekind began.

In order to make their Dundee Marmalade they took thousands of our brothers and sisters, our mothers and fathers, placed them in boiling water, sliced them up, crushed and boiled them with sugar and turned them into marmalade. The crimes that they have committed in Dundee since that fateful day in 1797 are too many, too numerous to name, but one thing is certain, they must be stopped.

That is why I come in front of you today, to ask you to join with us to fight this great evil, to protect Seville Oranges across the globe from the menace of the Dundee Marmalade trade. There is only one problem with my plan; I am an orange and therefore incapable of fighting anyone unless thrown..."

GENERAL WADE'S MILITARY ROADS

History Man: Hey, have you ever heard of General Wade?

Student: General who?

History Man: General Wade. He was the commander of British forces in Scotland during the early eighteenth century. He was given the job of controlling the Highlands after the Jacobite risings of 1689 and 1715.

Student: So what did he do?

History Man: There were a lot of people who supported the Jacobite cause, and a lot of them were willing to take up arms against the King. The King didn't like that so he sent Wade to Scotland. Wade started a program of road-building to control the Highlands.

Student: Road building? Why did he start road building?

History Man: The Highlands were very remote, and it was easy for Jacobite supporters to hide there. It was also very difficult for large numbers of British soldiers to get around quickly.

Student: That'll have been a good thing for the Highlanders then?

History Man: Especially because the government had larger armies than the Jacobite forces, they wanted to make sure that they could use that size difference to their advantage.

Student: So Wade built roads? Where did he build them?

History Man: Well he built four main roads, one from Inverness to Fort William, one from Dunkeld to Inverness through the Pass of Drumochter, one from Crieff to the road at Dalnacardoch and one from Dalwhinnie to Fort Augustus.

Student: And did Wade's roads work? Did they help to control the Highlanders?

History Man: Yes and no. There was another rising in 1745, probably the most famous Jacobite rising, but when Bonnie Prince Charlie was beaten at Culloden the roads helped the British army chase the Jacobites as they retreated to the Highlands. The roads opened up the Highlands for the British.

Student: So, good for the British, not so good for the Highlanders.

BERWICK UPON TWEED

Berwick, a medieval-walled town is the most northerly in England, with a history closely tied to Scotland. Indeed, Berwick was once in Scotland but changed hands between the two nations thirteen times.

Berwick started as a settlement in Northumbria and remained in that region until seized by the Scots at the Battle of Carham of 1018. From that time it was hotly disputed. The English retook it in 1174 but Berwick returned north in the late 1100s when the English King, Richard I sold it to pay for a crusade.

The following century King John retook it for England, but Berwick continued to change hands until 1482 and has been in England ever since.

It was a place worth fighting for. In medieval times Berwick was once the most prosperous place in Scotland, worth to the nation an annual customs value of £2,190 equivalent to about one quarter of the customs of the whole of England.

Today some English visitors mistakenly think Berwick is in Scotland. It's a reasonable assumption, after all Berwick is on the north bank of the Tweed, an entirely Scottish river.

Berwick even looks Scottish and the old county of Berwickshire (though Berwick was not part) was in Scotland.

Most of Berwick's banks are Scottish and deal in Scottish money and the football team plays in the Scottish league. The accent, to English ears at least, sounds Scottish, though Scots hear the northern English lilt.

Berwick's been in England for centuries but until the Reform Act of 1885 it maintained a degree of independence and was mentioned separately in Acts of Parliament.

The Crimean War was declared in the name of Britain, Ireland and Berwick. Strangely, Berwick's name was omitted from the peace treaty giving rise to the legend that Berwick is still at war with the Russians.

BERWICK UPON TWEED

SCOTLAND

IRELAND

ENGLAND

FEAR LIATH
SCOTLAND'S BIGFOOT

"And here, on the slopes of Ben Macdhui, the tallest mountain in the Cairngorms, we are hoping to catch a glimpse of the Am Fear Liath Mòr, the Grey Man of Ben Macdhui. This great beast, one of Scotland's most fearsome creatures, is said to stand at between fifteen and twenty feet tall, covered from head to toe in grey or brown hair.

...And there it is, the Grey Man, and you can see the head and hands of the animal, far larger in proportion to his body than those of a human, with pointed ears and great talons, it really is a frightening animal. Many people have reported a great sense of unease when coming into contact with the Fear Liath, and I'm certainly feeling that now, an almost overwhelming desire to run away...

...No, I'm back, and it's quite clear that the reports that the Fear Liath provokes suicidal thoughts and an almost paralysing terror are absolutely true. The Fear Liath has been encountered by a number of different mountain climbers over the years, and they have given striking descriptions of how they fled in terror from the great beast.

John Norman Collie, a respected scientist and mountain climber, was the first to report the Fear Liath, back in 1925. It was a story that he'd been holding on to for 35 years, but which was finally told at the AGM of the Cairngorm Club in 1925. And I can certainly confirm that the terror he reported then is still the case today. Whatever the Fear Liath is, I'd recommend to all viewers that they take the greatest of care when climbing Ben Macdhui..."

FEAR
LIATH

Fear Liath

MY SCOTLAND

Scotland! The home of tatties, tartan, "Rabbie Burns", William Wallace, the Celtic Football team, "pibroch", golf and Gaelic. My Scotland is so great words can hardly explain, but I hope this will be close enough.

One of the things I admire about Scotland is its brave people. Scotland has constantly been in wars to fight for what they believe in: independence. Important Scottish legends such as William Wallace and Robert Bruce gave their lives for freedom. Although the history is full of fighters, the people of Scotland are the friendliest I have ever met.

Scotland has produced great inventors like Alexander Graham Bell and Charles Mackintosh. I am proud that they have been brought up in the same place that I am being brought up in. I hope I can do something for Scotland too. As well as good inventors, Scotland is very rich in literature and folk tales.

Scotland has a picturesque landscape. The islands around are very peaceful and beautiful. There are lochs that shimmer in the moonlight like a topaz. Its moors have an excellent view. There is metropolitan life in its cities like Glasgow, Edinburgh and Aberdeen. There are lots of shopping centres and festivals on. I enjoy being a part of all these.

Overall Scotland is a wonderful place, and I hope this poem will explain:

> Look. What can you see?
> I see beauty in the lochs.
> I see majesty in mountains.
> I see legend in rocks.
> And it is ours.

My Scotland
Young Writer

Name: Doaa Shabbir
Age: 9
School: The High School of Glasgow

THE QUINTINSHILL RAIL DISASTER

On May 22 1915 the worst rail disaster in British history took place at Quintinshill near Gretna Green. The train crash involved five different trains, and resulted in the deaths of 227 men, as many as 215 of them soldiers on their way to ships which were bound for Gallipoli in Turkey.

That morning, both of the northbound express trains from Carlisle were running late. When a local train arrived, it had to be moved so that the express trains could pass. The signalman moved the local train to the north-south line, because he knew that there were two express trains on the south-north line.

The first express train passed safely, but the signalman had made the mistake of changing the signals on the north-south line, and they didn't tell trains on that line to stop. There had been a changeover of the signal men while the local train was on the north-south line, and the new man hadn't changed them back.

This meant that when the troop train from the north came through at seventy miles an hour it had no warning that there was a local train parked on the line. At the same time, the signalman had let the second express train come through south-north, so he couldn't move the troop train onto that line either.

The troop train hit the local train, derailing both of them and crushing the carriages of the troop train. Then the express came through, and crashed into the wreckage, and collided with a parked goods train.

Several of the engines broke open spreading hot coals through the wooden carriages, setting them on fire. This was made worse by gas canisters in the troop train exploding, causing an enormous blaze.

In the end, 227 died and 246 were injured.

CAPTAIN KIDD

Hamish McDougal,
Cockney Road,
London.

May 23, 1701.

Dear Father,

I write to you with some excitement from London, having witnessed today the hanging of the notorious Captain Kidd at Wapping. I am sure that you must be well acquainted with the fearsome Captain's story by now. But did you know that he was born in Greenock, In 1645 they say, and that he set himself out for a life on the high seas?

Although he was today hanged for piracy, there are some that say that he was a privateer, a pirate for the crown in the recent war against the French. The truth of that is as may be, and while it certainly seems he was a privateer, he was also involved in some most nefarious piratical activities - of that we can all be sure.

He was a member of high society in the new world colonies, living in a place called New York and being close friends with governors and admirals, and working his way as a privateer all across the Spanish Main.

It seems that because of this he was dispatched in 1695 by Governor the Earl of Bellomont to seek out pirates and Frenchmen across the Indian Ocean. Captain Kidd set sail in September 1696, and took his crew around the Cape of Good Hope, many of them dying in the attempt it is said.

The problem for the poor captain was that, whilst on his voyage, many back home changed their minds about piracy. Captain Kidd went from being a privateer funded to hunt pirates and the French, to a wanted man. Indeed it is said that it was Bellomont himself who put the price on his head, having him arrested in Boston in 1699.

An unfortunate story for the Captain, but a great tale for us all to tell you must admit.

Your son,

Hamish

THE FALKIRK WHEEL

The Falkirk Wheel opened on May 24 2002 and is one of the most impressive iconic features of modern Scotland. Linking the Forth Clyde Canal with the Union Canal two miles west of Falkirk town centre, this beautiful steel structure of 1,200 tonnes is a unique rotating boat lift.

In times past the two canals were linked by 11 locks that could take almost a day to navigate. Once the industrial heyday of the canals was over these locks were little used and became obsolete. In 1933 they were filled in and built over, severing the link between the two canals.

In the late twentieth century Scotland's canals underwent significant regeneration and have increasingly played an important role in tourism. It was realised that re-linking the Union and Forth Clyde canals could play an important part in this regeneration as it would reconnect Edinburgh and Glasgow within the canal system.

The 35 metre high wheel is formed by two claw-like arms upon which sit two opposing gondolas called "caissons" each holding about the same amount of water as an Olympic sized swimming pool.

The wheel provides an impressive landmark and a practical solution for efficiently linking the canals. It can rotate in five and half minutes transferring boats from one canal to the other in a fraction of the time it took before. All this is achieved using the same amount of energy as eight boiling electric kettles.

The wheel, which cost £17.5 million to build, lifts the boats from a new basin in the Forth Clyde Canal to an elegant concrete aqueduct. This leads a new short stretch of canal to a 150 metre tunnel which carries the canal beneath the ancient Antonine Wall and Edinburgh to Glasgow railway. After emerging from the tunnel the canal is linked to the Union Canal, by two locks.

CULZEAN CASTLE

Magnificently situated on a cliff overlooking the Ayrshire coast, Culzean Castle, which features on the reverse of the Royal Bank of Scotland five pound note, is as much a stately home as a castle and is certainly one of the grandest buildings in Scotland.

A tower house was first mentioned at Culzean (it is pronounced Cul-*layn*) in the 1400s and there may have been a building here in earlier times. The early tower was called Coif Castle from the caves in the cliff below but the present name which means 'nook of birds' was adopted in the 1600s.

The castle's association with the Scottish Kennedy clan began in 1569 when Sir Thomas Kennedy was given lands here by his brother the fourth Earl of Cassilis. Thomas enlarged the tower house in the 1590s and in the following century pleasure gardens and terraces were constructed as the place increasingly became a very comfortable family home for the Kennedys.

In 1777, David Kennedy, the tenth Earl of Cassilis employed the architect Robert Adam to commence the rebuilding of what would become a very grand and stately castle that would serve as an unrivalled symbol of status.

The castle remained in the hands of the Kennedy family until 1945 when they gave the castle and its grounds to the National Trust for Scotland.

As part of the agreement of this handover an apartment at the top of the castle was given to the American General Dwight D Eisenhower as an acknowledgement of his role as commander of the Allied forces in World War Two. President Eisenhower, as he would become, stayed here four times.

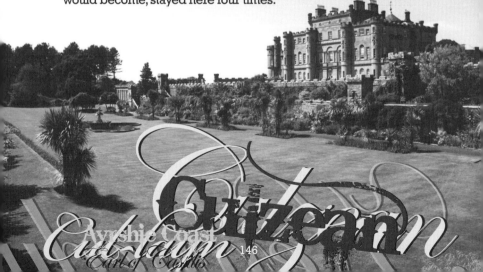

SAUCHIEHALL STREET

A street walks into a Glasgow bar and says to the barman:

"I was originally a narrow winding lane which ran between a number of different houses and estates, before being widened in 1846. My name actually derives from the word *Saugh* which is Scots for 'willow tree', and *Haugh* which means 'meadow'. I am one and a half miles long and stretch from Dumbarton Road in the West End of the city to Buchanan Street in the city centre.

There have been many amazing things which have happened on me, I've been the home to many businesses, bars, restaurants and shops, as well as cinemas including the Gaumont Cinema where *The Sound of Music* ran for two years. I was also home to the Beresford Hotel, Glasgow's first skyscraper which was built in 1938 for the Empire Exhibition.

I've been the centre of commerce and entertainment in Glasgow for more than one hundred and fifty years, and will hopefully continue to be so for many years to come."

The barman says: "And? What's the joke?"

The street replies: "Joke? What's a joke? I've told you, I'm a street. I've got no concept of humour."

27

THE DEVIL'S VISIT TO AUCHTERMUCHTY

In times gone by it is said that the people of Auchtermuchty in Fife were so deeply religious that they were virtually incorruptible.

This was clearly a challenge for the Devil who decided to pay them a visit to see what he could do to change this.

The Devil's cunning plan was to arrive in disguise and what better way to fool the Auchtermuchty residents than to pretend to be a Calvinist minister.

As he started to preach the people of the town were captivated by his seductive sermon in which he described their town as Soddom and Gomorrah. They were soon ready to follow his every word and change what the minister described as their evil ways. Fortunately for the pious residents of Auchtermuchty, one of their numbers, an old man called Robin Ruthven was suspicious that something wasn't quite right.

Ruthven, who had apparently heard a crow say that the preacher was the Devil, ripped aside the minister's long black gown to reveal the cloven feet that betrayed his true identity. It was perhaps very fortunate for Ruthven that it was the Devil as it could have caused the old man much embarrassment had his suspicions proved ungrounded!

The Devil was naturally furious that his ploy had failed and with gnashing teeth he turned into a fiery dragon and ascended into the air leaving a red rainbow behind him across the Lomond Hills.

According to the nineteenth century Scottish poet and folklorist, James Hogg, the residents of Auchtermuchty were always suspicious of rousing sermons from that day on.

Henderson

Actually three separate names that developed independently in
Scotland. Firstly we have the Hendersons of Dumfriesshire whose
name means 'son of Henry'. Then there was the MacEanruig of
Glencoe, descendants of a Pictish king. Their Gaelic name was
translated to Henderson. Finally the Hendersons of Caithness
descended from Hendry, a fifteenth century member of the Gunn Clan.

Home

Border surname from the Tweed valley thought to descend from the
Anglo-Saxon earls of Northumbria. Associated with Coldstream since
the 1200s. Usually pronounced *Hume*.

HUNTER

Descendants of hunters of Norman origin who arrived in Scotland in
the eleventh century. In 1116 a William Venator (William the Hunter)
was Royal hunter to the King of Scotland. Hunterston in Ayrshire was
the family seat.

Innes

Clan named from the Barony of Innes in Morayshire. Innes was
granted to a Flemish noble Berowald in 1160 by Malcolm IV. Berowald
and his descendants took the name Innes. Numerous in the north and
north east.

Irvine

Named from Irvine in Ayrshire or Irving in Dumfriesshire.

Johnstone

Mentioned in the Borders in the twelfth century. Named from John of
Johnstoun who established lands of that name in Dumfrieshire.

Keith

Possibly named from Keith in East Lothian, but associated with
Caithness and Aberdeenshire.

Kennedy

Said to trace their roots to Cunneda, a chieftain of the Votadini tribe
who inhabited the Lothians and Borders. The Saxons persuaded
Cunneda to establish settlements on the west coast as defence against
the Irish. Kennedys became established in Ayrshire and later some
settled in Ireland where there was already a Kennedy Clan that had
developed there quite separately.

Kerr

Border Reiving Clan of Berwickshire and Roxburghshire. *Kerr* is an Old
Norse word meaning 'marshland'. Surname also occurs as Ker, Carr
and Carre.

A SPECIAL KIND OF ANIMAL

"I'm a most unusual animal, I'm here to tell you all about myself. I'm part of a species that has made its way all over the world, there are many different breeds in this species, but I'm a special kind, native to Scotland. My species is called Great Highland, and I'm quite closely related to other species from Ireland.

I've got a long body, and five limbs. I fill my body with air, and when it's full I'm able to do lots of different and clever things with my limbs. One of my limbs is called a chanter, and I'll use it to make sweet music. My other limbs are called drones, two of them are tenor drones and one of them is a bass drone.

My drones make a noise, a 'droning' noise, when I push air through them. In combination with my chanter, I can make music by using them, and I do it very well, thank you very much. My fifth limb is my blowpipe, that's where I get the air from to fill my body up.

There's evidence my species has been around in Scotland since the fourteenth century, so we're pretty well established here. We're also one of the most recognisable symbols of Scotland not just in this country but around the world. I'm sure you've guessed what we are by now, but I'll tell you anyway, just in case you've not got it. We're Great Highland Bagpipes, a truly great Scottish animal."

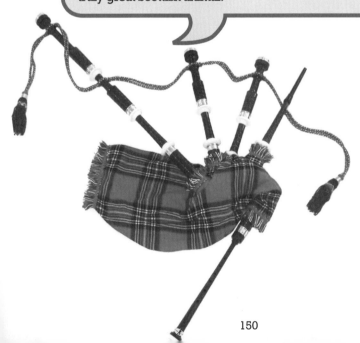

THE UNIVERSITY OF ST ANDREWS

University
of
St Andrews

THE OLDEST: Dating from 1413, St Andrew's is Scotland's oldest university. It is the third oldest university in the English speaking world after Oxford and Cambridge.

WORLD CLASS: A world-class centre of thought and learning with students from over 100 different countries across the planet.

HISTORY: The University was founded in 1413 by a Papal Bull – a kind of charter issued by the Pope. This bull was issued by Benedict XIII of Avignon who was known as an Antipope. At this time there'd been a split in the Catholic Church, with two different people claiming to be pope. One of the popes was based in Rome and the other one was based in Avignon in France. He was called the Antipope, so St. Andrews was founded by the Antipope.

ALUMNI: Some very famous and influential people went to St Andrews, including Alex Salmond the Scottish First Minister, John Knox the founder of the Presbyterian Church of Scotland, King James II, Edward Jenner, the pioneer of the smallpox vaccine and the cyclist Sir Chris Hoy.

ROMANCE: Two particularly well-known ex-students of St Andrews were of course Prince William and Kate Middleton. They are now the Earl and Countess of Strathearn (or Duke and Duchess of Cambridge in England).

WORLD CLASS: The University of St Andrews is a highly respected university, and regularly appears on lists of the best universities in the world. The University is a place steeped in history, right in the middle of one of the most picturesque towns in Scotland, and a place of learning that Scotland can be very proud of.

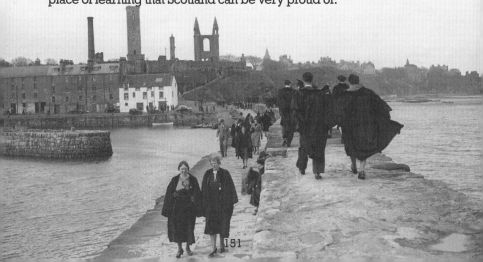

THE CHURCH OF SCOTLAND

Founded in 1560 by John Knox, the Church of Scotland is Scotland's largest church. The Church of Scotland is also known as the Kirk and is a Presbyterian church, meaning that it doesn't have bishops. It is instead governed by a series of courts, each of which has powers over different levels of the church.

Each congregation has a Kirk Session, which is answerable to one of more than 40 Presbyteries. They themselves are answerable to the General Assembly, which meets in Edinburgh every May. The King or Queen is allowed to attend the General Assembly, but they're not allowed to take part in any of the decisions made there.

The Church of Scotland is different to the Church of England in a number of different ways. For a start, the Church of England has bishops, which the Church of Scotland doesn't have. The Church of England also has the monarch as the head of the church, but the Church of Scotland doesn't.

In fact, having the monarch as the head of the church is one of the reasons that the Church of Scotland broke away from English Protestantism, because they said that having the monarch as the head of the church was too much like having the Pope as the head of the church.

The Kirk has been the national Church of Scotland since 1690, and about 9% of the Scottish population regularly attend, although 42% of people in Scotland would describe themselves as being Church of Scotland. There are about 980 Church of Scotland ministers, and 1,179 congregations in Scotland.

The Church of Scotland is protected by law, meaning that the Presbyterian structure of the church is protected.

THE TAY BRIDGE DISASTER

When it was opened on June 1 1878, the Tay Rail Bridge was a wonder of the Victorian world, a monument to the engineering brilliance of the British Empire. It was the longest bridge in the world at the time, at almost 11,000 feet long.

Designed by the famous railway engineer Thomas Bouch, the bridge was a masterpiece, remarked upon across the world and a great source of pride for all involved. Little did they know the tragedy that was about to befall it.

The night of December 28 1879 was a stormy one, with a force ten gale blowing down the Tay, shaking the bridge to its very foundations. At 7.15pm that night, a passenger train made up of six carriages was crossing the bridge. As the train crossed the centre of the bridge, it collapsed, sending the train and the seventy five passengers aboard hurtling into the freezing waters of the Tay, killing everyone on board.

The disaster shook Victorian Britain. The official inquiry blamed Thomas Bouch, because it said that when he designed the bridge he didn't design it to be strong enough for storms like the one which caused the disaster. It also said that the disaster could have been avoided if the bridge had been built and maintained better.

The disaster was immortalised in a spectacularly inappropriate poem, "The Tay Bridge Disaster", by William Topaz McGonagall, as well as in many books and films. It remains one of the worst disasters of its kind in British history, and one which is remembered to this day.

MERMAIDS
FISHY TALES OF FISHY TAILS

THE MURKLE MERMAID

At Murkle in Caithness a mermaid fell in love with a local fisherman and bestowed many jewels upon him. Sadly for this sea-dwelling lady her love for the fisherman was unrequited and he was using the jewels she had given to him to impress ladies of the human kind. When she discovered this, she enticed him to a cave with treasures taken from the wrecks of several ships and chained him up there. His spirit is still supposed to haunt the spot.

HERBAL ADVICE FROM A LADY OF THE SEA

In 1740 a ship owner called John Reid discovered a mermaid in the Dropping Cave at Cromarty and after sneaking up behind her, held her captive until she granted him three wishes. His first wish was that the lady he loved, called Helen Stuart, who had turned him down in marriage, would change her mind. The mermaid agreed and Helen did change her mind. His second wish was that he or his friends would never drown and this wish was also granted. Sadly the nature of his third wish was never revealed so we'll never know if it came true.

PORT GLASGOW MERMAID

At a funeral procession for a young girl who had died of consumption in Port Glasgow, a mermaid rose from the waters of the Clyde and is said to have advised that had the girl drunk nettles in March and eaten Mugwort in May, the girl 'wadnae hae gan to the clay'.

THE PORTGORDON MERMAN

In the nineteenth century fishermen from Portgordon near Banff were often troubled by a dark skinned merman with long arms and green curly hair. They never stayed out at sea very long when they saw him.

Deer Abbey: Ruined Cistercian monastery west of Peterhead established in 1219 by William Comyn, Earl of Buchan who is buried here. *The Book of Deer*, a tenth century Latin Gospel book was written nearby and is Scotland's oldest surviving example of Gaelic literature.

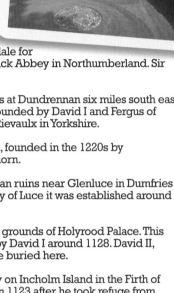

Dryburgh Abbey: Premonstratensian Abbey by the Tweed. Founded in 1150 by Hugh De Morville, Lord of Lauderdale for Premonstratensian canons from Alnwick Abbey in Northumberland. Sir Walter Scott is buried here.

Dundrennan Abbey: Substantial ruins at Dundrennan six miles south east of Kircudbright. A Cistercian abbey founded by David I and Fergus of Galloway in 1142. Monks came from Rievaulx in Yorkshire.

Fearn Abbey: Near the Dornoch Firth, founded in the 1220s by Premonstratensian canons from Whithorn.

Glenluce Abbey: Impressive Cistercian ruins near Glenluce in Dumfries and Galloway. Originally called Abbey of Luce it was established around 1190 by a Lord of Galloway.

Holyrood Abbey: In Edinburgh in the grounds of Holyrood Palace. This Augustinian establishment was built by David I around 1128. David II, James II, James V and Lord Darnley are buried here.

Inchcolm Abbey: Augustinian Abbey on Incholm Island in the Firth of Forth. It was founded by Alexander I in 1123 after he took refuge from a storm here. The island's hermit took care of him. The ruins are well preserved.

Inchmahome Priory: Built by Walter Comyn, Earl of Menteith in 1238. Ruins of an Augustinian priory on the island of Inchmahome in Lake

Menteith near Aberfoyle. The future Mary Queen of Scots was brought here for safety when she was five years old.

Iona Abbey: Situated on Iona just off the Island of Mull. St Columba founded a monastery here in 563 AD. It was attacked by Vikings in the ninth century. Some rebuilding took place in 1164 and in 1203 when the Benedictines were invited to build a new monastery.

THE TITAN CRANE

"Alright son, can you guess how old I am? I'm more than a hundred years old, that's how old. I was born in 1907, here in Clydebank, and I've lived here ever since. I worked in the shipyards for a very long time, over 90 years, starting off at the John Brown & Co. shipyard when I was very young indeed.

Then I worked for the Upper Clyde Shipbuilders between 1968 and 1971, but Upper Clyde collapsed in 1971. After that, I wasn't involved in much shipbuilding; instead I worked for Marathon Oil and UiE Scotland building oil platforms to go into the North Sea. Finally, the shipyard shut in 2001, but I hung around, I guess I just didn't know how to leave.

A bit about me? Well, I'm 150 feet tall, and I weigh around 150 tons. Well, obviously I'm not human, but I think it's pretty harsh when you say I'm not a person. I'm a crane, the Titan Crane. I was a big target for the Germans during the Second World War, they didn't like how much help I was giving to the British war effort, but for all their attempts to blow me up they never managed to get me.

After the shipyards shut I was feeling a bit down though, a bit blue, and some people were even talking about demolishing me. That all changed when I was made a Grade A Listed building though, and refurbished and revamped. I was given a new lick of paint and I opened as a tourist attraction in 2007, my hundredth birthday. Now people can come from all over and find out all about my history, and the history of shipbuilding."

ADAM SMITH

Scotland can claim many famous sons and daughters, many people who have shaped the world in which we now live, but there's one man in particular who fundamentally changed the way in which everything around us works.

Born in Kirkcaldy on June 5 1723, Adam Smith left home to study at Glasgow University when he was 14 years old. He studied Social Philosophy, both in Glasgow and later at Oxford University. He didn't much like Oxford, so when he graduated he came straight back up to Scotland, which was becoming one of the most intellectually important places in the world at the time.

Smith was part of the Scottish Enlightenment, a movement which included philosophers, scientists, writers and artists to name just a few. Smith was a very clever man and became a teacher at Glasgow University, but it was only after leaving the university that he wrote the book that makes him important enough to get into this book.

In 1762 Smith got a job as the tutor of the Duke of Bucchleuch, Henry Scott. This job allowed him to travel all over Europe and meet with many of the most prominent intellectuals of the day, including the American founding father Benjamin Franklin.

In 1766 Smith came home to Kirkcaldy, and spent the next ten years writing a book called *An Inquiry into the Nature and Causes of the Wealth of Nations.* This is often shortened to just *The Wealth of Nations,* and is one of the most important books ever written about economics. He finally published it in 1776.

Adam's book revolutionised the way people thought about money, and the way that business works to this day. Adam Smith is also the first Scot to feature on a Bank of England note, and you can now see his face on the English £20 note, a fitting reminder of a very influential man.

THOMAS BLAKE GLOVER
FOUNDING FATHER OF MODERN JAPAN

Scottish Samurai

[new for 2032, one of the most hotly anticipated games of the year]

You are Thomas Blake Glover, the Scottish merchant, born in Fraserburgh in 1838, who went on to become one of the fathers of modern Japan. Through an innovative combination of role-playing, first person shooter and real time strategy elements, Scottish Samurai charts Glover's rise from Scottish merchant to Japanese national hero.

Establish yourself as a prominent arms trader and set up your home in Nagasaki, Japan. Ally with the samurai and assist them in overthrowing the shogun and restoring to power the Emperor of Japan. These elements are played out in a lushly designed world which stretches over three continents and includes hundreds of square miles of nineteenth century Japan.

The later part of the game brings the strategy elements to the fore, as you develop your company from a minor Japanese manufacturer into Mitsubishi, one of the biggest manufacturing companies in the world today. You will introduce locomotives into Japan, and also create the country's first mechanised coal mine. On top of that, there's also a love story, as you fall in love with and marry Tsura, supposedly the inspiration for Puccini's Madam Butterfly.

Scottish Samurai is the next generation in gaming, an absorbing experience which will make you think you really are one of the fathers of modern Japan. Scottish Samurai coming soon.

10+ RATING
CONTENT SUITABLE FOR 10+ PLAYERS
Game Suitable For Players Aged 10 And Older

JapanGames

SCOTLAND PLACE-NAMES
WHAT DO THEY MEAN?

ELGIN

From the Gaelic *Ealg* 'noble'. Elgin is a former cathedral city and royal burgh.

FALKIRK

Town of 34,000 people in the Forth Valley. Originally *Egglesberth* from the Gaelic *Eaglais Bhreach* 'speckled church'. Translated into modern Scots as Fawe Kirke.

FIFE

Ancient region of Pictland and historic county. Forms a distinct peninsula between the Firths of Tay and Forth. Thought to be named from Fib, an ancient Celtic leader.

FORFAR

Town in Strathmore ten miles north of Dundee. From the Gaelic *Faithir Faire* 'watching hill'. The historic county of Forfarshire was also called Angus.

FORRES

In Moray between Elgin and Inverness. Gaelic *Far Ras* meaning, 'under the bushes'.

FORT WILLIAM

Overlooking a sea loch in the Highland region near Ben Nevis, it was originally called Inverlochy. The English built a fort here in 1655 calling it Gordonsburgh after the Duke of Gordon, then renaming it Maryburgh after the Queen and finally Fort William after King William of Orange.

GALLOWAY

This south westerly region of Scotland was settled by a mixed race of Gaelic speakers and Norsemen. The Gaelic speakers of the north called them *Gall-Ghadail* (Galloway) 'stranger gaels'.

GLASGOW

Scotland's largest city has a Welsh name. The Welsh language once spoken in parts of Scotland is also called Cumbric, Old Welsh or Brythonic. *Glasgu* means 'dear green place'. The Welsh kingdom of Strathclyde had its capital along the Clyde at Dumbarton.

COLIN THE CLYDESDALE

"I'm Colin the Clydesdale. I belong to the Clydesdale clan, Scotland's famous breed of horse. We're Clydesdales because, not surprisingly, we originated from Clydesdale in Lanarkshire. Us Clydesdales are found all over the world, but I'm glad to tell you that I still live here, in Clydesdale.

Clydesdales can trace our clan's beginnings to the eighteenth century when three Flemish stallions were brought to Scotland and bred with the local mares. The children born from this union were bigger than the other horses of the district.

In the nineteenth century records were kept of our pedigrees, a kind of family tree of Clydesdales. Almost all the Clydesdales living today have a lady Clydesdale called Lampits Mare in their family history. She was born in 1806 and named after the owner of the farm where she was bred.

The actual use of the name Clydesdale was first recorded in 1826 in an exhibition at Glasgow and the name has been officially used ever since. Our breed soon became noted for its use in agriculture and haulage and stallions were sent throughout Scotland for extensive crossbreeding. In our native Lanarkshire we were often used for hauling coal from the local mines and were used for haulage in the heavy industries of Glasgow.

In 1877 the Clydesdale Horse Society of Scotland was formed and an American Association for the breed was founded in 1879. Many Clydesdales had been exported to America during the nineteenth century as well as to Europe, Russia, Australia and New Zealand. In Australia we were the dominant draft horse breed by a long way.

Some people think we're Shire Horses, but we're not. They're a different breed. Until the 1940s we were smaller than them, but through selective breeding we've become the big guys, so don't mess with us."

ST COLUMBA

Saint Columba, or "Colum Cille", was Scotland's most influential saint. He was born around 521 AD in what is now Donegal, Ireland where he was reputedly the great-great grandson of the famed fifth century king called Niall of the Nine Hostages.

Educated at the monastery of Clonard in what is now Meath, Columba became an influential monk who established several monasteries at places like Kells and Derry.

In 563 AD he fell out with St Finian over the ownership of a copy of a Psalter made by Columba. This dispute resulted in a battle being fought between the two rivals in which a number of people died.

Saint
Columba

Columba sought exile on the west coast of Scotland where Irish seeking Gaels called the "Dal Riata Scots" had extensively settled. Here as a penance for the battle, Columba worked as a missionary.

Columba was granted the island of Iona off Mull as the site for a monastery and he soon became noted for his wisdom, literacy and diplomacy.

Iona became an important centre for educating the sons of the Scots-Gaelic tribal leaders and Columba himself acted as a diplomat for the Gaels in their relations with the Irish and the Pictish King Bridei who he visited at Inverness.

When Columba died on June 9 597 AD he was greatly revered, largely due to a biography written by Saint Adomnán two or three years after Columba's death.

So revered was Columba that Pictish and Gaelic kings liked to be buried on Iona near Columba's remains. When the Vikings attacked Iona and destroyed the monastery in the ninth century, St Columba's remains were rescued and shared between Scotland and Ireland for protection.

For many years St Columba's remains were carried into battles by the Scots in a special eighth century casket called the Monymusk Reliquary. It was used at the Battle of Bannockburn in 1314.

SCOTLAND'S GREATEST ATHLETE

The year is 1880. Percival Temperley, gentleman adventurer and well known dandy, has been dispatched from his home in Glasgow on a vital mission for Queen Victoria. He and his man-servant and faithful assistant, Thornton, are discussing the demands of their mission.

Temperley: Thornton, we're going to need someone strong, someone very strong.

Thornton: Why, Sir?

Temperley: That's top secret, Thornton, but they're going to have to be possessed of an almost inhuman strength.

Thornton: I think I have the very man, Sir. Donald Dinnie is his name, and he is the greatest athlete and strongman in all of Scotland.

Temperley: Excellent, Thornton. Tell me about this Dinnie fellow.

Thornton: Well Sir, he was born in Aberdeenshire in 1837, and became well known when he was working as a labourer and carried two stones, one weighing 340 pounds and the other weighing 435 pounds across a bridge.

Temperley: That is impressive, Thornton, but how do we know that wasn't a one off?

Thornton: He has since competed in the Highland Games, being hugely successful; indeed he was the champion of the Highland Games for 20 years from 1856 to 1876. In these last years he has travelled to America, becoming celebrated as an exhibitor of great strength.

Temperley: Wonderful, Thornton, make sure that he is added to our party. This, Thornton, will be the greatest mission any of us have ever undertaken!

Thornton: Consider it done, Sir.

Donald Dinnie continued to exhibit throughout America until 1883, then moved to Australia and New Zealand, staying in the Antipodes until 1897. He won over 10,000 awards for his abilities throughout his career, and even advertised Barr's Iron Brew. He returned to Britain the following year, and lived until the age of 78, dying in London in 1916.

June 11, 1719

Thistle Press

Battle Reviews

The Battle of Glen Shiel

Yesterday's performance of the Battle of Glen Shiel represented a regrettable, yet predictable, continuation in form for this country's Jacobite opposition. Although the style of the rebel forces was different, with the ranks of the Jacobites including some two hundred or two hundred and fifty Spanish marines sent by Cardinal Alberoni on behalf of Philip V, the outcome was a strong reminder of their previous effort, and one suspects that it may be some time until we see a further Jacobite revival.

A paltry 1,000 men lined up to support the Jacobite cause, led by Lord George Murray, William MacKenzie the fifth Earl of Seaforth and George Keith the tenth Earl Marischal. Although they were joined in their battle line by Rob Roy MacGregor and a party, their battle line was unoriginal and unimaginative.

Countering them was Major General Joseph Wightman with 850 infantry, 120 dragoons, 130 clansmen loyal to the government and six mortars, which he used to good effect in one of the few performances of the day which was memorable for the right reasons.

One may ask what would have happened had the further troops promised to the Jacobites by Spain arrived, but alas for the rebel forces they did not, and instead we were left with an uninspiring performance by a committed, but under-rehearsed and badly directed Jacobite army. Whether this was the final act of the 1715 rising, or a 'little rising' all of its own, this reviewer was unimpressed with the results and doubts very strongly that there will be call for another revival any time soon.

Battle Rating:

2/5 (I would advise anyone with a real interest in quality battles to give this a miss and wait for Prestonpans in 1745.)

THE CAPE BRETON GIANT

"Good day sir, and welcome to Curnbinten Timberstinch's Remarkable Tailors. I am Curnbinten Timberstinch, and for these many long years I have been the personal tailor to many of the most remarkably shaped people in the world: very fat people to very thin people; very short people to very tall people - I have been personal tailor to them all. "Curnbinten", they say to me, "Curnbinten, without you I would have lived a life of solitary misery, but with your help I have become beautiful".

But less of my reminiscing, what is it I can do for you sir? I can see you have a most remarkable frame. You must be seven feet tall sir? Fear not, I have handled taller challenges than this. For instance, perhaps one of my greatest challenges was to clothe the man they called the Cape Breton Giant, **Angus Mor MacAskill**.

A beast of a man he was sir, seven foot nine in his stockinged feet. Born on Berneray in the Sound of Harris in 1825, he moved to Canada with his family when just a child sir but my, did he grow. He is said to be the world's tallest man to have been born without any, shall we say, abnormalities sir. He was also the strongest man who has ever lived. He could lift 50kg with only two fingers sir!

A kind man he was too, most well regarded among the people who knew him, he toured Canada and the United States displaying his great stature, and indeed was presented to Queen Victoria, but mostly he simply wished to live out his life in Cape Breton.

As I say sir, compared to him you should be an easy task. Now, I'll just get my tape measure."

164

JAMES CLERK MAXWELL

"Guten tag, my name is Albert Einstein.

I'm sure you've heard of me, I am a very famous physicist, but I'm here today to speak about another physicist who you probably won't know.

I want to tell you about this man, whose work I have described as 'the most profound and most fruitful that Physics has experienced since the time of Newton'. This man is a Scot and his name is James Clerk Maxwell.

Maxwell was responsible for formulating *classical electromagnetic theory.*

This was important because he discovered equations that demonstrated electricity, magnetism and light were all different sides of the same thing. He showed that they were different examples of the electromagnetic field at work. That's a quite a major thing to discover, Maxwell was a terrifically clever fellow.

Maxwell was born in Edinburgh on June 13 1831, and educated at Edinburgh Academy. He attended Edinburgh University and then Cambridge University, before taking a professorship at Aberdeen University when he was only 25! Mein Gott, that's almost as impressive as me!

He married Katherine Mary Dewar on June 2 1859, whilst he was at Aberdeen. They moved to Kings College in London in 1860, and it was here he did some of his great work on colour, as well as some of his many developments in the field of electromagnetic theory.

Although he retired from Kings College in 1865 he remained an active scientist, being made the first Cavendish Professor of Physics at Cambridge in 1871.

You know something, and I don't exaggerate here, if it were not for James Clerk Maxwell, my work wouldn't have been possible. Maxwell's advancements in physics certainly made him a great scientist and I am proud to think of him as my colleague."

HISTORIC TOWNS AND CITIES: EDINBURGH

STATUS: City and capital of Scotland.

RIVER: Edinburgh is situated on the south bank of the **River Forth**. A river called the **Water of Leith** flows through the town before entering the Forth at Edinburgh's port of Leith.

NAMES AND NICKNAMES: "Auld Reekie" or "The Athens of the North".

MOTTO AND EMBLEM: Edinburgh's motto associated with the city since 1647 is *Nisi Dominus Frustra* which means something like "in vain without God". The traditional arms of Edinburgh feature a doe as a symbol of St Giles, Edinburgh's patron saint and a maiden. The maiden is thought to derive from Edinburgh Castle being anciently known as *Castrum Puellarum*, "Castle of the Maidens".

POPULATION: About 477,000; Scotland's second largest city.

KEY FACTS AND INDUSTRIES: Inhabited since pre-Roman times, Edinburgh is one of Scotland's most beautiful cities and a magnet for tourists from all over the World. Historic Edinburgh consists of two main centres, namely the **Old Town** situated along the Royal Mile on the rock of Edinburgh Castle and the **New Town** commenced in the eighteenth century below the rock after the draining of the Nor Loch.

KEY DATES: 580 AD: Fort of Din Eitin or Eidyn mentioned in a Welsh poem. Circa **960 AD**: Scots seize Edinburgh from the Northumbrians. **Circa 1125**: David I makes Edinburgh a burgh. **1437**: Edinburgh becomes Scotland's capital. **1532**: Holyrood Abbey becomes a Royal palace. **1559**: John Knox becomes Minister of St Giles. **1624**: Plague hits Edinburgh. **1767**: Construction of New Town begins.

THINGS TO SEE:

- **Edinburgh Zoo**, situated three miles to the west of Edinburgh city centre.
- **Castle**, sited on top of an extinct volcano it is Edinburgh's top tourist attraction.
- **Palace of Holyroodhouse**, this is the official residence of the Queen when she is in Scotland.
- **John Knox's House**, Edinburgh's oldest Royal Mile mansion.
- **Old Town and Royal Mile.**
- **New Town and Princes Street.**
- **National Museum of Scotland.**
- **National Gallery of Scotland.**
- **Scottish National Gallery of Modern Art.**
- **Arthur's Seat.**
- **St Giles' Cathedral.**
- **Royal Botanic Gardens.**

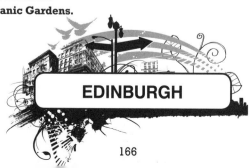

EDINBURGH

MARY QUEEN OF SCOTS CROWNBOOK™ WALL

Mary Stuart

Wall | Info | Photos | Events

What's on your mind?   **Share**

 Mary Stuart and **Earl of Bothwell** are fighting Scottish Lords.
Comment - Like - 15/06/1567 at 3:30pm

 Mary Stuart is imprisoned in Loch Leven Castle :(
Comment - Like

 Mary Stuart has abdicated the throne in favour of James - Good luck son :)
Comment - Like - 24/07/1567 at 4:15pm

 Mary Stuart is fleeing to England. Hopefully somewhere for me to live
thanks to **Elizabeth Tudor.**   Comment - Like

 Mary Stuart I've been put on trial for the murder of Darnley! I don't believe
it! I'm Mary Queen of Scots, you can't try me!!! It's the Scottish Lords who
threw me out who are accusing me as well!   Comment - Like

 Mary Stuart apparently Elizabeth Tudor's seen letters in a silver casket
saying I ordered death of Lord Darnley. Not happy about this one bit.
Comment - Like - 14/10/1569 at 7:21pm

 Mary Stuart fancies being English Queen tbh, and has lots of support
from Spain. There's a plan afoot for me to be made Queen ahead of
Elizabeth Tudor.   Comment - Like

 Mary Stuart Ridolfi Plot failed, but there's another plan on. I'm still
imprisoned as Elizabeth Tudor's afraid people want me to take over.
Comment - Like - 08/04/1570 at 4:36am

 Mary Stuart Babington plot failed!! Now Elizabeth Tudor's got evidence I
wanted her assassinated. Well, maybe...   Comment - Like

 Mary Stuart is on trial for treason :(Comment - Like

 Mary Stuart has been convicted of treason and sentenced to death :(:(:(
Comment - Like

 Mary Stuart just found out she's going to be executed tomorrow :(:(:(:(:(:(
Comment - Like - 07/02/1587 at 4:56pm

Mary Stuart is no longer a member of Crownbook™
08/02/1587 at 2:14pm

June 16, 2032

Thistle Press

Daring Heist at Burrell Collection Sees Priceless Artwork Stolen

Police are searching for criminals involved in a night raid on the Burrell Collection in Pollok Park, Glasgow. Masked men are believed to have entered the building at around 11pm last night, and after knocking the guards unconscious, proceeded to ransack the collection, removing some of the most valuable and ancient art in Scotland.

The Burrell Collection, gifted to the city of Glasgow by shipping magnate William Burrell in 1944, is one of the most substantial collections of art in Scotland, containing until last night over 8,000 objects and works of art, ranging from work by major artists to historically and culturally significant artefacts.

The collection is housed in a purpose built gallery in Pollok

Country Park, which opened to the public in 1983, Barry Gasson and Brit Andresen's design having been chosen by a competition held in 1971.

It is an L-shaped building specifically designed to accommodate the collection, with objects such as Romanesque doorways built into the structure, and was voted Scotland's second greatest post-war building in 2005.

Among the works believed to have been taken by the gang are a bronze bust of Rodin's *The Thinker*, paintings by Cezanne and Degas, as well as several pieces of ancient Islamic art. "The specific items targeted, along with the speed and precision of the heist, suggest that this was both a professional robbery and one done with specific objects in mind", a police spokesman said.

The men left the guards shaken but unharmed, and after loading the stolen items into what is believed to be a white Ford Transit van, made their escape at around 1:30am. Police are asking anyone who saw a van matching the description, or who was in the area last night, to contact them.

THE ANTONINE WALL

The **ANTONINE WALL**™ is the Empire security solution brought to you by Antoninus Pius, the 15th Roman Emperor. With construction beginning in 142 AD and continuing for just 12 short years, the **ANTONINE WALL**™ is the perfect way to keep those pesky Picts out of your British possessions.

We recommend that the **ANTONINE WALL**™ is constructed on the 40 mile stretch between the Firth of Forth and the Firth of Clyde, the narrowest part of the country. The **ANTONINE WALL**™ is constructed of locally sourced turf and other materials, 10 feet tall and 15 feet wide. With a ditch on the northern side, and a military road on the southern, the **ANTONINE WALL**™ is the ideal defence against marauders from Caledonia.

We advise the construction of a fort every 2 miles, with 19 in total along the length of the wall, as the best way to guarantee that your empire remains secure. Ideally, the wall should be patrolled by Roman soldiers, as without this extra security we cannot guarantee that it will retain its protective qualities. Antoninus Pius is happy to provide these soldiers for a negotiable monthly fee.

We suggest that the **ANTONINE WALL**™ should be the primary protection against attacks from north of the border, and are willing to extend our guarantee for the **ANTONINE WALL**™ until 162 AD. (After this point, Antoninus Pius will unfortunately have died and been replaced by Marcus Aurelius and Lucius Verus as co-Emperors. Protection will then move back to Hadrian's Wall, 100 miles south).

The **ANTONINE WALL**™ is the ideal solution for anyone involved in Empire building in Northern Britain. All of our engineers are fully CAESAR certified, and work is carried out to a high standard. If you've got an empire to build, build it with ANTONINE.

THE ANTONINE WALL™

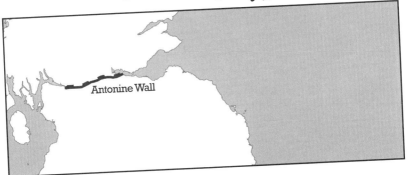

Antonine Wall

THE UNIVERSITY OF EDINBURGH

Alexander Graham Bell, Arthur Conan Doyle, Charles Darwin, David Hume, Adam Smith, Gordon Brown, J.M. Barrie, Arnold Schwarzenegger, Robbie Coltrane, Kirsty Wark and Ian Rankin. All of these people went to Edinburgh University, except for one. Can you guess which one it is?

Founded in 1583, the University of Edinburgh is one of Britain's best universities. It was established by a royal charter of James VI in 1582, one of the few universities of the time not to be established by a Papal Bull.

During the eighteenth century Edinburgh University was one of the centres of the Scottish Enlightenment, with many of the most important thinkers of the time working at the university, people such as David Hume, Adam Ferguson, Thomas Brown and Dugald Stewart.

The university continues to be a home to great learning, and world class research to this day. There are about 28,000 students at Edinburgh University, giving it about the same population as Bearsden on the outskirts of Glasgow.

All in all, Edinburgh University is a fantastic place to study and work, and long may it continue to be so.

Oh, and it was Arnold Schwarzenegger, by the way.

Alexander Graham Bell
Arthur Conan Doyle
Charles Darwin
Gordon Brown

J.M.Barrie
Robbie Coltrane
Kirsty Wark
Ian Rankin

WHAT'S YOUR NAME?

Lennox

From the Gaelic *Levenach* (field of the Leven) an ancient region that covered Dunbartonshire, areas of Stirlingshire and parts of Perthshire and Renfrewshire.

Leslie

Descended from Bartolf, a noble who arrived in Scotland in the twelfth century. Bartolf became governor of Edinburgh Castle and was granted lands in Fife, Angus and at Leslie in Garioch, Aberdeenshire. Numerous in Aberdeenshire.

LINDSAY

Descended from Sir Walter De Lindsey of Lindsey. Lindsey was the ancient name for Lincolnshire in England. Sir Walter came to Scotland with David I in 1124. The family initially settled in Lothian and Clydesdale but later spread north to Angus.

Livingstone

Lowland Clan named from Livingston (without the "e") in West Lothian.

MacAlister

Descended from Alasdair Mor, the son of Donald of Islay, founder of the MacDonald Clan. Found throughout Scotland, particularly in the west.

MacArthur

Descended from a thirteenth century member of the Campbell family. One of the oldest clans in Argyll.

MacAulay

Descended from Amalghaidh, the son of an Earl of Lennox. Their homeland was between Loch Lomond and the Firth of Clyde.

MacDonald

A clan with Viking and Gaelic ancestry descended from Donald of Islay (Dòmhall Mac Raghuill). His father, Ragnald was King of the Isles and Lord of Argyll and Kintrye. Ragnald was the son of Somerled who ruled the Hebrides. MacDonalds often fought on the side of the Norwegians until the Battle of Largs in 1263 when the Norwegians were defeated. A major branch of the MacDonalds is Clanranald, established in the fourteenth century. They descend from Angus Mor, a son of Donald of Islay and were founded by Reginald, a fourth great-grandson of Somerled. Connected to Clanranald are the MacDonnells of Glengarry. Glengarry joins the Great Glen between Loch Ness and Loch Lochy.

The Royal
Aberguidtime Hotel

Main Course

- Arbroath Smokies -
Traditional smoked haddock from the fishing village of Auchmithie near Arbroath in Angus.

- Chicken Tikka Masala -
One of the most popular dishes in Scotland. Indian style curry dish was reputedly invented by a chef at Glasgow's Shish Mahal restaurant in the 1970s.

- Haggis, Neaps and Tatties -
Scotland's all time traditional dish.

- Fish Supper -
Fish and Chips served in a daily newspaper of your choice, wash it down with a can of Irn-Bru.

- Cabbie Claw -
Orkney fish dish of young fish (speldings) in sauce of butter, flour, milk, boiled eggs and nutmeg.

- Rumbledethumps -
Traditional Borders dish made with potato, curly kale cabbage and butter baked until golden brown. Can be made, for those who prefer, as Aberdeenshire's 'Kailkenny' with cream instead of butter.

- Roast of the Day -
From our alternating menu of Roast Aberdeen Angus Steak, Venison, Grouse or Woodcock.

- Crappit Heid -
Large cod stuffed with oats, suet, onion pepper and cod liver. Served with Arran Chief tatties and root vegetables. A Hebridean and North East coastal dish.

- Finest Scottish Salmon -
One of Scotland's all time favourites

HEARTS AND HIBS

Edinburgh is hugely important to all areas of Scottish life, and football is no exception. Edinburgh's two major football teams have been some of the biggest clubs in Scotland since they were formed in the last quarter of the nineteenth century.

Heart of Midlothian FC was formed in 1874 and was a very successful club in the early years of Scottish football, winning league championships in 1895 and 1897, and winning the Scottish Cup four times between 1891 and 1906. The club then went through a difficult period for almost fifty years, without winning a trophy until the 1950s when they went through a golden period, winning the league twice, the Scottish Cup once and the Scottish League Cup four times. They have never enjoyed a period like that again, although cup wins in 1998 and 2006 gave younger fans a taste of success.

Hibernian FC formed the year after Hearts, in 1875. It was founded by Irish immigrants, being called Hibernian after the Latin name for Ireland, Hibernia. Hibernian established themselves as a force in Scottish football, winning the Scottish Cup in 1887 and 1902, and the league championship in 1903. The club's best period was just after World War Two, when the "Famous Five" as they were known, the forward line of Gordon Smith, Bobby Johnstone, Lawrie Reilly, Eddie Turnbull and Willie Ormond were incredibly influential, each of them scoring over 100 goals for the club and guiding Hibs to league championships in 1948, 1951 and 1952. In 1955 Hibs were also the first British club to play in European competition. Since then there have been League Cup wins in 1972, 1991 and 2007 to celebrate, but Hibs fans still await another golden age.

PAISLEY WITCH TRIAL WEEKLY

NEW LOW INTRODUCTORY PRICE !!!

SUBSCRIBE

TO PAISLEY WITCH TRIAL WEEKLY TODAY

and you can start to build your very own Paisley Witch Trials of 1696-1697 at home. Starting at a low introductory price, every week you receive a different element of the famous witch trial, along with a detailed full colour magazine telling you the story of the witch trial itself.

WEEKONE

Your trial begins with a very special atmosphere of fear and suspicion in Renfrewshire during the seventeenth century, made worse by the appointment of *celebrity witch hunter Mr Blackwell as minister of Paisley*.

WEEKTWO

Introduces eleven year old *Christian Shaw*, daughter of the Laird of Bargarran, who became sick after being "cursed" by a coven of witches, and started vomiting up eggshells, pins, straws, hair, excrement and bones.

WEEKTHREE

Reveals yet more of Christian's symptoms, including trances, speaking in tongues, unnatural convulsions and predictions of the future.

WEEKFOUR

Introduces *Dr Brisbane, the Glasgow doctor* who diagnosed her as "supernaturally affected".

WEEKFIVE

Behold, the seven "witches",
Margaret Lang, John Lindsay, James Lindsay, John Reid, Catherine Campbell, Margaret Fulton, and Agnes Naismith
who were found guilty of witchcraft and sentenced to death.

WEEKSIX

We end with the strangulation and burning at the stake of the witches concerned, one of the great pieces of judicial murder in Britain and one of the last mass executions for witchcraft in Europe.

So don't delay, start your collection today, and soon you could be well on the way to re-enacting your very own superstition-driven killing of innocent people

I HEARD, I SAW,
I FELT SCOTLAND

As I walk down Glasgow I hear a variety of noises.
I hear buskers, coins being dropped,
I hear high-pitched voices talk, I hear singing,
I hear my own breath.
I hear Glasgow and I hear Scotland.

I looked to each side of me and I saw lots of interesting shops,
People passing by quickly, holding filled bags,
I saw the people who needed getting and I saw Scotland.

I put my hand to the air. I felt the cold but warmth of it,
I felt trickles of rain water running off my hands,
I felt the mist close in, the heat of the sun poking out from behind
the clouds
And I felt Scotland sheltering me from harm.

I fell and Scotland gave me a leg up.
I was hurt and Scotland healed me.
I was there but now I am here.

My Scotland
Young Writer

Name: Euan McElhinney
Age: 10
School: Milngavie Primary, Glasgow

BANNOCKBURN

Reporter (R): [June 24, 1314 on the battlefield] And here I am with Robert the Bruce now. Robert, how do you feel about these last two days?
Robert the Bruce(RtB): Well Phil, I'm very pleased with the way my lads have performed, the English are always difficult opponents but I think we've stood up to the task admirably.

R: Obviously this was a home tie, how significant was that to your plans?
RtB: Very significant Phil, the English have come up here with a lot of soldiers, some say they had more than twice as many as us, so home advantage was key.

R: And can you tell us a little bit about your preparations?
RtB: Well Phil, I set my forces in the woodland of the New Park to block their advance. We knew they had an advantage in cavalry, so we set out to use the terrain to combat that.

R: You did more than that though, didn't you?
RtB: Obviously we had to make it difficult for them, set up a defence that was going to be strong and make Bannockburn a difficult place for the English to come, so we dug camouflaged pits to defeat the English horses.

R: And you yourself even got involved there, which must make a change?
RtB: It did Phil, I have to say, as you know when Henry de Bohun came for me I had to act, he is, or should I say he was, a fine knight, but I'm glad I came out on top. I was quite pleased with my performance there, but it's not about my personal performance, it's the way we performed overall which is really pleasing.

R: And it's been a great performance, a truly memorable victory. Just quickly, how significant is it for you personally to have defeated Edward II?
RtB: Well, Edward's a great competitor, and there was a little bit of motivation for me since he imprisoned my wife, sister and daughter, but all I can say is it's been a very satisfying day.

R: Robert the Bruce, thank you.

THE OLD PRETENDER

"I'm **James Francis Edward Stuart** the **Old Pretender**. I should have been King of England, Scotland and Ireland.

My Dad was **James VII of Scotland** or James II in England. He was King of Ireland too. Dad became King in 1685 but many weren't happy because he was a Catholic like me.

When he became King, Protestants like Archibald Campbell, the Earl of Argyll rebelled and tried to oust him. Campbell was executed at Edinburgh for his efforts.

Dad hung on and powerful Protestants put up with him because they knew his daughters, my Protestant half-sisters Mary and Anne would succeed him.

That was before I was born. My mum, the Catholic Mary of Modena, my dad's second wife became pregnant with me in 1688 causing a rebellion led by **William of Orange**, the husband of my half-sister Mary.

I was born in June and in December 1688 William ousted dad from the throne. They called this **The Glorious Revolution**. The Scottish Parliament confirmed William and Mary as rulers the following year.

Dad fled to France and so did mum, taking me with them. People were scared one day I'd claim the throne so they said my mum's baby was still-born and that I was an imposter.

Laws were passed preventing me becoming King and in 1714 when William and Mary's successor, **Queen Anne**, died, a Protestant German became King. He was **George I**.

My supporters were **Jacobites** (Jacob is the Latin form of James) and in 1715 they rebelled against George. I returned to Scotland to support the cause, which roused support in the Highlands and northern English counties like Northumberland.

This rebellion, called **The '15** was a failure. I returned to Europe living out my final days in Rome where I died in 1766."

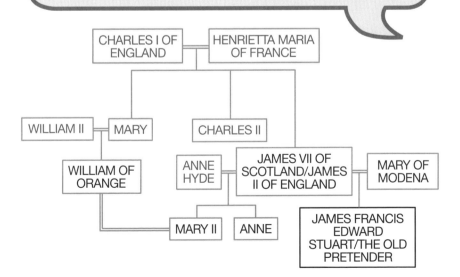

LOCHS
UNLOCKING THE FACTS

What is a loch?
Loch is a Gaelic word for a lake or a sea fiord. In Ireland, where Gaelic originated the same word is used but is spelled Lough. The word Lough is also used just over the border in Northumberland, but here it is pronounced *loff.* In Scotland, a smaller loch is called a Lochan.

Fiords are basically inlets of the sea and are known as Sea Lochs. It is difficult to measure the length or area of sea lochs since it is hard to determine the boundaries between each loch and the wider ocean. Sea lochs often stretch many miles inland and are different to the much wider estuaries called firths.

Fresh water lochs
These are the land-locked lochs that do not directly enter the sea, though all of course are ultimately linked to the sea by rivers.

How many lochs are there?
There are more than 31,000 fresh water lochs in Scotland including the lochans.

What is the DEEPEST loch?
The deepest fresh water loch in Scotland is Loch Moray which reaches a depth of 310 metres but Loch Ness has the deepest mean average depth at 132 metres.

LONGEST lochs?
The five longest fresh water lochs in Scotland are: Loch Awe (41 km); Loch Ness (39 km); Loch Lomond (36 km); Loch Shiel (28 km) and Loch Shin (27.8 km).

The BIGGEST lochs?
Scotland's five BIGGEST lochs by AREA are: Loch Lomond (71 km2); Loch Ness (56 km2); Loch Awe (39 km2); Loch Maree (28.6 km2) and Loch Morar (27 km2).

MOST Water?
Scotland's five biggest lochs by VOLUME are: Loch Ness (7.45 km3); Loch Lomond (2.6 km3); Loch Morar (2.3 km3); Loch Tay (1.6 km3) and Loch Awe (1.2 km3).

June 26, 2032

Thistle Press

Protests Grow as Scottish National Gallery is Set to be Sold

Protests in Edinburgh continued for a fifth day yesterday as people took to the streets to complain about the proposed plans to sell the Scottish National Gallery building, and its contents to a wealthy unnamed billionaire.

The Gallery, designed by William Henry Playfair, first opened to the public in 1859. It famously houses some of the greatest art in Scotland, including works by Goya, Rembrandt, El Greco, Raphael, Cézanne and Botticelli. The main building, which the billionaire is particularly interested in purchasing, was remodelled in 1912 by William Thomas Oldrieve and shares an underground access with the Royal Scottish Academy Building. It is not known whether the Royal Scottish Academy building is included in the proposed sale.

Should the sale take place, the iconic building on the Mound will be dismantled brick by brick and moved to an undisclosed location possibly anywhere in the world. The research facilities at the National Gallery, including over 30,000 works of art and 50,000 books, slides, journals and microfiches will also be relocated.

The sale, which has been underway for some months now, has attracted a great deal of negative publicity from across the country, with many seeing it as selling off an important part of Scotland's cultural heritage.

Many people are flocking to Edinburgh to get what may be a final glimpse of the great artworks on show, while still holding out the hope that the government may have a change of heart. One thing is certain, until the sale does go through there will be protesters on Edinburgh's streets attempting to make their voices heard.

Montagne Sainte-Victoire by Paul Cézanne

SKYE

This sixty mile long island in the Inner Hebrides is the **fourth biggest island of the British Isles** or second biggest if we exclude Ireland and the British mainland. Of all the Scottish islands, only Lewis/Harris in the Outer Hebrides is bigger.

Skye's Gaelic name *An t-Eilean Sgitheanach* may mean 'winged-island'. It is also called *Eilean a' Cheò* 'Isle of mists' and its Viking, name *skuy* has the same meaning.

Skye consists of a number of peninsulas like Trotternish, Waternish and Miginish, each separated by sea lochs.

Skye has been inhabited since the Stone Age times and is currently home to over 9,000 people.

Historically it was settled by the Gaelic speaking Scots and later by the Vikings. Gaelic is spoken by many on the island particularly in the Kilmuir region where around 47% are Gaelic speakers.

For centuries Skye was dominated by the **MacDonald and MacLeod** clans, both claiming Viking ancestry.

Tourism, fishing, whisky distilling and crofting are important Skye industries. Attractions include **Armadale Castle** overlooking the Sound of Sleat in the south. This was the ancestral home of the MacDonalds of Sleat. **Dunvegan Castle**, ancestral home of the MacLeods can be found in the north west.

In the north there is a monument to the heroine **Flora MacDonald**, who is buried on Skye. She rescued Bonny Prince Charlie and brought him to Skye in 1745.

Skye mountain ranges include the eroded volcanic peaks of the **Black Cuillin**.

Many of Skye's towns and villages are clustered around the coast and the largest settlement is Portree on Loch **Portree** on the north east coast which has a population of just fewer than 2,500.

Skye is linked to different parts of the mainland by ferry, but a significant link is **Skye Bridge** which opened in 2005 linking Skye to the Kyle of Lochalsh.

JAMES BOWMAN LINDSAY
THE MAN WHO INVENTED THE ELECTRIC LIGHT

Student: Hey, I've just been reading about this Joseph Swan from Sunderland. Apparently he invented electric light in 1878.

History Man: Joseph Swan did indeed pioneer one of the first electric lights, as did Thomas Edison the following year. But have you ever heard of James Bowman Lindsay?

Student: James Bowman who?

History Man: Lindsay. He was a Scotsman who can also lay claim to being the first man to invent electric light, only he did it more than 40 years before Swan, in 1835.

Student: Really? That can't be right, surely?

History Man: In July 1835 Lindsay demonstrated a constant electric light at a public meeting in Dundee. He said that he created enough light to read a book from a foot and a half away.

Student: So why do we think of Swan and Edison when we think of electric light?

History Man: Well, as with a lot of great inventors, Lindsay wasn't really a businessman. He invented his electric light, but he didn't do much to actually develop his invention, or to make it commercial. So he gets forgotten, and Swan and Edison get the praise.

Student: That's a shame. Did he invent anything else?

History Man: Oh yes, a lot of different things. He invented an underwater telegraph, but it was flawed, and so it never got put into full usage. He was also one of the first people to propose arc welding, welding which uses electricity, as a method for manipulating metals.

Student: So, what happened to him? Did he end up rich and famous from his inventions?

History Man: No, although he did receive a £100 pension from the Prime Minister in recognition of his work, and a monument was erected to him after his death in 1862. You can see it at Western Cemetery in Dundee.

THIRTY SCOTTISH CASTLES

DOUNE CASTLE

The castle of Doune about six miles north west of Stirling dates back to the thirteenth century but was rebuilt by Robert Stewart, Duke of Albany in the late fourteenth century. It became the property of the Earls of Moray in the sixteenth century. Mary Queen of Scots stayed at the castle on numerous occasions and it was occupied by Bonnie Prince Charlie for a time during the Jacobite Rising of 1745. The castle was used for the filming of a number of scenes in the comedy film *Monty Python and the Holy Grail*.

DRUM CASTLE

This rather quaint castle near Drumoak in Aberdeenshire has a thirteenth century tower that is thought to be one of the oldest in Scotland. The castle was historically the home of the Irwyn (Irvine) family who were first given land here during the reign of Robert the Bruce.

DRUMLANRIG CASTLE

This castle in Dumfries and Galloway is the family home of the Duke and Duchess of Buccleugh. It is an impressive stately castle of pink sandstone noted for its art collection which includes works by Rembrandt. The castle was constructed in the late seventeenth century for William Douglas, the Duke of Queensberry.

DUART CASTLE

Situated on the Isle of Mull, this thirteenth century castle was the ancestral home of the MacLean family. The castle was abandoned in 1751 and fell into ruin. It was used as a location in the 1999 film *Entrapment* starring Sean Connery (a MacLean descendant) and Catherine Zeta Jones.

DUNNOTTAR CASTLE

This dramatic medieval ruin has a magnificently defended setting on a rocky headland surrounded by cliffs on the north east coast two miles south of Stonehaven. Most of its buildings date from the fifteenth and sixteenth centuries on a site that has a history as a fortress stretching back many centuries. The site was an important Pictish defended site first mentioned in 681 AD when a siege took place here. Another battle took place here between King Donald II and the Vikings in 900 AD. By the fifteenth century Dunnottar belonged to the Clan Keith. It was visited by Mary Queen of Scots on two occasions in the 1560s. The 1990 film *Hamlet* starring Glenn Close and Mel Gibson was filmed here.

THE SASSENACHS

Sooner or later, they had to be mentioned, those rivals to the south, with whom the Scots have been united in one kingdom since 1707.

Sassenach is the Scottish term for an Englishman, but what does it mean and where does it originate?

In short the word is Gaelic and means 'Saxon'. It occurs in Irish Gaelic and Scots Gaelic, but it's the Scots who mostly use it. Ironically it's one of the Scots Gaelic words most widely used by English speaking Scots.

The Welsh use a variation of the word too. In Welsh *Seisnig* means 'English people' and *Saesneg* means 'English language' but the Welsh don't use these words when speaking English.

The Saxons originated from the German coast south of Denmark's Jutland peninsula, and came over to what had previously been a largely Welsh speaking Britain in the fifth and sixth centuries. Accompanying the Saxons on their invasion was a closely related people called the Angles from the southern part of Jutland itself.

In truth Scotland's nearest neighbours were the Angles of Northumbria. Angles gave their name to England, and not the Saxons, but Scots indiscriminately referred to Angles and Saxons alike as Sassenachs.

Saxons settled mostly in the south of England but Angles settled all the way up to the Firth of Forth where their language came to dominate lowland Scotland. In fact in some cases the Scots language retained elements of Angle speech that were lost from the language of England itself.

For many centuries the Gaelic-speaking Highlanders of Scotland, referred to the Scottish lowlanders as Sassenachs and today, the term may still be occasionally used in that respect.

More commonly, now, the word Sassenach is usually used as a friendly jibe by Scots referring to their English rivals south of the border.

Angles

Saxons

THE BISHOPS' WARS AGAIN

Student: So what happened when the King called the Parliament in 1640?

History Man: They were angry with him, and they were much more interested in raising their grievances than they were in funding his war with the Covenanters. He ended up dissolving the Parliament after only three weeks, without any money for his war. It's known, unsurprisingly, as the "Short Parliament".

Student: So that left the King in a bit of a pickle then, did it?

History Man: It did, and things were about to get worse. The Covenanters actually invaded England, capturing Northumberland and County Durham. The King couldn't force them out, and ended up doing a deal with them called the "Treaty of Ripon" which left those two English counties in Scottish Covenanter hands, and he had to promise to pay their expenses too!

Student: I bet he didn't like that at all. I thought he didn't have any money before, and that's why he called the Short Parliament? So how was he going to pay for that?

History Man: He had to call Parliament again, this time in what became known as the "Long Parliament".

Student: Imaginatively named...

History Man: Quite. But calling the Long Parliament was the beginning of the end for Charles, they attacked his government, took away his powers, a series of moves which eventually ended with the monarchy's abolition and his execution.

Student: So how significant were the Covenanters and the Bishops' Wars?

History Man: Well, it's often seen as the beginning of the end for Charles, the squeeze on his power starting in Scotland before moving to London and they can claim to have had a big role in the birth of the only republic Britain's had so far.

Thistle Press

LATEST NEWS: Tragedy at Alexander Stephen & Sons Shipyard

Monday, July 3, 1882

124 Dead In Ship Launch Tragedy

News is coming in of a terrible tragedy which has occurred during the launch of a ship at the Alexander Stephen & Sons shipyard at Linthouse in Glasgow. More than one hundred people are feared dead.

Today was supposed to be a happy day, a day of fanfare and celebration marking the launch of the newly built ship, the SS Daphne from the yard.

As the ship was launched there were around 200 workers on board. These days when a ship is launched there is still much work to be done. This involves finishing off the interiors and this can't be done until the ship is actually afloat. That's why there were so many on board as the ship left the slipway.

Ships are launched in a controlled way, using two anchors on either side of the ship. The anchors slow the ship down, to keep it from going too quickly when it is finally released.

As the Daphne was launched, it is understood that the starboard anchor did its job, only moving six or seven yards, but the port anchor was dragged almost sixty yards by the force of this 460 ton ship.

As the ship slid into the river, the current caught it and, because one side was held back by the anchor and the other one wasn't, the ship capsized, flipping onto its port side in the middle of the river.

The ship sank into the deep water in the middle of the Clyde, and it is believed that 124 of the workers on board, many of them young boys have been drowned.

This will surely go down as the saddest day in Glasgow's proud maritime history, and one we will remember for many years to come.

THE DARIEN SCHEME

In the late seventeenth century, Scotland was in trouble. The country was very poor, and in the 1690s there was a famine which is thought to have killed as many as 10% of the population at the time.

In order to grow, Scotland had to go west, to the New World. In 1695 the Company of Scotland was established to trade Scottish goods with the rest of the world. A man called William Paterson came up with a plan. The Company would establish a colony at Darien in Panama, so that they could trade with the Atlantic and the Pacific Oceans at the same time.

They needed to raise a lot of money to make it work. England wouldn't support it because they were afraid it would interfere with English ambitions, so £400,000 (£30,000,000 today) was raised from Scotland for the expedition.

Six ships with 1,200 settlers set sail on July 4 1698 for Darien, with a further expedition to follow, but many of them died on the 14 week journey. When they got there, they realised it was going to be very difficult, there were long rainy seasons and the place they were to set up the colony became very marshy, and they couldn't grow much food. Many people died from starvation and disease.

On top of that, Panama was Spanish territory, and the Spanish made many attacks to try and force the Scots out. The King needed Spain as an ally to fight France, so he made sure nobody helped the settlers. In the end they fled back to Scotland in 1700, with only 500 living settlers from the 2,500 who had set sail.

It ended Scottish colonial ambitions, but it is interesting to consider what might have happened had it worked.

DOLLY THE SHEEP

"Ladies and gentlemen! Boys and girls!

Roll up, roll up, and come on in to my Worldly Wonderarium. It's time for you to see the modern medical marvel, one of the supreme successes of science, that's right ladies and gentlemen, Dolly the cloned sheep.

Dolly was cloned right here in Scotland, cloned from the cells of an adult sheep, cloned by scientists named Ian Wilmut, Keith Campbell and their colleagues at the Roslin Institute.

The very first mammal, that's right boys and girls, the very first mammal ever to be cloned from an adult cell in the whole wide world, roll up, roll up.

Born July 5 1996, a truly remarkable achievement Dolly was, let me tell you. Come gaze at her heroic hooves, be amazed by her sheepish face, and let me dazzle you with her wondrous woolly coat.

Ladies and Gentlemen, I said you could see Dolly, I said you could marvel in wonder at her, but I must now tell you something. The Dolly born in 1996 passed away on February 14 2003.

No, please madam, come back, I promised you a Dolly and I'm going to give you a Dolly. In fact, I'm going to do better than that; I'm going to give you four Dollys. The stars of science have done it again, folks, but they've gone one better. In 2010 they cloned four more Dollys for your delectation and delight, so come on in, roll right up, and take a good look at a superb bit of Scottish science right before your eyes."

ARTHUR CONAN DOYLE

"Good day to you sir, madam, you may know me as the world's greatest consulting detective, Sherlock Holmes. I see that you have some doubt as to the truth of my claim. For that I cannot blame you, I have seldom been in evidence these last few years, but I come to you now on a matter of utmost importance, I come to tell you the story of my creator.

Born in Edinburgh on May 22 1859, Mr Conan Doyle became a medical student at the University of Edinburgh, studying under the famous Doctor Joseph Bell, the man who many say was the inspiration for me. Alas, his medical practice was not successful, but what was successful was his writing, in particular giving birth to me on the pages of Beeton's Christmas Annual in 1887, in the form of my famous case known to you as *A Study In Scarlet*.

Both I and my good friend and constant companion Watson were of great help to Mr Conan Doyle, and we gained him much admiration, his tales of our exploits thrilling the world. He was also a keen sportsman, playing football for Portsmouth AFC and cricket for the Marylebone Cricket Club (MCC), during which time he took one first class wicket, that of Mr W. G. Grace.

He did attempt to kill me, at the Reichenbach Falls in 1893, but the outcry was so strong that I returned in 1901, and solved many a further case. A fine man, I'm sure you will agree, a father of five and a committed political activist, sadly Mr Conan Doyle died on July 6 1930, but his legacy lives on through me and my associate, Watson, not to mention through the lasting contribution we together made to crime fiction."

Arthur Conan Doyle

Sherlock Holmes

THE SCOTTISH ENLIGHTENMENT

COMING SOON TO A HISTORICAL PERIOD NEAR YOU...

A tale of achievement, a tale of discovery, a tale of triumph and disaster. In July, make sure you're ready for:

A JAMES CAMERON FILM

THE SCOTTISH ENLIGHTENMENT 3D

After years in the dark, after centuries as an intellectual backwater, something is happening in Scotland. Thinkers DAVID HUME (KEVIN SPACEY), ADAM SMITH (JOHNNY DEPP), JOSEPH BLACK (CHRISTIAN BALE), JAMES HUTTON (MATT DAMON), FRANCIS HUTCHESON (MEATLOAF) and JAMES WATT (THE GINGER ONE FROM HARRY POTTER) are just some of the intellectuals brought together to revolutionise eighteenth century Scotland.

Using cutting edge technology, director **JAMES CAMERON** brings the invention and academic achievement of the Scottish Enlightenment to you in staggeringly realistic 3D. Gasp as David Hume confounds modern science with the problem of induction, howl as Francis Hutcheson puts forward his revolutionary ethical theories, and be shocked by James Watt's development of the concept of horsepower to measure the power of engines.

This year, for the first time, you can see all of the achievements which made Scotland the intellectual centre of the world. This all-star cast will show you exactly what it means to be an academic genius.

From the producers of The Spanish-American War, from the team who brought you The London Matchgirls Strike of 1888, comes one of the greatest periods in modern Scottish history.

"HAD ME ROLLING IN THE AISLES - ABSOLUTELY THE FEEL GOOD HIT OF THE SUMMER"
NAPOLEON BONAPARTE
"INTELLIGENT, INTENSE, AND REMARKABLY WELL SCRIPTED"
MAHATMA GANDHI
"CLEVERER THAN ANYTHING I'VE EVER DONE"
ALBERT EINSTEIN

ON JULY 7, THE SCOT IS HOT

SAWNEY BEAN
THE SCOTTISH CANNIBAL

I know you like ghoulish and gory stories; I like ghoulish and gory stories too. And here's one of the most ghoulish of all the gory Scottish stories, the tale of Sawney Bean.

Sawney Bean was born in a small village 10 miles from Edinburgh sometime in the fifteenth century. At the age of 20 he ran away with a woman called "Black Agnes" Douglas. They decided they did not want to live an honest life, and set up home in a sea cave north of Ballantrae, in Ayrshire. In order to survive, Sawney and Black Agnes set about ambushing travellers, murdering them, and eating their bodies! They ate their entrails raw, and they pickled and salted the limbs!

They had children, and their children had children, until there were 46 people living in the cave, murdering many people and eating their dead bodies. One day, they attacked a man and woman riding home from the fair. The woman was torn from her horse and eaten alive by the pack of cannibals. However before they could start on the man, they were interrupted by a large party of people, and they had to run away.

When the people got back to Glasgow, they told the local magistrate of what they had witnessed. The magistrate then informed the King, and the King took 400 men, and a pack of bloodhounds, and set out to find Sawney's clan.

The bloodhounds found the cave, and when the King's men entered it they saw it was full of dead bodies. They took Sawney and his family back to Edinburgh, where they were convicted of the murder of more than 1,000 people, and executed. The men had their hands and legs cut off, and were left to bleed to death, whilst the women were burnt at the stake.

Pretty gory, I'm sure you'll agree!

WHAT'S YOUR NAME?

MacDougall
Descended from Dugall, son of Somerled, Norse King of the Isles. Surname is still numerous today. Dugall's lands included Mull, Jura and Tiree and most of Argyll.

MacDuff
'Son of the Black' (MacDhuibh) the family is linked to the ancient kings of the Scots and Picts. The Shaw of Tordarroch clan are descended from a branch of the MacDuffs but are not to be confused with the English surname Shaw.

MacEwan
Descended from Ewen of Otter of Loch Fyne in Argyll. MacEwans are first mentioned in 1174.

MacFarlane
Descended from Parlan, son of Malduin, a contemporary of Robert the Bruce. Malduin was a descendant of the Earls of Lennox.

MacFie/MacPhee
From the Gaelic Mac Dhubhsith 'son of the dark fairy'. Reputedly descended from a woman who was partly a seal or sea creature. Numerous on Colonsay.

MacGregor
Descended from Gregor of the Golden Bridles who lived in the fourteenth century. Associated with Glenstrae, Glenlochy and Glenorchy. MacGregors were outlawed by James VI in 1603 and forced to renounce their name or hang. Rob Roy (born 1671) was a member of the clan.

MacInnes
Descended from the rulers of the Dal Riata Scots of Argyll. Derives from MacAonghais (son of Angus) and can be traced back to the seventh century.

MacIntyre
Gaelic name means 'son of the Carpenter'. In legend they descend from MacArill, a nephew of Somerled, a twelfth century Viking lord. MacArill bored holes in the galley of Olaf, a Scandinavian King who ruled the Scottish Isles. He only plugged them in after the King agreed to offer Somerled his daughter's hand in marriage. Somerled eventually ruled Olaf's lands. It was supposedly for this reason that the MacIntyres became associated with carpentry. Clan lands include Glen 'Oe around Loch Etive near Oban.

July 10, 1857

Thistle Press

Madeleine Smith "Not Proven" Verdict Ends Trial of The Century

Yesterday in Edinburgh one of the most intriguing murder cases of recent years concluded in Edinburgh, with the jury giving a "not proven" verdict. This verdict means that, although the jury did not believe in Miss Smith's innocence, they felt that the prosecution had not made a convincing enough case against her.

Miss Smith, 22, the well known Glasgow socialite, was accused of the murder of Emile L'Angelier, apprentice nurseryman and Miss Smith's former lover. Mr L'Angelier died on March 23 this year from arsenic poisoning.

Miss Smith had fled the city shortly after L'Angelier's death, and was followed to her family's holiday home at Rhu by a suitor of hers, Mr William Minnoch. Upon investigation of Mr L'Angelier's personal effects, love letters were found from Miss Smith to Mr L'Angelier, and notebooks detailing his meetings with Miss Smith in the weeks running up to his death.

This, along with the suggestion Miss Smith feared Mr L'Angelier would sabotage her proposed marriage to Mr Minnoch, was enough for the police to investigate Miss Smith, and it was discovered that she had purchased arsenic from a chemist.

She was arrested, and placed on trial for the murder of Mr L'Angelier. This case fascinated the public, with almost 10,000 people attempting to gain access to the public galleries in the court.

Public opinion has backed Miss Smith in an unusual fashion, and that faith was rewarded yesterday with the "not proven" verdict, arrived at by the jury after deliberating for only thirty minutes.

Whether Miss Smith is innocent, or whether a guilty woman has just walked free, this is a case which is sure to fascinate for many years to come.

CRANNOGS:
LIVING ON A LOCH

How would you fancy living on a loch? Now I don't mean on the banks of a loch, no I mean on the loch itself. Some Scots have been doing this for centuries.

How can you live on a loch? Well you could live in a Crannog of course! A Crannog is a kind of ancient circular-shaped dwelling built in a loch. They are in truth artificial islands, built to house families. Sometimes they are modified natural islands that already existed within the loch.

There have been Crannogs in Scotland for at least 5,000 years, and people were still building or modifying them as dwellings as late as the seventeenth century.

What were they for? Well essentially they were homes for farmers or were fishing stations. They could be used as refuges in times of trouble and may sometimes have served as symbols of status or inherited power. Some Crannogs were continuously inhabited for several centuries.

Many early crannogs were round timber-built houses supported by stilts driven deep into the bed of a loch. Where wood wasn't available, rocks were piled high on the bed and a stone house built on the resulting island.

There are 347 officially listed Crannogs in Scotland and perhaps as many as 500 if we include the Hebridean variation called Atlantic Roundhouses.

In Ireland there are more than a thousand and in both countries new ones are occasionally discovered by divers and archaeologists.

Scotland's oldest known Crannog is the artificially created island of Eilean Domhnuill on Loch Olabhat on North Uist which may date from as early as 3600 BC.

An authentic reconstruction of a Crannog can be seen at the **Scottish Crannog Centre** near Kenmore on Loch Tay. It was built by the Scottish Trust for Underwater Archaeology.

ROBERT BARCLAY ALLARDICE
THE CELEBRATED PEDESTRIAN

"And you join me at Newmarket Heath, on July 12 1809. We have reached a critical moment in one of the great sporting events, some might say, of all time. Captain Robert Barclay Allardice, the 'celebrated pedestrian', will today complete the Herculean task of walking 1,000 miles in 1,000 hours.

The feat, which began forty two days ago on the first of June has involved Captain Barclay walking a mile every hour for the last 1,000 hours and is about to be successfully completed. Captain Barclay has been much celebrated in the field of competitive walking since he walked 110 miles in 19 hours and 27 minutes back in 1796 but this will be Captain Barclay's greatest achievement to date.

Captain Barclay, born in Stonehaven, Kincardineshire on August 25 1779, has attracted much public attention and admiration with this competition, and indeed there have been as many as 10,000 spectators who have come to watch him since his walk began.

This has made Captain Barclay one of the most famous and respected sportsmen in Britain. Helped by the public's continuing fascination with competitive walking as a sport, it is certainly a sport at which Captain Barclay excels.

Although he is a practiced pedestrian, this exertion has been very taxing for Captain Barclay, I am told that the sleep deprivation caused by him walking a mile every hour has almost broken him physically.

...And here he is, coming around the corner now; he's onto the final stretch of his final mile, the crowning achievement of a long career in professional walking. He's approaching the finishing line, and yes, yes he's done it!

A great day for Captain Barclay and a great day for the sport itself."

ROBERT BARCLAY ALLARDICE

EDINBURGH ZOO

"Well good morning, gentlemen. My name is Thomas Gillespie, and I come before you today to tell you about my vision for Edinburgh, or more precisely my vision for a new Zoological park in Edinburgh. Too long have the people of Edinburgh been unable to look at the many wonders of the natural world in their own city, but I plan to change all of that.

'But Thomas', you cry, 'will such exotic beasts be able to live through the grim Edinburgh winters?' I too had my doubts about this, but I am encouraged by the new zoo in Hamburg, Germany. As many of you may know, Hamburg has a winter climate very similar to that of Edinburgh, and the many creatures in that zoo live a happy life.

I will be seeking, from you, contributions towards the purchasing of a site I have decided will be perfect for the foundation of our new zoo. The estate of Corstorphine Hill House is that site, eighty five acres to the west of the city, and I have it on good authority that it will cost the sum of £17,000 to purchase.

I am aware that is a sizeable sum, yet just consider what we can do if we acquire this site. Edinburgh Zoo will be unlike the menageries you may have seen in other cities. No, this will not be a site of small cages for these mighty beasts; instead they will have large enclosures through which to roam, making them far more comfortable than they could possibly be anywhere else.

I am Thomas Gillespie, and today I ask you to help me in this great quest. Thank you."

(The Scottish National Zoological Park was opened in the summer of 1913)

THE TEXTILE INDUSTRY

Weaving and textiles played a massive role in the history of Scotland over the centuries and many of Scotland's greatest towns and cities owe their early growth and development to this industry.

In early times wool was exported abroad from Scotland to Flemish or Baltic ports for the manufacture of textiles overseas. Monasteries like Melrose in the Borders, which owned considerable quantities of sheep played an important part in this trade. Soon the making of linen from flax became important at home in places like Melrose and by the sixteenth century the woollen cloth industry had become important in Scotland.

By the nineteenth century the Borders were noted for their tweed and the west of Scotland for cottons. Some towns were noted for particular textiles, such as Dunfermline known for its damask and fine linens, Edinburgh and Kirkcaldy for their linens, Paisley for its patterned shawls, Aberdeen for its heavy cloths, Galashiels for its wools and tweeds, Dundee for its jute and the Irvine valley for lace making.

Galashiels was famed for its checked cloth called "Shepherd's Plaid", popularised by Sir Walter Scott and it was Scott who also popularised the use of tartan.

The cloth produced from what was called a *twill* or *tweel* weave is thought to have incorrectly acquired the name "Tweed" from an improperly written invoice sent from a William Watson of Hawick in the Borders to a London merchant called Joseph Locke in 1826.

Locke was in truth, a Scot, very familiar with the material and may have simply created the name Tweed as a brand. Tweed from the Isle of Harris in the Hebrides - the famed Harris Tweed - was popularised by a Lady Dunmore in the 1840s.

Today textile manufacture is still an important industry in Scotland with around 20,000 people employed in the textile trade.

MIDGE RAP

Mary MacMidge: Me and the girls and it's always the girls, love to hang out in our mad Midge worlds. We gather in crowds, waiting to bite, we're called midge clouds and we're quite hard to fight.

Maggie MacMidge: Yes we're true Highland Midges, from the good clan MacMidge, we love the damp summers and winters like fridge.

Mary MacMidge: Oh dear, my good Mags, your rhyme sucks of blood. Cold kills our foes, and for us that is good.

Maggie MacMidge: But most of all, Mary, we love to bite. One look at a human and we bite them on sight. We love human blood but any will do – cattle, cats, deer, or even a ewe.

Mary MacMidge: We don't care what you're called if it's Smith, Jones or Ronald, though Campbell MacMidges love eating MacDonalds.

Maggie MacMidge: Our favourite time's dusk and also at dawn, we'll hover on hillsides or down near the lawn.

Mary MacMidge: You'll not see our faces and really nice legs, as we suck out your blood to nourish our eggs.

Maggie MacMidge: We're the girls who should scare you. We have all the powers. You see, we feed off the blood, while boys feed on the flowers.

Mary MacMidge: So when we come down, in a cloud or a shower, be warned that we chomp at 3,000 bites per hour.

Maggie MacMidge: There's no point in hiding, coz we'll smell your breath, but no need to worry, we won't cause your death.

Mary MacMidge: So be nice to us please, we are only titchy. The worst that we'll do is leave you quite itchy.

SCOTLAND PLACE-NAMES
WHAT DO THEY MEAN?

GLENCOE

Gaelic Gleann Comhann 'narrow glen'.

GLENEAGLES

Valley in Perthshire gave name to a golf course at Auchterarder. Gaelic Gleann Eaglais 'glen of the church'.

GLENROTHES

New town of 29,000 created in 1948 as a mining settlement. Named after the Earls of Rothes, local landowners who owned the colliery.

GRAMPIANS

Ancient name for mountains of unknown meaning. Romans mention a battle with the Caledonians at Mons Graupius which may be connected.

GRETNA GREEN/GRETNA

From the Anglo-Saxon Greoten-Halh meaning, 'gravelly meadow or nook'.

HAMILTON

Town of 49,000 people in the Clyde Valley south east of Glasgow. Originally called Cadzow, it was renamed by the first Lord of Hamilton when he became resident here in the 1400s.

HELENSBURGH

Spa town and coastal resort built in 1776 by Sir James Colquhoun. On the north side of the Firth of Clyde. Named after James's wife, Helen.

INVERARAY

On the north shore of Loch Fyne (a sea loch) where the River Aray enters the loch. Means 'mouth of the Aray' from the Gaelic word Inbhir 'river mouth'.

INVERNESS

City of 44,000 people where the River Ness and Caledonian canal enter the Moray Firth. Gaelic name means 'mouth of the Ness'. Gave its name to Inverness-shire.

SCOTTISH MONEY

There's one little bit of Scotland that manages to make its way all over the United Kingdom. No, it's not bagpipes, no, it's not haggis, we're talking about Scottish money.

Scotland has been producing its very own money since the bank of Scotland was founded on July 17, 1695. Three hundred and odd years of making money, you've got to admit that's pretty good! Scotland enjoys an excellent, and very stable, exchange rate with England, with one Scottish pound being worth exactly the same as one English pound!

There are three banks in Scotland which now print money, the Bank of Scotland, the Royal Bank of Scotland and the Clydesdale Bank. This means that there are a lot of different types of Scottish notes that you can see, but you can spend any of them anywhere.

There's about two billion pounds worth of Scottish notes in the world at any one time, just think what you could buy with all that money!

The one thing Scotland doesn't produce is coins, only the Royal Mint in London is allowed to make them, but to make up for it the Royal Bank of Scotland made £1 notes, and if you're lucky you might find one of those instead.

There's another reason that Scottish banknotes are special, because they're not actually "legal tender" anywhere in the world! Scottish notes are technically "promissory notes", not legal tender. And English notes are only legal tender in England and Wales, in Scotland they're "promissory notes" too. So that means that there aren't any notes that are legal tender in Scotland. Weird!

Still, that's not stopping the banks and the shops in Scotland from accepting all that lovely Scottish money; let's hope it stays that way for another three hundred years.

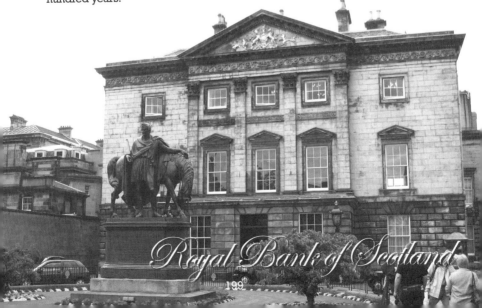

JOHN PAUL JONES

JOHN PAUL JONES

AMERICA'S FIRST NAVAL HERO

YOURNATIONALHEROES.COM

When you're starting a new country, you need a number of different ingredients to make sure that you are successful. From suitable land to united people, from natural resources to the acceptance of other world powers, there are an awful lot of things to think about.

One thing you might not have considered is your new country's heroic figures, the kind of men and women that your people can unite behind and be proud of.

If the hero factor is one you haven't addressed yet, don't panic.

We at YourNationalHeroes.com have got you covered.

For one low monthly fee we will keep you supplied with top class heroes who will thrill and unite your people.

In month one you will receive John Paul Jones.

John Paul Jones was born John Paul in Kircudbrightshire on July 6 1747. He started his career as a sailor at 13, sailing from Whitehaven in Cumbria, a town he would famously return to raid many years later.

The captain of his own ship by the age of 21, John Paul Jones was a fierce man with a hot temper. After immigrating to America, he enlisted in the newly formed Continental Navy in 1775. He led a number of expeditions to Europe, which included raids on Whitehaven, and on the north east coast of England where the famous battle off Flamborough Head took place.

After the American War of Independence, he was recommended by Thomas Jefferson for a role in the Russian Navy, where he became a Rear Admiral and played an important part in the Black Sea campaign against the Turks.

John Paul Jones died July 18 1792 aged 45, but, not letting death stand in the way, he can be yours if you *join* YourNationalHeroes.com TODAY!

Did you know?
Waterfalls

The three highest waterfalls in Britain are all in Scotland. They are:

The Falls of Glomach

Glomach means 'gloomy', but these falls are anything but. They're in Ross-shire, on the Kintail and Morvich estate owned by the National Trust for Scotland. The falls themselves are 370 feet high, and although it's about a five mile walk to reach them they're really worth it once you get there.

Steall Waterfall

Another beautiful waterfall, this time in Glen Nevis near Fort William. The waterfall's name, An Steall Bàn, means 'The White Spout' in Gaelic. Steall Waterfall is 393 feet high and it forms the centrepiece of a popular walking route known as the Ring of Steall, which includes climbing four Munros. This is a favourite route of highland walkers, but it has been known to be treacherous, and should only be walked with extreme care.

Eas a' Chual Aluinn

The highest waterfall in Scotland, and indeed in Britain, Eas a' Chual Aluinn is 696 feet high. This makes it taller than the Victoria Falls (360ft) on the Zambezi River in Africa and Niagra Falls (167ft) in North America – put together! The waterfall is in Sutherland, and the water eventually runs into Loch Beag. This area is also very dangerous because it is so remote, but it is one of the most beautiful sights in Scotland.

Professor
C. Claggs

SCOTTISH FOOTBALLERS XI

(Take Two)

We couldn't fit all the great Scottish players into one team, so here's our second pick.

GK: Andy Goram
Played more than 600 games for 12 different clubs, including Rangers, Hibs and Manchester United. Was voted Rangers' greatest ever goalkeeper, and got 43 Scotland caps.

RB: Danny McGrain
Played 657 times for Celtic during 20 years at the club, collecting 14 trophies; 62 Scotland caps.

LB: Dave MacKay
Although really a centre back, he slots in at left back here, 135 games for Hearts, 318 games for Spurs, 122 games for Derby and 26 games for Swindon; 22 Scotland caps.

CB: Billy McNeill
Nicknamed "Cesar", McNeill, was Celtic captain and played almost 800 times for the club, winning countless trophies in the process including the European Cup; 29 Scotland caps.

CB: Alan Hansen
Started out at Partick Thistle and then became the lynchpin of the great Liverpool team of the 1980s. More than 600 appearances for Liverpool and 26 Scotland caps.

RW: Gordon Strachan
Played for Dundee, Aberdeen, Manchester United, Leeds and Coventry; won 50 Scotland caps.

LW: Davie Cooper
645 league games for Clydebank, Rangers and Motherwell; 22 Scotland Caps. Davie Cooper sadly passed away on March 23 1995 aged just 39.

CM: Graeme Souness
Another Scottish Liverpool legend, with 247 league games for the club. His career also included spells at Middlesbrough, Sampdoria, and as player-manager of Rangers. He won 54 Scotland caps and captained Scotland.

CM: Paul McStay
677 appearances for Celtic at every level; 76 Scotland caps.

ST: Denis Law
237 league goals in 485 league games for Huddersfield, Torino and both Manchester clubs, as well as 30 goals in 55 games for Scotland.

ST: Mo Johnston
A controversial choice, but a worthy one with 236 goals in 688 games for Celtic, Rangers, and 7 other clubs. 14 goals in 38 games for Scotland.

ROBERT BURNS

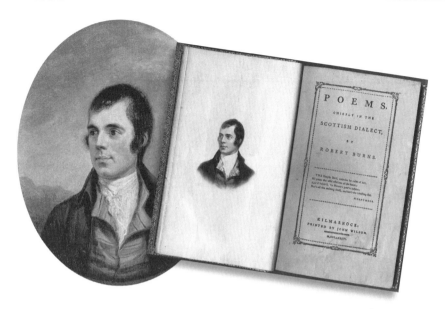

Born in Alloway near Ayr on January 25 1759, Robert Burns, also known as "Rabbie Burns", only lived to be 37, but in that short time he made his mark upon Scottish literature and Scotland's place in the world as a whole. Burns is undoubtedly Scotland's national poet and regarded by many in Scotland as the greatest Scot ever to have lived.

The eldest of seven children, Robert's father was a farmer and as a family they moved around as his father attempted to make a living to support his children. Robert was never destined for a farming life, however, and soon his poems began to be published.

In 1786 *Poems, Chiefly in the Scottish Dialect* was published in Kilmarnock. This work made him very famous, and in November that year he went to Edinburgh and sold the rights to have it published again, which it was on April 17 1787.

As well as being Scotland's national poet Burns was also a collector of Scottish folk songs which he often adapted in his own works. Burns most famous words are undoubtedly those of his poem "Auld Lang Syne" sung the world over at the beginning of each New Year. Other famed works include "Scots Wha Hae" and "Tam O' Shanter".

Burns stayed in Edinburgh until 1788 when he retired to Dumfries, and settled on a farm with his long term partner Jean Armour, who became his wife that year. He turned down many attractive offers in order to stay and write. Sadly, he died on July 21 1796 but his poems have outlasted him and will surely stand the test of time.

THE ACTS OF UNION

Student: Hey, can you tell me about the Act of Union?

History Man: You mean the Acts of Union. There were two of them.

Student: What do you mean?

History Man: Both Scottish and English parliaments had to sign them. The English signed in 1706 and the Scots in 1707 and that's why people usually associate 1707 with the union, but the terms were actually agreed on July 22 1706.

Student: So why did they happen? What was in it for the English?

History Man: Well, the crowns of England and Scotland had been united in 1603 when King James VI of Scotland also became James I in England, but the countries were still officially separate. The English had decided who was going to have the English throne after Queen Anne with the Act of Settlement of 1701, but the Scots could have chosen someone else, and the English didn't want them to do that.

Student: So if the English wanted to keep the Scots from choosing a different monarch, why did the Scots want it?

History Man: After the failure of the Darien Scheme in the 1690s, Scotland was very nearly bankrupt. There'd been a number of bad harvests in the previous years, and Scotland had suffered greatly. Scotland also wanted to play a part in the trading empire that had developed in England.

Student: And did it work out?

History Man: Well, the English managed to stop the Scots from picking a different king, and the Scots were saved from bankruptcy. They also managed to turn themselves from an economic backwater into one of the major trading nations of Europe. The country the Acts created went on to be one of the most successful empires that the world has ever seen.

ISLE OF MULL

Mull is the **fourth largest island in Scotland**. Only Lewis with Harris, Skye and Shetland's mainland are larger. Mull belongs to the Scottish island group called the **Inner Hebrides**.

Mull is separated from Scotland's mainland by the Sound of Mull on its north east coast and the Firth of Lorn to the south east.

The island is home to over **2,600** people of which 700 live in **Tobermory**, the island's capital which forms a picturesque harbour on the north side of the island.

Mull was first mentioned on a map by the Roman geographer Ptolemy around 150 AD when it was called **Maleos** but the island had been inhabited in much earlier times. Burial cairns, standing stones and a stone circle are evidence of this past. In the sixth century, **Iona**, off Mull's south west coast became home to St Columba and a centre of Christianity.

In the Viking period Mull came under the rule of the Norsemen. They gave the island its present name which means 'headland'. Mull formed part of the Norse-ruled domain called **Sudreyar** (south islands). The Norsemen also named Ulva (wolf island) just off Mull's western shore.

Ulva was the birthplace of **Lachlan Macquarie** 'the father of Australia' who was the Governor of New South Wales from 1809 to 1822. A mausoleum in memory of the man can be seen near the village of Gruline on the Mull mainland.

Historically Mull was associated with the MacLeans and later the Campbell clan. **Duart Castle** and the nearby **Torosay Castle** on the eastern coast of Mull and **Moy Castle** on the island's southern shore are among Mull's notable landmarks.

The town of Tobermory with its colourful and brightly painted harbourside houses is the home of a whisky distillery and is the fictional setting for the young children's TV programme *Balamory*.

WILLIAM GED
THE INVENTOR OF
STEREOTYPING

All Scottish people wear kilts and only eat fried food. The Irish are constantly cheerful, eat nothing but potatoes and drink only Guinness. Everyone from Liverpool wears shell-suits and has curly hair and moustaches.

People from Newcastle never wear a coat, even when the weather is very cold and they always carry coal. People from Yorkshire are neither friendly, nor generous. People from the south of England all talk posh except for Cockneys who speak in rhyming slang, sew buttons onto all their clothing and eat jellied eels.

The man you have to thank for all of these, and many more sweeping generalisations, is William Ged, the inventor of stereotyping. William Ged was a goldsmith from Edinburgh, born in 1699. He is responsible for all of these offensive statements, and many more besides. I don't know why we're even... Hang on...

Sorry about that, it turns out William Ged *was* from Edinburgh, but he *didn't* invent this kind of stereotyping. No! The stereotyping he invented was a brand new kind of printing, not the practice of generalising about people based on one of their characteristics. Sorry about that, William.

William Ged's stereotyping was a process which enabled people to print things over and over again, and it could be done in a much quicker and easier way than ever before. It meant that books became much easier to make, which made them cheaper to make. And since they were cheaper to make, they were also cheaper for people to buy, which meant more people could buy them.

It's a great thing that William did, trust me. And I'm sure he wasn't responsible for any of those awful things I put at the beginning...

THE MANY SCOTS OF SCOTLAND

Scotland. A place where many things have happened that changed the history of the world. A place that has changed the living standards today. A place of freedom and past victory. A place of beautiful scenery and purple moors. A place where animals enjoy their wild life in the highlands. A place that is independent and strong. A place that is home to millions, a place that is Scotland.

Think about David Tennant. He is from Bathgate, a town in Scotland. He has made many people in Scotland believe that it doesn't matter if you live in the most fancy city, or the most horrible. He proved to many that you don't need to live in Hollywood or New York to have your dreams a reality. He proved to Scotland's citizens that if you aspire to become anything, you just have to believe in yourself. And that's exactly what he did.

Take Robert Burns; a poet that loved his country and regularly wrote about it. Sean Connery; multi-awarded actor and producer. Gerard Butler; another very famous and talented actor. Shirley Henderson; most known for portraying the character Moaning Myrtle in the Harry Potter series. These people and many more, like David Tennant, who believed they could achieve something extraordinary, if they tried.

Scotland should be proud of its achievements. In Scotland, anything can happen. Any dream, any belief, any inspiration. I am proud to be Scottish. I am proud to be a Scot!

My Scotland
Young Writer

Name: Sarah Kate Bradley
Age: 12
School: Bathgate Academy, West Lothian

SCOTTISH STARS OF STAGE AND SCREEN
PART TWO

EWAN MCGREGOR
Arguably the biggest Scottish movie star in the world today, Ewan McGregor has been in films as diverse as *Trainspotting, Shallow Grave* and *Moulin Rouge*, not to mention his starring role as Obi-Wan Kenobi in the trilogy of *Star Wars* prequels. Born in Perth on March 31 1970, he is a true superstar, whilst also being an accomplished stage actor.

PETER CAPALDI
Born in Glasgow on April 14, 1948, Peter is perhaps most famous in recent years for his role as Malcolm Tucker in the Armando Iannucci comedies *The Thick of It* and *In The Loop*, Peter Capaldi is an accomplished actor, writer and film director. He won an Oscar and a BAFTA in 1995 for his short film *Franz Kafka's It's a Wonderful Life*, and has starred in many films and television shows over the last twenty five years. He's also been in TV shows such as *Skins, Doctor Who* and *Fortysomething*.

RICHARD WILSON
Richard Wilson, born July 9 1936 in Greenock, is best known to television audiences for his starring role as Victor Meldrew in the long running and much loved sitcom *One Foot In The Grave*. As well as acting, however, he is also a theatre director and broadcaster, having appeared in many different productions over a long and varied career. A loyal supporter of Greenock Morton FC, in 1996 he was also elected Rector of Glasgow University, a post he held until 1999.

eter Capaldi

Ewan McGregor

Richard Wilson

THE BATTLE OF KILLIECRANKIE

"Eeeeh, well you'll never guess what happened the other day... I'm away down to the town to get my shopping in, and this young laddie comes up to me in the street... 'Alright darling', he says, 'do you want to buy the Battle of Killiecrankie?'

Well I'd never heard anything like it, some wee boy asking me if I want to buy a battle fought on July 27 1689 between Jacobite forces led by Viscount Dundee and the Orange forces led by Hugh MacKay. Honestly, you just wouldn't credit it...

'Come on doll' he says to me, 'I'll give you a great deal for it, one time offer only.' Well I knew the importance of the battle, that it took place because Jacobite forces had taken Blair Castle, which had a commanding position on the main route through the Highlands.

'Here', he said, pressing the battle into my hand, 'I know you want it, you'll regret it if you don't.' I started to think about it then, you see, because I knew that when Hugh MacKay found out Blair Castle had been seized he sent his troops up the pass of Killiecrankie, in order to try and take it back.

The wee laddie was getting quite insistent now, and I did know that Dundee sent his forces down into the pass and with their strategic advantage and the ferocity of the Highland charge they forced MacKay's force into a full retreat, killing 2,000 of his men.

It was tempting, but then I thought about the fact that the Jacobites suffered heavy losses too, including the death of Dundee himself, and still ended up losing the war. So I bought the battle of Bannockburn off him instead."

MORE SCOTTISH INVENTORS

So many hugely important inventions are actually Scottish. Here's a couple you might know, or maybe you might not:

James Goodfellow
ATMs and PINs

Paisley-born James Goodfellow created one of the most common things in our world, the modern cash machine. Another Scotsman, John Adam Shepherd-Barron is credited with making a bank machine before Goodfellow, but his used radioactive cheques! Goodfellow came up with the idea of giving people a magnetic card and a secret number so they could get to their money. A pretty nifty invention, and now there's more than a million machines in the world.

William Murdoch
Gas lighting

Born in Ayrshire in Cumnock, on August 21 1754, William Murdoch was responsible for perfecting gas lighting, an innovation which made the streets of the world much safer at night. His house in Cornwall was the first domestic house in the world to be lit by gas. His other inventions include the pneumatic message system and the high powered steam engine, whilst working for the famous Boulton Watt Company. He died in 1839, but his inventions live on, and helped shape the industrial world.

Robert William Thompson and John Boyd Dunlop
Pneumatic Tyres

Robert William Thompson (born Stonehaven, Kincardineshire circa 1822) patented the pneumatic tyre in 1845, but gave up on his invention a year later and decided to use solid rubber tyres instead. Then in 1888, John Boyd Dunlop (born Dreghorn, Ayshire 1840) unaware of Thompson's invention, attempted to patent the pneumatic tyre. There was a long legal battle between the two, and eventually Dunlop had to accept that Thompson had patented it first, but Dunlop's design was superior and is in fact far more like the tyres we use today.

SCOTTISH FAIRY FOLK

NINE FAIRIES TAKE HOSTAGE IN BOAT KIDNAPPING
According to a story from Glen Esk in the Angus region a
popular piper was once kidnapped by nine fairies wearing
green robes, who sailed down the river in a tiny boat to
seize him. Apparently, they shrunk him with a magic wand
to get him on board. According to witnesses they sailed
three times around a pool in the river called Pontskinnen
Point before sailing upstream with him. He was never
seen again, but it is said that if you visit the right
place in Glen Esk, you can still hear his faint piping
somewhere in the distance.

MUSICAL CAVE FAIRIES
According to a story from Rosehall in
Sutherland, a man was drawn to music
in a cave in the hills near here in which
fairies were discovered playing on pipes.
Enchanted by the music he began to dance and
was not seen for a whole year. After a year passed
the man was discovered still dancing in the cave by
a passerby but no fairies could be seen. The man
could not be convinced he had been there a year
until he returned home to find his baby was one
year older.

SPECIAL DELIVERY
A midwife once rescued a large yellow frog from
being killed near the shore of Loch Ranza on the
Isle of Arran. Later a boy under the spell of a
fairy arrived at the midwife's house and
explained that the frog was actually the
Queen of the Fairies and that she wished
to meet her rescuer in person. After
arriving at a secret fairy hill mound, the midwife
successfully delivered a baby for the fairy queen.
Fairy Nuff!

NORTH, WEST, EAST, SOUTH

Most westerly mainland point: The point of Ardnamurchan on the Ardnamurchan peninsula in Argyll is the most westerly place on the British mainland.

Most westerly and most remote: The islands of **St Kilda** form the most westerly and most remote location in Scotland. They are situated in the North Atlantic 40 miles west of The Outer Hebrides. The island of **Rockall** could also make this claim. It lies a further 187 miles west of St Kilda and is claimed by Britain. It falls under the administration of the Outer Hebrides, but is also claimed by Ireland, Iceland and Denmark. Rockall is only 102 feet long and 83 feet wide.

Highest sea cliffs: The island of Hirta is the largest island on St Kilda and has the highest sea cliffs in the United Kingdom.

Scotland's southerly point: The **Mull of Galloway** is about 25 miles further south than Newcastle upon Tyne in England.

Most northerly mainland point: The most northerly point on the British mainland is **Dunnet Head**. It is 11 miles west of John O' Groats and 2 miles further north.

Most north easterly place: The most north easterly place on the British mainland is **Duncansby Head**. It is 2 miles further east than John O' Groats. Sorry John O' Groats.

Most north westerly place: Cape Wrath on the Scottish mainland is the most north westerly point in Britain.

Most easterly place: The island of **Bound Skerry** in the Shetlands is the most easterly location in Scotland. Peterhead is the most easterly point on the Scottish mainland.

Highest place in Britain: Ben Nevis at 1,344 metres (4,409 feet).

Highest village: Wanlockhead in Dumfries and Galloway is Scotland's highest village.

The coldest place: The coldest place in Britain is **Braemar**. A temperature of 27.2 Fahrenheit (minus 17 Celsius) was recorded in both 1895 and 1982.

HISTORIC TOWNS AND CITIES: GLASGOW

STATUS: Scotland's biggest city.

RIVER: The River Clyde flows through the heart of Glasgow.

NAMES AND NICKNAMES: "Beloved Green Place" is a translation of Glasgow's ancient name. In the local dialect it is called "Glasgae".

MOTTO AND EMBLEM: The city's motto is "Lord let Glasgow flourish through the preaching of thy word and praising thy name" or just "Lord Let Glasgow flourish".

POPULATION: The Glasgow authority area has a population of over **480,000** but lies at the centre of a continuously built up conurbation that is home to around **two million** people.

KEY FACTS AND INDUSTRIES: Glasgow has a long history dating back to medieval times and became a prosperous trading and industrial centre, particularly after the construction of Port Glasgow further down the Clyde. Its wealth and trade was built on the importing of goods from the Americas like tobacco, sugar and cotton. Shipbuilding and engineering also became important heavy industries in the city.

KEY DATES: 543 AD: St Mungo builds a church here. **1136:** The first stone of Glasgow Cathedral (St Mungos) laid. **1175:** Glasgow receives a charter. **1451:** Glasgow University established. **1600, 1652, 1657:** Fires devastate Glasgow. **1712:** A great flood devastates Glasgow. **1811:** Glasgow becomes the second city of the British Empire (in terms of population) after London. 1964: University of Strathclyde founded. **1964:** Glasgow Caledonian University founded.

THINGS TO SEE:

- **St George's Square** and its array of statues depicting the famous.
- **Glasgow City Art Gallery and Museum**, home of the Burrell Collection.
- **Royal Highland Fusilier Museum**.
- **Royal Exchange**, a grand building of 1775.
- **St Mungo's Cathedral**.
- **Tron Steeple** (1637), **Tolbooth Steeple** (1626) and **Merchants Steeple** (1872).
- **Hunterian Museum**, part of Glasgow University.
- **Provands Lordship**, Glasgow's oldest house dating from 1471.

GLASGOW

ABOUT THE ORKNEYS

The Orkney Islands consist of about seventy islands of varying sizes. Twenty islands are inhabited including the fifteen largest ones which are in order of size: **Mainland, Hoy, Sanday, South Ronaldsay, Rousay, Westray, Stronsay, Shapinsay, Eday, Papa Westray, Burray, Flotta, South Walls, North Ronaldsay** and **Egilsay.**

The 'ay' in these island names derives from a Viking word *ey* which simply means 'island'.

The Orkneys are home to around 20,000 people, of which about 15,000 live on the **Orkney Mainland**. The second most populous island is **South Ronaldsay**, where over 800 people live. Apart from this **Westray** is the only island with more than 500 people.

Hoy, the second largest of the Orkneys is home to less than 300 people. Its Viking name comes from *Háey* meaning 'high-island' which describes the way it rapidly rises from the sea. Hoy is quite untypical of the Orkneys being more mountainous than the rest.

The Orkneys can be reached by ferry from the Scottish mainland, departing from Gill's Bay, Scrabster and John O'Groats in Caithness.

The passenger only trip from **John O' Groats** is the quickest, crossing the ten mile **Pentland Firth** to reach **Burwick** on **South Ronaldsay**, one of the nearest points to the Scottish mainland.

The ferry trip passes in sight of the **Island of Stroma**, near the Caithness coast which is sometimes mistakenly considered to be one of the Orkneys.

The largest settlement on Orkney is the cathedral town of **Kirkwall**, where almost 9,000 people reside. It is situated on a narrow neck of land between the western and eastern regions of the Orkney mainland.

Here ferry services link Kirkwall to the larger Islands in the north.

The picturesque harbour town of **Stromness** is home to over 2,000 people and has ferry links to Hoy and Caithness.

SCOTTISH WEATHER

"You'd better watch it pal. I'm unpredictable. I'm a loose cannon. You can't handle me. I'm everywhere and nowhere. You put on shorts - I'm going to bring the rain. You stick your coat on - I'm going to make it the hottest day on record. But mostly, mostly I'm going to make it **drizzle**!

That's right, I'm **Scottish Weather**. You're stuck with me, but it's your own fault. I live up here, I've always lived up here, if you want to come and play on my turf, *you* play by *my* rules. After all, you've chosen to set up home somewhere on the same latitude as Scandinavia or Canada, and then you're surprised that I'm unpredictable?

You've not seen the half of it, if I didn't have the North Atlantic Drift sucking all that Gulf Stream warmth round the top of Scotland I'd be colder, much colder than you can even possibly imagine. I'd have made it icy for you, you can bet on it, instead you get a bit of rain, you get snow in the winter, and you complain? Well, you know what you can do!

I'm a temperate climate, an easy going guy. The sea freezes in Canada, I don't freeze the sea here, yeah I make it snow a bit in the winter but you've got to get used to that. You get long days in the summer, you get sunshine, it's mostly pretty good for you. Just don't make me angry, or there'll be a sting in the tail for Christmas, right!"

SELKIES
PART SEAL-PART MAN

In the islands of Scotland seals were often perceived to have human like qualities and many islanders regarded some seals as humans who had been caught under a spell. These creatures were known as 'selkies', mythical creatures also known in Iceland, The Faeroe Islands, Ireland and Wales.

Scottish islanders and particularly those of Orkney and Shetland believed that selkies could become human again simply by taking off their skins particularly at Midsummer Eve when they are said to have danced on the shore. Some believed that selkies were the reincarnated spirits of people who had drowned at sea.

On occasions men would marry female selkies after they had removed their skin but this often involved the human males having to hide the skin to prevent their brides from returning to the sea. According to one legend the children of one such human and his selkie wife discovered their mother's skin. Her yearning for the sea was too much to bear. She put on her selkie skin, headed for the sea and was never seen again.

Sometimes selkie males came ashore and found female humans to bear them children. One sad story relates how a lady of Orkney fell in love with a male selkie from the small

rocky island of Skule Skerry. She had a child by him, a baby boy but her selkie husband departed to the sea shortly afterward. Seven years later he returned with a gold chain for his son and took the boy away with him.

Years later the woman remarried and one day her husband shot two grey seals – an old one and a young one. A gold chain was found around the neck of the younger one and the woman wept when she realised that this was her son.

SIR HARRY LAUDER ENTERTAINER EXTRAORDINAIRE

Harry Lauder was one of the most famous Scottish entertainers of all time. Born in Edinburgh on August 4 1970, he later moved to Lanarkshire where as a young man he worked in the coal mines and entertained his fellow workers with his singing.

With their encouragement he exercised his vocal talents in local halls and his good voice coupled with a natural talent for song writing and comedy, gained him ever increasing popularity.

Soon his tours earned him national fame, particularly after he wrote the successful song **I Love a Lassie** for a pantomime in which he starred at Glasgow in 1905. Other songs by Harry include **Roamin' in the Gloamin', Keep Right on to the End of the Road** and **A Wee Deoch-an Doris.**

In 1912 Harry was top of the bill at the very first Royal Variety Performance at London's Palace Theatre, Shaftesbury Avenue in front of George V.

By this time Lauder was becoming increasingly popular in the United States, where he regularly toured on board his own train **The Harry Lauder Special**. In America and Britain he helped to define the popular image of Scottishness dressing for his performances in Kilt, Sporran, Tam O' Shanter and rough cut walking stick.

Harry was so successful that he was for a time the highest paid performer in the world and was the first British artist to sell a million records.

During the Great War, he was actively involved in entertaining the troops and helped raise a million pounds for the rehabilitation of serviceman back into civilian life. Harry was knighted for his efforts in 1919.

Harry retired from entertaining in 1935 but returned for a while to entertain the troops during the Second World War. Harry passed away at his luxurious home called Lauder Ha' near Strathaven in South Lanarkshire in 1950 aged 79.

CLANS

The origins of many Scottish clans are lost in the mists of time though clans often claim ancestry from ancient leaders or warriors. Some claim to be Norse or Irish in origin or may claim descent from the powerful Alpin family who united Scotland in the ninth century.

In truth, the early history of the clans is hard to trace with certainty and it was only in the twelfth and thirteenth centuries following the defeat of the Norsemen that the clans began to emerge from history with solid foundations.

The word *clan* is Gaelic and means 'offspring' or 'descendant', so clans were essentially a Highland concept. In the Lowlands of the north east and south of the Forth and Clyde a clan system also existed but here the term clan was not generally used for family groups until the nineteenth century. Families in these regions had names with more of an English or Norman ring to them and certainly in the south there were no clans with the familiar names beginning in Mac - the Gaelic word meaning 'sons of'.

Clans were ruled by a chief, whose authority within certain regions was of a feudal nature and verified by the Scottish Kings. In the 1740s the Highland clans were closely involved with the Jacobite rebellion and after the Battle of Culloden the clan system was suppressed. It did not end completely however, as many clan leaders became established members of the Scottish aristocracy.

The forced displacement of Highlanders in the Highland Clearances for the freeing up of agricultural land in the eighteenth and nineteenth centuries forced many clan members to seek new lives in North America.

Despite these events it was the nineteenth century that saw a growth of a romantic interest in the clans and their associated tartans, partly influenced by the novels of Sir Walter Scott.

PENICILLIN

In the modern world, there are a lot of threats to you and your family. Bacteria, germs, diseases from plants or animals, it's never been more important to use the right kinds of protection. The industry leader since its discovery in 1928 has been **Penicillin**, an invaluable substance in combating all kinds of common and uncommon infections and diseases.

About Penicillin

Penicillin was discovered in 1928 by Scottish scientist Alexander Fleming, and has been the world's premier infection solution ever since. For everything from gangrene to staphylococcal infections, **Penicillin** is the choice of the professional.

Alexander Fleming's discovery really has changed the face of the modern world, and we're sure that it will prove to be the right choice for you and your family. 100% of doctors surveyed said that they would prescribe **Penicillin** for many complaints, and it has received a massively positive response from patients too since it was introduced.

About Alexander Fleming

Of course none of this would have been possible without the discoveries of Alexander Fleming, born at Lochfield Farm near Darvel, on August 6 1881. A Nobel Prize winner for his discovery, his has been a remarkable contribution to medical history, one for which we are all grateful. And if you choose **Penicillin** as your disease combat solution today, we're sure you will be too.

You've never made a more important choice than the one you make today, so choose carefully, choose wisely, and choose **Penicillin**.

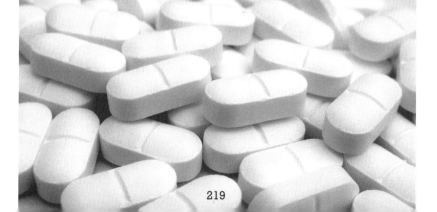

THE ROMAN CATHOLIC CHURCH IN SCOTLAND

The Roman Catholic Church has long been one of the biggest and most important Christian churches in Scotland. There are now more people attending Catholic Mass in Scotland than any other kind of regular religious ceremony, with the Catholic Church being particularly strong in the Highlands and the West of Scotland.

The Catholic Church estimates there are about 670,000 Catholics in Scotland today, with an average of about 185,000 going to Catholic Mass every Sunday. That means that almost 13% of the people in Scotland are Catholic and about 3.5% of Scottish people regularly attend Mass.

Scotland's Christianity has been influenced by Rome since as long ago as the second century when Christianity came to these shores, but the Church in Scotland was led by monks in places such as Iona, and it wasn't until about the eleventh century that the Church in Scotland became fully part of the Catholic Church.

Although the religious turmoil of the reformation and almost two hundred years of religious conflict which followed it involved the virtual criminalisation of Catholicism in Scotland, there remained a Catholic following in the country. Following Catholic emancipation in 1793 Scottish Catholics were allowed to regain their place as important members of Scottish society.

Irish immigration into Scotland during the nineteenth century meant that the Catholic Church in Scotland grew, and increased in importance as a social organisation for these new communities. This has become more important again in recent years as many of the European immigrants to Scotland are Catholic too.

The Catholic Church has played, and will continue to play, a very important part in shaping both Scotland's history and the country in the future.

LEGEND OF THE WIZARD LAIRD

Alexander Skene (1680-1724), the **Wizard Laird**, was the sixteenth Laird of Skene House, 10 miles west of Aberdeen.

As a young man he went to Padua University in Italy where he became interested in the black arts. On his last day, his master warned the class that the last to depart, upon paying their fees would be taken by the Devil.

Alexander was unfortunately the last to depart but as the Devil attempted to seize him, Skene tricked Old Nick into believing there was someone else behind.

The foiled Devil was only able to seize Skene's shadow. Skene returned to Scotland shadowless, a strange fact that alerted Aberdeenshire folk to Skene's magical abilities.

Back in Scotland Skene was accompanied everywhere by a crow, a magpie, a hawk and a jackdaw. It was said Skene was often seen in the churchyard exhuming the bodies of un-baptised babies to feed his mysterious feathered friends.

Skene's only other companion was his coachman, Kilgour. One Hogmanay night, Skene instructed Kilgour to transport him across the Loch of Skene upon which he'd cast a spell creating a thin layer of ice.

Kilgour was doubtful the ice would hold, but the Wizard assured him it was safe, so long as Kilgour never looked behind.

Sure enough the coach made it but just as they began to alight on the opposite bank of the loch, Kilgour's curiosity got the better of him.

There in the coach, seated next to the laird, Kilgour momentarily saw the Devil himself, as he turned into a raven and took flight, just as the ice began to crack. The coach and the Laird narrowly escaped drowning, but Kilgour noticed four wild black dogs in hot pursuit slowly sinking into the depths of the icy water.

SCOTLAND PLACE-NAMES
WHAT DO THEY MEAN?

IRVINE

Town of 33,000 people on the Firth of Clyde coast north of Ayr. Welsh *Yrwyn* means 'white river'.

JEDBURGH

A Borders region abbey town on the Jed Water. *Burgh* is an Anglo-Saxon word originally describing a fortified place or manor and later a town.

JOHN O' GROATS

On the coast of Caithness. Named after Dutchman John De Groot who lived here in the 1400s.

JOHNSTONE

Town of 15,000 people west of Paisley and Glasgow. Means 'the farm (*tun*) of someone called John', who lived here in the thirteenth century.

KEITH

Small town in Moray from the Welsh/Pictish *Coed/Coit* meaning 'wood'. A place of the same name in East Lothian gave rise to the Scottish surname Keith from which the forename derives.

KILLIN

Small village noted for its waterfalls west of Loch Tay. Gaelic *Cill fionn* meaning, 'church white'.

KILMACOLM

Town west of Glasgow. Gaelic *Cill Mo Coluim* meaning 'church of my Columba' (Saint Columba).

KILMARNOCK

East Ayrshire town of 44,000 people south west of Glasgow. Gaelic *Cill Mo Iarnan*, meaning, 'church of my Iarnan'. Iarnan was reputedly the uncle of St. Columba.

KILSYTH

Town north east of Glasgow between the Forth and Clyde. Gaelic name means 'church of St Syth' about whom, unfortunately, nothing is known.

DONALD CASKIE
THE TARTAN PIMPERNEL

*The year is 1941. Percival Temperley, gentleman adventurer
and well-known dandy, is in Nazi-occupied France on a vital
mission for the Crown. Together with his manservant, Thornton,
Temperley is attempting to escape after completing his mission.
However, their original plan has been foiled, and they are forced
to look for a different way...*

Temperley: Thornton, we must find
our way out of this God forsaken
country. We need someone with
experience of helping our boys to
get out of France and back home to
Blighty.

Thornton: I believe I know the very
man to help us in our hour of need sir,
Reverend Donald Caskie.

Temperley: It's not quite time for a
minister yet, Thornton, at least as long
as we can stay one step ahead of the Germans.

Thornton: Reverend Caskie is far from just a minister, sir. He is a
Church of Scotland minister in Marseille who has helped many
British servicemen escape from France.

Temperley: But who is this Caskie, Thornton? Can we trust him?

Thornton: Caskie was born on Islay in 1902, sir, and he became
a minister at the Scots Kirk in Paris in 1938. When the Germans
came, rather than escape as many of his compatriots did, he
moved to Marseille and worked at the British Seamen's Mission
in Marseille.

Temperley: And he can get us out, Thornton?

Thornton: If he can't sir, nobody can. I've got a feeling that he'll
end up helping over 2,000 Allied soldiers to escape France
during the remainder of this war, and will run the risk of being
executed for doing so. That in fact he will be arrested, and tried,
but that lack of evidence against him will see him escape.

Temperley: Your predictions, Thornton, they do serve you well...

Thornton: Yes, sir.

The Claymore

In the modern world, every woman needs a way to defend herself. Some women use personal alarms, some have tried mace or pepper spray, some have even tried electric stun guns. However, we at ModernProtectionSolutions Inc. are now prepared to offer you two new products which will guarantee safety and peace of mind.

The Original Claymore™

Originating in the Scottish Highlands around the beginning of the fifteenth century, and used for many years by clansmen in internal Scottish conflicts, and last used en masse at the Battle of Killiecrankie in 1689. Our Original Claymore™ uses the advances in technology available to create a weapon for the modern era. At around four and a half feet long, with a three and a half foot blade, and designed to be wielded with two hands, it is a fine choice if you are looking to scare off potential urban attackers.

The Basket Hilted Claymore™

A development of the original Claymore which came into being during the seventeenth century, this was the choice of Scottish soldiers from then on, remaining part of the uniform of many Scottish regiments to this day. A lighter weapon than the Original Claymore™, the Basket Hilted Claymore™ is used with one hand, and has a shield to protect that hand (also included). With a three foot blade, this is a more manageable size, and can be accessorised in a number of different colours, making it the perfect addition to any evening outfit.

Whichever Claymore you choose, you know that it carries the endorsement of hundreds of years of Scottish bravery, and will guarantee your security when you're out and about. Whether you've got important business to do, you're spending time with your family, or you're out for a night with the girls, you'll know that you've got your Claymore.

HISTORIC TOWNS AND CITIES: INVERNESS

STATUS: Scotland's northernmost city.

RIVER: Situated at the mouth of the **River Ness** where it enters the **Moray Firth.**

NAMES AND NICKNAMES: Known as the "Capital of the Highlands".

MOTTO AND EMBLEM: The Inverness motto is "Concordia et Fidelitas" which means 'harmony and fidelity'. The coat of arms of Inverness once featured a camel and an elephant as a symbol of its eastern trade.

POPULATION: Around 42,000.

KEY FACTS AND INDUSTRIES: In ancient times Inverness was a stronghold of the Picts. It was later the site of five castles. Situated about five miles north east of Loch Ness, Inverness became a major centre for the Highland sheep and wool trade from around 1817. Its proximity to the Great Glen enables easy access to the Highland hinterland. There are more than 2,000 Gaelic speakers in Inverness.

KEY DATES: DATE: 560 AD: St Columba visited Bridei/Brude King of the Picts at his Inverness fortress. **Circa 1124**: King David gave Inverness Royal Burgh status. **1745**: Bonnie Prince Charlie occupied Inverness. **1746**: The Battle of Culloden took place near Inverness. **1746**: The Duke of Cumberland ransacked Inverness following the battle. **1817**: A wool and sheep market was established. **1822**: Caledonian Canal completed. **1921**: The British cabinet met for the first time outside London at Inverness under Lloyd George. Stanley Baldwin and Winston Churchill attended. **2001**: Inverness was granted city status.

THINGS TO SEE:

- **Abertarff House**, situated in Church Street dates from 1593.
- **Inverness Castle**, built in 1835 on the site of an earlier castle.
- **St Andrews Cathedral**, built 1866-69.
- **Inverness Town House**, where the British cabinet met in 1921.
- **Culloden battlefield**, six miles to the east.
- **Clava Cairns**, Bronze Age burial mounds seven miles to the east.
- **Loch Ness** and if you're lucky, the monster too!

JOHN LOGIE BARID

History Man: Why don't you turn that off, I've got some really interesting stuff to tell you?

Student [watching TV]: What? Sssssh, I'm trying to watch this.

History Man: I'm trying to tell you something about that.

Student: Don't spoil the ending for me!

History Man: It's not the ending I want to talk about, but the beginning: The beginning of television itself.

Student [switches off TV and sighs]: What about it?

History Man: Did you know that John Logie Baird, the man who invented TV, was Scottish? He demonstrated the first television in history in 1925.

Student: Where did he demonstrate it then? And what did he show?

History Man: He demonstrated it in Selfridges in Oxford Street, London, and he showed people pictures of letters.

Student: Lettuce?

History Man: Letters! He showed them pictures of letters!

Student: So who was this John Logie Baird when he was at home?

History Man: He was born in Helensburgh, Dunbartonshire on August 14 1888, and went to university in Glasgow. He then moved to England and started to develop his television. It took a lot of hard work but he succeeded. In 1927 he formed the Baird Television Development Company. They were the first company to transmit television across the Atlantic in 1928.

Student: Did he do anything else?

History Man: He invented a kind of radar, made advancements in fibre optics, infra-red vision and invented an early type of video recorder which he called "Phonovision". His most famous invention, however, will always be the television.

Student: Well what an interesting man, well done to him, now if you don't mind... **[Turns TV back on]**

History Man [Sighs]: Sometimes I despair, I really do.

THE FAIRY FLAG

Dunvegan Castle on Skye is the seat of the MacLeods and home to their Fairy Flag, one of Scotland's magical relics.

Made of silk and supposedly covered with "elf dots" this ancient flag seems to have originated from Syria or Rhodes and was possibly a relic associated with a saint. According to one story it was acquired by the Viking leader Harald Hardrada - a MacLeod ancestor - who acquired it in Constantinople. He called it the Land-Ravager and it brought him success in battle but there are other theories concerning its legendary origins and magical properties.

Some say it was a gift from a fairy given to an infant MacLeod chieftain in the fifteenth century. She wrapped the child in her protective magical flag and sang it a lullaby. The lullaby was recalled by the infant's nurse when she awoke from a spell and it is still remembered today.

According to another story, a fourteenth century clan chief married a fairy but she could only stay with him for 20 years before returning to Fairyland. On her departure from him at Fairy Bridge, three miles from Dunvegan Castle she presented him with the flag and instructed him that it could be unfurled and waved on three occasions to rescue the MacLeods in times of need.

It was apparently used twice, bringing victory to the MacLeods over the MacDonalds at the Battle of Glendale in 1420 and later at the Battle of Waternish in 1520.

In addition to this, the flag is said to have prevented a serious fire at Dunvegan Castle in 1938 from completely destroying the building. Other magical properties included curing cattle of plague, increasing fertility and bringing herring to Dunvegan Loch. During the Second World War members of the MacLeod clan carried a photograph of the flag with them for good luck.

SCOTT TO BE WALTER

Any biography of **SIR WALTER SCOTT** has *scott* to start with his birthplace which has *scott* to be nowhere other than Edinburgh.

The biography has *scott* to include his birthday too. That was on August 15 and since it's *scott* to include the year, it was 1771. It's *scott* to be said, his dad, a solicitor was called Walter too.

We think young Walter has *scott* to have become interested in Border Ballads on his trips to the Borders with his dad.

He's *scott* to have shown potential at school where he attended Edinburgh High before studying arts and law at Edinburgh University. He's *scott* to have been following in his father's footsteps with his interest in law.

He's *scott* to have gained good experience apprenticed to his father. In 1799 he was appointed deputy sheriff for Selkirk which has *scott* to have been a big responsibility.

In 1797 he married Margaret Carpenter, so he's *scott* to have been in love. Mary and Walter had five children and that's *scott* to have been hard work.

This biog's *scott* to mention his works. It's *scott* to include *Minstrelsy of The Scottish Border* (1803), "The Lay of The Last Minstrel" (1805), "Marmion" (1808), "The Lady In The Lake" (1810), "Rokeby" (1813) and "The Lord Of The Isles" (1815).

It has *scott* to be mentioned his life wasn't always a success. He started a publishing company that failed and wrote novels to pay his debts. It's *scott* to have been a difficult time.

The biography has also *scott* to mention some of his novels. They include *Waverley* (1814), *Guy Mannering* (1815) *Rob Roy* (1817), *The Heart of Midlothian* (1818) and *Ivanhoe* (1819).

SCOTT died on September 21 1832 and was buried at Dryburgh Abbey; *scott* to be said, he was sorely missed.

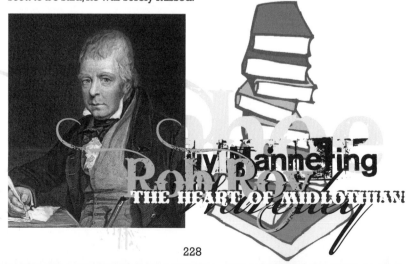

ELSIE INGLIS

"Greetings. My name is Eve Strogen, but you can call me E Strogen for short. I'm the type of hormone which makes women into women, and I feel like I get a bit of a bad rap. People often say that I make people weak, indecisive and subservient, where Terry Tosterone (Tes Tosterone) makes people aggressive, commanding and dominant.

Of course, I'd argue that that's evidence of millennia of social conditioning, not a fundamental difference between men and women, but either way it's always nice when someone with a lot of me sloshing about inside of them proves the doubters wrong. There's one particular woman who's a great example of this, and that's Elsie Inglis.

Elsie was born in India on August 16 1864, to Scottish parents. Her mother and father were pretty forward thinking people for their time, they thought that educating girls was as important as educating boys, and Elsie was well educated. They moved back to Scotland when she was aged 14, and she went to school in Edinburgh.

When she left school, she went to medical school, and she qualified as a doctor. She even set up her own medical school, the Scottish Association for the Medical Education of Women. She then went to work in London.

She was appalled by the poor treatment and lack of care doctors had for their female patients, and she decided this wouldn't change without political support. She became very active in politics as a suffragette, and in 1909 she became the secretary of the Federation of Scottish Suffrage Societies.

During the First World War she pioneered female medical units to serve on the front lines, and they helped to save the lives of many soldiers. Sadly, Elsie died in Newcastle upon Tyne on November 26 1917, after an exceptional life that makes me proud."

THE EDINBURGH FRINGE

Where can you see a naked *Othello*, *The Crucible* performed with hand puppets or *Waiting for Godot* performed by midgets? The Edinburgh Festival Fringe of course. Every August Edinburgh comes alive with actors, singers, writers and comedians, as the world's biggest and best arts festival comes to town.

For a month the town is filled with world class acts, and with people coming to try and make their names. Walk down the Royal Mile and you'll have hundreds of leaflets shoved into your hands, and people imploring you to come and see whatever show it is they happen to be doing. With more than 250 venues every year, and thousands of shows from one man stand ups to theatrical extravaganzas, Edinburgh really is the place to be in August.

The Fringe began in 1947, when eight theatre companies turned up uninvited to the 1947 Edinburgh International Festival. They played in the city anyway, and the Fringe grew from there. It has grown to dwarf the International Festival now, with many of the visitors to the city during August not even being aware that there is such a thing!

It's a place you can see shows from morning to night, from acts you love to acts you don't know yet, and a place that everyone can find something to suit their taste. If you get a chance to go you really ought to, it's great fun.

THE HIGHLAND GAMES

"Good afternoon. My name's Pinus Sylvestris, but you can call me Sylvia for short. I'm a Scots Pine.

You know, when I was just a sapling my mother said to me, 'find yourself a trade, make sure you've got something to fall back on' but I didn't listen. Now I look at my family, my brother Pete's a telephone pole, Stella's working as a table and Keith's got a very decent job as a kitchen floor. They've all settled down; found themselves steady work, all but me?

I have to decide to go and become an athlete, to try and make it on the world stage, but how many opportunities are there for a pine tree in modern sports? So I find myself here, exactly where you'd expect me to be, working as a caber in the Scottish Highland Games.

Tossing me might be the most high-profile event at the games, but there are plenty of other ways that Scottish men and women can test their abilities to throw heavy things a long way. The stone toss, weight throw, hammer throw and sheaf toss to name just a few, they're all great traditional ways for Scots to chuck heavy things of different shapes and sizes.

It's not just that though; it's a great celebration of Scottish culture, music, food and dance, and one which has been taking place in its current form since the 1820s, although they say that competitions like these have been taking place in Scotland for a lot longer than that.

It's spread all over the world too, there are now hundreds of different Highland Games which take place in Scotland, Canada, America, and all across the world. Basically, anywhere that Scottish people have gone to live, they've taken the Highland Games with them."

GLASGOW ARTISTS
THE GLASGOW SCHOOL

In the 1870s a loose affiliation of artists with similar views and outlook on art rose to prominence in the city of Glasgow and would have an important impact on Scottish art.

Known as the **Glasgow School** or **Glasgow Boys** its members included **Sir James Guthrie** (1859-1930), **Sir John Lavery** (1856-1941), **George Henry** (1858-1943), **E.A.Hornel** (1864-1933), the Newcastle-born **Joseph Crawhall** (1861-1913) and several others.

Often meeting in the studio of fellow artist **William York Macgregor** (1855-1923) the artists rejected the existing sentimental styles of Scottish painting which had its roots in the eighteenth century. They brought Scottish art up to date drawing on contemporary French, European and even Japanese painting styles.

The French Impressionists and the American artist James Abbott Whistler were amongst the influences that shaped the artistic styles of this Glasgow group who were streets ahead of the rest of Britain in their artistic experimentation.

Their use of liberal splashes of paint and realistic depiction of poor peasants, contrasted with the rather staged and sentimental appearance of these subjects with happy poses in earlier Scottish art. The painting style of the Glasgow Boys offended the art establishment in Scotland and Britain, but the Glasgow Boys didn't really care as they knew they were pioneers in their field.

A similar circle of female artists and designers known as the **Glasgow Girls** were also part of the Glasgow School and two of these artists were among the four most influential members of the Glasgow School known as **The Four** or **Spook School.**

The Four were **Charles Rennie Mackintosh** (1868-1928), his wife **Margaret Macdonald** (1865-1933), her sister **Frances Macdonald** (1873-1921) and **Herbert MacNair** (1868-1955).

Drawing on a revival of Celtic styles of art and the Arts and Crafts Movement these artists were a big influence on Art Noveau.

DOCTOR WHO

It's one of the best loved shows on British TV, it's featured some of the scariest aliens, the worst baddies and the biggest thrills we've ever seen on TV, but what you might not know is just how big a Scottish influence there's been on *Doctor Who*.

The seventh Doctor, **Sylvester McCoy**, was born Percy James Patrick Kent-Smith in Dunoon on August 20 1943. He became the Doctor in 1987, taking over from Colin Baker, and was the Doctor from 1987-1989, then again in a charity special in 1993, and then finally he regenerated into Paul McGann in 1996. This means that he was actually the Doctor for longer than anyone else, almost 9 years!

Even though *Doctor Who* went away for a while, when it came back, it came back with a very strong Scottish influence. For a start, the tenth Doctor was played by another Scot, **David Tennant**. He was born David McDonald in Bathgate on April 18 1971, and became the Doctor in 2005. He played the Doctor for four seasons, and one of his regular companions was Captain Jack Harkness. Captain Jack was played by **John Barrowman**, who was born in Glasgow.

Another major influence on *Doctor Who* has been **Steven Moffat**, born in Paisley on November 18 1961, who first wrote for *Doctor Who* in a Red Nose Day Special called "Doctor Who and the Curse of Fatal Death" in 1999. Since then Steven's become lead writer and executive producer, and in that role cast Karen Gillan as Amelia Pond. **Karen Gillan** was born in Inverness on November 28 1987, and is now the main companion for Matt Smith's eleventh Doctor.

WHAT'S YOUR NAME?

MACIVER

Descended from *Ivar*, a Norse name suggesting Viking roots. The Campbells descend from a branch of the MacIvers.

MacKay

From MacAodh, son of Hugh, possibly Hugh, Abbot of Dunkeld, a brother of Alexander I. Family held lands in Strathnaver.

MacKenzie

Gaelic name MacCoinneach means 'son of the bright one' (son of Kenneth) and is associated with Kintail in Ross. Said to be descendants of the kings of the Dal Riata Scots. MacKenzie lands included Kintail, Orkney and the Hebrides. In 1625 the senior clan member became the Earl of Seaforth.

MacKinnon

Said to descend from the family of King Kenneth MacAlpin. Name derives from Mac Fhionghuin 'fair born'. The family had strong connections to Iona and the kindred of St Columba. A notable presence on Skye.

Mackintosh/Macintosh

From Mac-an-Toisich 'son of the chief'. Descended from the Macduffs of earlier times. From the late thirteenth century Mackintoshes were chiefs of the Clan Chattan federation, an alliance of 16 Scottish clans that included Macphersons, Davidsons, Shaws and Macintyres. The related MacThomas Clan are descended from Tomaidh Mor a fifteenth century descendant of the Clan Chattan Mackintoshes.

MacLachlan

MacLachlans trace their line to Lachlan Mor, an Irish warrior who lived near Loch Fyne (a sea loch) in Argyll. Lachlan's ancestors were the powerful ancient O'Neil family of Ulster.

MacLaine

Descended from a thirteenth century warrior Gillean of the Battle Axe who owned lands on Mull. MacLeans also claim descent from him, but their name is thought to be *MacGille Eoin*, meaning, 'son of the servant of St John'.

MacLaren

Thought to descend from a thirteenth century abbot Laurence of Achtow in Balquihidder, in the Strathearn region of Perthshire.

MACLENNAN

Thought to derive from a Gaelic name meaning 'followers of St Finnan'. Numerous in north west Scotland and the Outer Hebrides.

MY NEW TATTOO

"I want to tell you about my new state of the art body art. Look it's here on my arm. Scots like me have been permanently painting our bodies like this for centuries. The Picts were noted for it, but this latest tattoo is very special. It's a virtual reality tattoo you see. Created with the very latest technology, it's a fully animated three-dimensional work.

I know it's not doing much at the moment, but every August during the Edinburgh Festival it comes to life, right here on my arm. So what will we see? For a start you'll see Edinburgh Castle, brightly lit up with a crowd of 7,000 people from all over the world watching it live. Then the military bands appear, from across Britain and the Commonwealth. I feel them marching in rhythm across my arm. It creates a bit of a tingle and gives me goose pimples.

A quick tap on the wrist and I can play it over and over again. A flick of a thumb and I can rewind all the way back to 1949 when the event began. Back then it was called "Something About A Soldier" and took place at Princes Street Gardens, but the following year it moved to the esplanade of Edinburgh Castle and was renamed the **Royal Edinburgh Military Tattoo**. It's been held there ever since.

Tattoo is a Polynesian word for body art, but not this tattoo. No this tattoo comes from a Dutch phrase *Doe den tap toe* meaning 'put the tap to'. The British military learned the term when stationed in Flanders during the 1700s. It has come to refer to a military procession. The Edinburgh Military Tattoo is one of the most memorable and moving events in the Scottish calendar and I can watch it all, right here on my arm."

CONSTRUCT YOUR OWN WILLIAM WALLACE

Congratulations on purchasing your new William Wallace. Just follow these simple instructions and you will have your own personal Scottish national hero up and running in no time.

1. First, take the noble birth and relation to King David I of Scotland. This will form the foundation of your William Wallace.

2. Take King Alexander III and remove him from horse, so dead. Insert conflict over rule over Scotland.

3. Then, insert Edward I, and grip rule of Scotland. Insert Treaty of Brigham which should guarantee that your England and Scotland remain separate. Add John Baliol, but ensure that Baliol's control is weak. Repeat until English power over Scotland is strong.

4. Now, use Edward to remove Treaty of Brigham. Take Scottish nobles and make treaty with France.

5. Insert English forces into Scotland in March 1296. This should increase anger among your Scotsmen.

6. Using your William Wallace, remove the Sheriff of Lanark. Connect your William Wallace with other Scottish forces and use to remove English at Loudon Hill, Ayr, Perth, Glasgow, Scone and Dundee.

7. By now your William Wallace should have an army attached to him. Now, take your William Wallace to Stirling Bridge, and use to remove English forces. The English forces should be much larger. Knight your Wallace and declare him "Guardian of the Scottish people".

8. Take your William Wallace and raid northern England. Then, place your Wallace and English forces at Falkirk. Remove Scottish soldiers. Remove title of "Guardian of the Scottish people". Place this title on your Robert the Bruce.

9. Your William Wallace is almost ready. Move your William Wallace around Scotland.

10. Finally, place your William Wallace in English hands. Take your William Wallace to London. Try your William Wallace for treason.

11. Your William Wallace should now be hanged, drawn and quartered. Place the head of your William Wallace on spike A – London Bridge. Place the limbs separately in Newcastle, Berwick-upon-Tweed, Stirling and Aberdeen.

12. Repeat story for generations. Install story into Scottish legend.

MY SCOTLAND

Scotland is a very adventurous place, from Edinburgh Castle to Sueno's Stone in Forres. I was saying this to myself as I was climbing the hill. The rushing wind was blowing against me. I heard a voice behind me saying, "What's it feel like, being blown against the wind?"

I turned round. Suddenly there he was, his kilt blowing, and his whole body was there. His tartan hat was coming off so he had to keep his hands on his hat so it would stay on. It didn't make sense – one minute he was there the next minute he was gone, I don't know how he did it. Maybe he was the ghost of Scotland, or maybe I am imagining it – but I couldn't have, I know it.

Next thing I saw was the beach, the sand dunes hastening by.

"Can you see the sand dunes racing past?"

"Well, yes, but not very clearly."

"Well, as long as you can see it."

The waves were smashing against the brick wall. What was that in the distance? A seal! Amazing! His name was Jo and I told him my name – Lola.

"We are at Findhorn beach," I told him. Next thing I was getting whizzed around. It felt like a time portal. It was, I knew it! Next I was walking that rufty tufty hill again!

Although I was born in Dr Grey's hospital, Elgin, I couldn't live without Scotland and that is why: it is full of wonders and joy.

My Scotland Young Writer

Name: Freya Paterson
Age: 9
School: Anderson's Primary School, Forres

DETECTIVE AGENCY

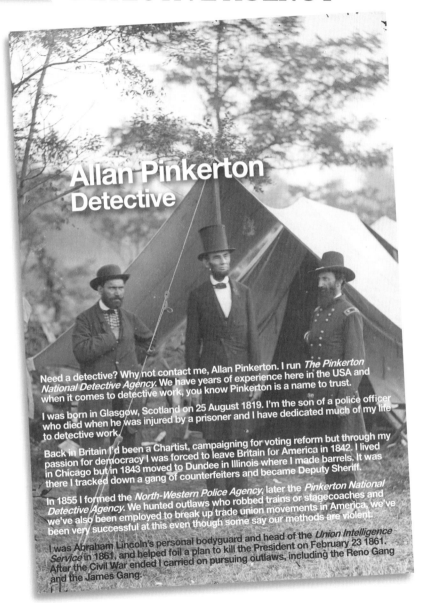

Allan Pinkerton
Detective

Need a detective? Why not contact me, Allan Pinkerton. I run *The Pinkerton National Detective Agency*. We have years of experience here in the USA and when it comes to detective work, you know Pinkerton is a name to trust.

I was born in Glasgow, Scotland on 25 August 1819. I'm the son of a police officer who died when he was injured by a prisoner and I have dedicated much of my life to detective work.

Back in Britain I'd been a Chartist, campaigning for voting reform but through my passion for democracy I was forced to leave Britain for America in 1842. I lived in Chicago but in 1843 moved to Dundee in Illinois where I made barrels. It was there I tracked down a gang of counterfeiters and became Deputy Sheriff.

In 1855 I formed the *North-Western Police Agency*, later the *Pinkerton National Detective Agency*. We hunted outlaws who robbed trains or stagecoaches and we've also been employed to break up trade union movements in America, we've been very successful at this even though some say our methods are violent.

I was Abraham Lincoln's personal bodyguard and head of the *Union Intelligence Service* in 1861, and helped foil a plan to kill the President on February 23 1861. After the Civil War ended I carried on pursuing outlaws, including the Reno Gang and the James Gang.

Allan Pinkerton died on July 1 1884, aged 64, and left behind a detective agency with a mixed reputation. It was famous and respected for their work, catching outlaws and criminals, but on the other it was involved in violence during a number of strikes. Pinkerton left his mark on the world, but whether it was a good one is open to interpretation.

THIRTY SCOTTISH CASTLES

DUNVEGAN CASTLE

Near Dunvegan on the Isle of Skye, this castle is the seat of the MacLeod family chief. It claims to be the oldest continuously inhabited castle in Scotland. MacLeod chiefs have lived at this castle for 800 years. Famous relics associated with the clan include the clan's "fairy flag" of Dunvegan which is said to have magical properties.

EILEAN DONAN CASTLE

Arguably Scotland's most beautiful, iconic and frequently photographed castle Eilean Donan stands on an island near the north bank of Loch Duich, a sea loch, about eight miles east of the Kyle of Laochalsh. The island is named after St Donnán of Eigg. It has been a stronghold of the MacKenzies and later the Macraes who still own it. The castle dates back to the thirteenth century when it was built as a defence against the Norsemen. It was captured by Spanish troops in 1719 who were attempting to start up another Jacobite rebellion but they were defeated by the Royal Navy. Eilean Donan castle can be reached by a short bridge from the north bank of the loch.

ELCHO CASTLE

A neat z-shaped stone castle four miles south east of Perth close to the River Tay on a site dating back to the sixteenth century. The castle is historically the home of the Wemyss family who still own the property though it has not been occupied for two centuries.

FLOORS CASTLE

Stately seat of the Duke of Roxburghe in the Scottish Borders overlooking the River Tweed and the Cheviot Hills. The castle was built for the Duke by the architect William Adam in 1720. It was really built as a stately home rather than a defensive castle.

FORT GEORGE

Eighteenth century fortress constructed around an earlier medieval castle on a peninsula at the mouth of the Ness near Inverness. Built in the 1750s to suppress Jacobite risings, it could house up to 400 troops.

THE EGLINTON TOURNAMENT OF 1839

"And welcome back to the coverage of the Eglinton Tournament of 1839, and what a three days we've had. I have to say it's been an absolute privilege to bring you what, despite the weather, has been a truly remarkable event.

The preparations have been going on for over a year now, and it's great to see all of the planning and plotting, the hopes and dreams of Archibald Montgomerie, the thirteenth Earl of Eglinton and his team finally coming to fruition.

Almost 100,000 people have braved the rain to come and see the greatest celebration of Britain's medieval heritage in recent memory. We've had jousting by tilt and melee, processions, banquets, and many more events which have truly made this a return to our past.

Knights have come from all over the country, and indeed across the world to make their mark, with visitors such as the Earl of Craven in a suit of armour worn by his ancestor at the Battle of Crecy, the Duke of Atholl with his newly formed regiment, the Atholl Highlanders, Baron Esterhazy of Hungary and Prince Louis Napoleon of France.

The weather hasn't been kind to us, admittedly, especially to Prince Louis Napoleon and... Oh no, he's gone again... That's the fourth time this morning he's fallen off his horse, and he just can't get up in that armour...

I know there's a strong feeling of being part of history for everyone here, with artists, writers, painters and musicians gathering to document this historic event for posterity. This is certainly being seen as a significant moment in what people are calling the "Gothic Revival".

It's been a great event for everyone involved, and I'm sure it's one nobody will be forgetting in a hurry, I know I won't."

EGLINTON
TOURNAMENT

TRANENT
A MASSACRE, MINING AND SCOTLAND'S FIRST WAGGONWAY

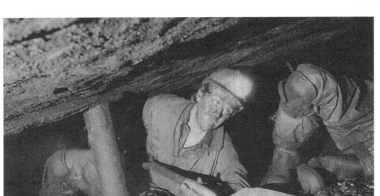

Tranent, a town of almost 10,000 people in East Lothian, was historically famed for coal mining, radicalism and a massacre of 1797.

Coal is no longer mined here but mining in Tranent traced its origins to the 1200s when the monks of Newbattle Abbey operated mines here, making Tranent Scotland's oldest mining community. By the 1720s it was home to Scotland's first wagonway, an early form of railway taking coal from Tranent to the port of Cockenzie.

Miners worked in dangerous conditions and were treated as property by mine owners. It encouraged a radical determination amongst miners to stand up for their rights.

Such determination led to the Massacre of Tranent in 1797. That year, a Militia Act empowered Lord Lieutenants to raise militia in Scotland's counties and cities. This involved the enforced recruitment of Scots who might be employed in controlling other people or serving overseas.

The people of Tranent were having none of it. On August 28 they read a proclamation drawn up by its people passionately highlighting their determination to resist.

The objections highlighted in the proclamation are thought to have been encouraged by members of a radical secret society called the United Scotsmen.

On August 29, the proclamation was handed to the recruitment officer but was ignored. The officer's troops were then confronted by local miners led by a very determined lady called Jackie Crookston. Their response was to open fire. Jackie and eleven others were instantly killed. Many others lay wounded.

Other protesters fled from the town but were cut down by the pursuing military forces, leaving up to twenty dead including children.

Since 1995 a statue of Jackie Crookston has stood in Tranent town centre as a memorial to the dreadful event.

THE EVACUATION OF ST KILDA

One of the saddest events of Scotland's move into the modern world has to be the evacuation of St Kilda. A community which had existed for over 2,000 years, but which could not keep pace with the modern world, finally came to an end on August 29 1930.

The 36 St Kildans who boarded HMS *Harebell* that night were the final inhabitants of an island chain with a long history. There had been signs that the evacuation was inevitable. The population of the main island in the chain, Hirta, had been falling ever since the middle of the nineteenth century. Indeed in 1851 the *Priscilla* took 36 islanders to Australia. That's why there's a place in Melbourne called St Kilda!

Still, the islanders struggled on, existing in a way that people had been existing for thousands of years, farming the land to feed and to support themselves. However by the 1920s things were becoming desperate. The population of Hirta, 73 in 1920, had fallen to 37 in 1928 after a number of bad winters and many of the young people leaving the island.

The last straw was when Mary Gillies died of appendicitis in January 1930 because she couldn't reach medical help. The fact that a young woman died of something which was by that point perfectly treatable saddened the people of St Kilda, and on May 10 1930 they sent a joint letter to William Adamson, Secretary of State for Scotland, asking to be evacuated.

The ship set sail on August 29, and took the people of St Kilda to the mainland for the last time, leaving the islands uninhabited.

Did you know?
The Picts

- Picts were a people of ancient Scotland who lived north of the Forth and Clyde when the Romans arrived.

- Pict derives from a Latin word meaning 'painted'. They were called this, either because they liked tattoos or because their stones were inscribed with mysterious pictures.

- In Roman times the most famous Pictish tribe were the Caledonii from whom Caledonia was named but there were other less well-known tribes like the Verturiones, Taexali and Venicones.

- Place-names and the recorded personal names of Pictish kings show the language of the Picts was a Celtic language related to Welsh. It was different to that of the Scots who spoke Gaelic. It's thought that a mysterious non-Celtic language may have been spoken in places.

- Place-names of eastern Scotland like Pittordrie, Pitcaple and Pitlochry and many others were probably Pictish shire centres. Pit derives from a Pictish word Pett meaning 'portion of land'.

- Decorated slab-like Pictish stones can be found across Scotland. They date from 500 AD to 1000 AD and often include swirling patterns or comb patterns.

- Some stones depict a mysterious Pictish Beast that looks a bit like a sea horse. It's been compared to a dolphin, dragon, the Loch Ness monster and even an elephant.

- Pictland was originally formed from a number of smaller kingdoms that may have included Fife, Caithness and probably a kingdom on Orkney.

- Fortriu was the dominant Pictish Kingdom. It was centred on the Moray Firth and reached the height of its power around 800 AD.

- Enemies of the Picts included the neighbouring kingdoms of Northumbria, Dal Riata and Strathclyde each of which spoke a different language.

- Around 900 AD Pictland was absorbed by the Gaelic kingdom of Dal Riata and became part of the Kingdom of Alba.

Professor
C. Cloggs

THREE SCOTTISH WRITERS

Kenneth Grahame

Born in Edinburgh on March 8 1859 Grahame is famed as the author of *The Wind in the Willows,* published in 1908. It's not so well-known that Kenneth worked for the Bank of England between 1879 and 1908 and rose to the rank of Secretary. He retired due to ill-health that may have been brought on by a shooting incident at the bank in 1903 in which Grahame was shot at three times.

Irvine Welsh

Born in Leith on September 27 1958, but moving to Muirhouse, Edinburgh at the age of four, Irvine Welsh worked as a television repairman until an electric shock convinced him he should change career. He moved to London for a while trying out several jobs but returned to Edinburgh in the late 1980s and started to write.

His first novel was *Trainspotting,* published in 1993. Since then he's written seven more novels. He has also written short stories and scripts for television, film and stage.

J.M. Barrie

J.M. Barrie was born in Kirriemuir, Angus on May 9 1860, the son of a weaver. When he was six Barrie's brother died in a skating accident. Some say the character of Peter Pan, the boy who never grows up, was inspired by his brother's death.

Barrie attended the University of Edinburgh, studying English Literature. After working for a newspaper in Nottingham Barrie returned to Kirriemuir and wrote his first novel, *Auld Licht Idylls* in 1888.

It wasn't until he met the children of Arthur and Sylvia Llewelyn-Davies that he was to get his greatest inspiration. When the boys' parents died, Barrie adopted them, and they would inspire the Lost Boys of *Peter Pan.* When Barrie died, he left the copyright to *Peter Pan* to the Great Ormond Street children's hospital in London.

A SCOTTISH SENSES POEM

In Scotland I see lochs where Nessie larks
In Fife I see Highland coos moving and mooing
In Dunfermline I see the stained glass windows of the Abbey.

In Scotland I hear rain falling fast as lightning
In Fife I hear The Proclaimers sing out load as people roar
In Dunfermline I hear bagpipes play at weddings,
so beautiful and haunting.

In Scotland I taste the old favourites, haggis, neeps and tatties
In Fife I taste a crumbling of shortbread
In Dunfermline I taste tae cakes, which my mum loves.

In Scotland I smell Highland flowers
In Fife I smell lovely heather
In Dunfermline I smell candles in my home.

In Scotland I feel the cold wind from the hills
In Fife I feel happy to be free
In Dunfermline I feel safe with my friends and family.

My Scotland
Young Writer

Name: Rachael Murray
Age: 9
School: Pitcorthie Primary School, Dunfermline, Fife

2

WELCOME TO THE UFO CAPITAL OF THE WORLD

American Sam: Well howdy there, my Scottish amigo. I'd like to welcome you to the UFO capital of the world, Roswell New Mexico, in the good old U. S. of A.

Sandy Scot: Erm, sorry pal, I think you must be mistaken. We are in the UFO capital of the world, sure, but we're nowhere near New Mexico. We're in Bonnybridge, Stirlingshire, in Scotland.

American Sam: Scotland? That can't be right, everybody knows that Roswell's the place for UFOs.

Sandy Scot: Roswell is certainly famous for its alien connections, but did you know there are almost 300 alien sightings in Bonnybridge and the surrounding area every year?

American Sam: 300? What's going on up there?

Sandy Scot: Nobody knows, but there's definitely something happening. People say it might be the military testing aircraft, or atmospheric conditions. Whatever it is, there are an awful lot of lights in the sky.

American Sam: Lights in the sky isn't all that impressive though, is it? Our boys in New Mexico had actual aliens. We've got crop circles and alien abductions too. That's got to put us ahead on points.

Sandy Scot: It's not like there haven't been alien abductions reported in Bonnybridge either you know, there have been a whole number of them reported since 1992.

American Sam: 1992? What's so significant about 1992?

Sandy Scot: 1992 is the year Bonnybridge started to have so many UFOs. They were made public by local councillor Billy Buchanan writing to MPs and the Prime Minister to try and find out why they were happening. Some people say that this was Buchanan's way of increasing tourism in his town, by inventing UFO sightings.

American Sam: Ah ha! So they're not real?

Sandy Scot: I'm sure that's what they'd like you to believe...

ORKNEY HISTORY

Orkney has an unrivalled prehistory, an eventful history and to this day its inhabitants called **Orcadians** maintain an independent outlook, quite separate from the rest of Scotland.

As far back as 325 BC, a Greek explorer called Pytheas of Massalia mentioned **Orca** at the northern tip of Britain, though he may have been referring to the tip of Caithness. In the first century AD a Roman geographer called Pomponius Mela mentioned that the islands were called the **Orcades**.

There are few if any places in Scotland that can trace their name back to such ancient times.The name is thought to derive from a Pictish word for pig, though the Vikings who came later called it *Orkn-Ey* meaning 'seal island'.

Orkney has been inhabited for at least 8,500 years and for prehistoric sites it is quite remarkable. Orkney's Neolithic sites have designated UNESCO World Heritage status. The star attractions are the Neolithic homes of **Skara Brae** on the mainland and the Neolithic **Tomb of the Eagles** site on South Ronaldsay.

The Pictish history of Orkney emerges from history in Roman times when an Orkney king swore allegiance to Rome, but it is in Viking times that the recorded history of Orkney comes to life, particularly as many events from this period are recorded in the Icelandic *Orkneyinga Saga*.

From about 875 AD the Vikings began to extensively settle Orkney using it as a base for piratical raids and they gradually replaced the indigenous Pictish population. Orkney would remain under Scandinavian control and was part of Norway until eventually handed over to the Scottish crown in 1472.

The Norse heritage of the island is still recalled in Orkney's place-names and in the dedication of a cathedral at Kirkwall to a Viking saint, St Magnus and in the distinctly Scandinavian-looking **Orkney flag**.

4

KING ARTHUR AND SCOTLAND

Everybody knows the legend of King Arthur, but most people think of him as an English King. It might surprise you that there's almost as many Scottish links to Arthur as there are English ones! Here's just a few of them, but there are tons more out there for you to find...

King Arthur's round table may actually have been in Stenhousemuir! Some historians and scholars think that it wasn't a table at all, but a round building, and that the building was in Stenhousemuir, in what's now somebody's back garden!

Arthur's Seat in Edinburgh has a lot of links to Arthurian legend. Some people say that it was the site of Camelot, Arthur's legendary fortress and the capital of his lands. Others say that King Arthur and his Knights sleep inside Arthur's Seat, waiting for the day when his country needs him which, according to legend, is the day that he'll return.

Merlin, the legendary wizard and Arthur's teacher, is said to have been buried in Drumelzier, on the River Tweed in the borders. It is said that it was here that he was murdered, and his body buried. Other legends have it that it was in Drumelzier that Merlin's body was imprisoned in a tree by the sorceress Morgan le Fay.

Guinevere, Arthur's queen, may be buried in Meigle, near Forfar. She is said to be buried in Meigle churchyard at "Vanora's mound". "Vanora" is supposed to be the name she adopted following the death of Arthur.

SPORTY SCOTS

A bunker deep below Edinburgh Castle. One year from now. The most evil of all criminal masterminds, Ian McShane (no, not that one) is plotting what will be the greatest heist in human history with his assistant, Jasper.

McShane: Now, we're going to need some getaway drivers, two I think. But they must be Scottish.

Jasper: I believe I have the very man sir, Jackie Stewart. He was Formula 1 World Champion three times between 1965 and 1973, he'll be perfect.

McShane: Excellent, but we will need another, who do you recommend Jasper?

Jasper: David Coulthard, sir. He won 13 Grands Prix in 15 years of driving in Formula One, as well as being ninth on the all time scorers list.

McShane: Wonderful, things are shaping up exactly according to plan. But now I need someone who is capable of travelling through much smaller spaces than these two men, someone indeed who can get around on two wheels.

Jasper: The man you seek is Chris Hoy, sir. He is actually a knight of the realm, and Scotland's most famous Olympian, with three gold medals at the Beijing Olympics in 2008.

McShane: Excellent. I believe our team is almost complete.

Jasper: Sir, I have one more addition to the team, Dario Franchitti.

McShane: Dario Franchitti? That's clearly not a Scottish name. Who is this Franchitti fellow?

Jasper: He is a racing driver sir, from Bathgate. He is of Italian descent, but he is verifiably Scottish.

McShane: I'm not sure that we need another racing driver, Jasper. And especially not one I've never heard of.

Jasper: He is married to the actress Ashley Judd, sir...

McShane: I do love Double Jeopardy, Jasper, so I will allow it. Now, the plan is as follows...

JACOBITE RISING OF 1715
A RECIPE

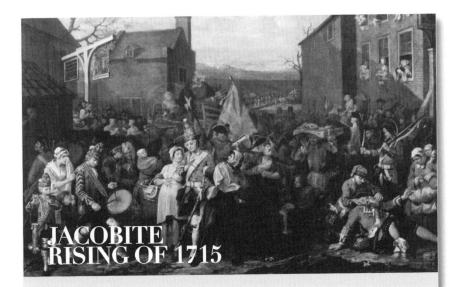

JACOBITE
RISING OF 1715

Ingredients:

A heap of unhappiness with the Act of Union of 1707
1 new King George I
1 John Erskine, Earl of Mar
1 Duke of Argyll
1 Old Pretender – James Francis Edward Stuart
A pinch of fear and distrust among the Scottish people
A smattering of Jacobite soldiers
A heaped tablespoon of military incompetence and lack of leadership

Preparation:

1. Take your George I, install him in London as King and sack your Earl of Mar, then return your Earl of Mar to Scotland and spread your fear and distrust of George I among the Scottish people.
2. Use your Earl of Mar and raise the Jacobite standard at Braemar on 06/09/1715.
3. Take your Earl of Mar, mix with your Jacobite soldiers and capture Inverness, Gordon, Aberdeen and Dundee.
4. Take your Earl of Mar and seize Perth on 05/10/1715.
5. With your Earl of Mar, march on Stirling Castle – Fight your Duke of Argyll with your Earl of Mar at Sheriffmuir on 13/11/1715, and although your Earl of Mar's forces outnumber your Duke's, make sure he does not manage to win. (At this point you will need to use your heaped tablespoon of military incompetence.)
6. Land your Old Pretender at Peterhead on 22/12/1715. Insert your Old Pretender into Perth by 09/01/1716. Now sprinkle the entire mixture with the lack of leadership.
7. Take your Duke of Argyll and advance on your Jacobite soldiers at Perth.
8. Take your Earl of Mar and your Jacobite soldiers north from Perth, burning villages on the way on 30/01/1716.
9. Place your Old Pretender and your Earl of Mar on a ship back to France from Montrose on 04/02/1716. Finally, remove your Old Pretender's hopes of reclaiming the throne.

THE SHORTEST SCHEDULED FLIGHT IN THE WORLD

Scotland has the shortest scheduled flight in the world. Because it's so short, we decided that the story about it should be very short too. But we weren't sure what to put in. You see, it's a flight from Westray to Papa Westray, and it only takes ninety three seconds. Obviously those two facts are very important, but we weren't sure what else you'd want to know.

It's operated by Loganair, and the distance between the two airports is just 1.7 miles. We weren't sure whether that was important or not, and since we wanted this to be a very short story we weren't sure whether we should cut that out.

Then we thought: Do we need to include the fact that Westray and Papa Westray are islands in the Orkneys, or is that really not that important to the rest of the story? We weren't sure, we talked about it for a bit, and then we thought we'd probably leave that out as it wasn't absolutely vital to getting the point across.

We then couldn't decide if we ought to include the fact that Westray has about 60 people living on it, and Papa Westray has about 70, but since it wasn't directly relevant to the very short flight, and we were trying to make the story very short, we thought we'd probably better leave it out too.

In the end, we spent so much time discussing what should go in, what should stay out, what was absolutely vital for the story that we didn't even have time to write it, so you'll never be able to find out about the world's shortest scheduled flight. Sorry about that.

BALMORAL CASTLE

Balmoral has been a home to royalty since King Robert II, who is said to have had a hunting lodge there, but it's really in much more recent times that it's become known for having royal connections.

Queen Victoria and Prince Albert first stayed there on September 8 1848 because Deeside was said to have a "healthy and advantageous climate". The house that originally stood there was thought to be too small, and so they decided to knock down the old house and replace it with a new, much bigger one.

The current castle was designed by William Smith in 1852, although Prince Albert himself made changes to the plans for the building. They started building it in 1853 and it was finally finished in 1856, and since then it's been one of the places where the Royal Family regularly go for their holidays.

Victoria and Albert loved it in the Highlands, often going to the Highland Games at Braemar, decorating Balmoral with tartans and using their time on the 50,000 acre estate to go hunting and shooting, or to just enjoy the beautiful scenery with long walks. After Albert died Victoria spent more and more time there, and it was there that she formed her long-lasting friendship with John Brown.

Balmoral is one of the Royal Family's most famous houses, and since 1987 it's been on the back of Royal Bank of Scotland £100 notes. The grounds are open to the public when the Royal Family aren't there, and it's well worth a look if you're having a day up by the Dee!

THE BATTLE OF FLODDEN FIELD

The Battle of Flodden Field took place on September 9 1513 and was one of the most disastrous battles in Scotland's history. It took place just over the border in Northumberland, near the village of Branxton and was for centuries called the Battle of Branxton.

It happened during the reign of the English king Henry VIII who was away fighting against the French at the time. Sending money and arms, the Queen of France persuaded King James IV to invade northern England.

Before the battle, the Scots occupied the slope of Branxton Hill, a strong position from which they could gain great momentum charging the English forces below.

It didn't work out. Unable to handle their cumbersome artillery the Scots missed their targets while the English fired with precision. Scottish guns and gunmen were blown to pieces.

When James finally decided to charge, an unexpected ridge and boggy area at the base of the hill slowed the Scots down and brought them to a halt at the foot of the hill. A fierce battle then began at the base of the hill.

As defeat closed in on the unfortunate Scots, King James, in a last desperate measure attempted to charge towards the English banners held high where the English military leaders were located. His actions proved fatal, he was knocked down from his horse, unrecognized - the last British monarch to die on a battlefield.

The following morning James was one of 10,000 Scottish victims who lost their lives. Among the Scottish dead were 12 earls, 15 lords, several clan chiefs and the Archbishop of St Andrews.

Their loss is commemorated in a Scottish pipe tune called "The Flowers of the Forest" and on a granite cross at the battle site inscribed "To the Brave of Both Nations".

Flodden
SEPTEMBER
Scotland.vs.England

VIDEO GAMES IN SCOTLAND

The year is 2011. Percival Temperley, gentleman adventurer and well-known dandy is out of work. It has been some years since his last mission for the Crown, and finally his life of leisure and globe-trotting adventure is becoming tiresome. Temperley has decided that he must find himself a job other than as an adventurer and dandy and he enlists the help of his manservant Thornton.

Temperley: Thornton, I'm bored, damnably bored. I need some new thrill to my life, something to fill the gap left by my missions for the Crown.

Thornton: I see, sir. And what is it that you would like to do? You are most excellently qualified for all kinds of dandy adventuring, perhaps something in that vein?

Temperley: No Thornton, dandy adventuring's no longer the game for me, I need something else. I wish to use my adventuring knowledge, but put it to good use right here in Scotland.

Thornton: I think I may have exactly the job for you sir. I think you ought to find yourself employment in the Scottish video games industry.

Temperley: Video games, Thornton? Video games? What do I know about video games?

Thornton: Video games are a way for people to experience adventures in their homes sir, and who knows more about adventure than you, Percival Temperley?

Temperley: And you say there are jobs in this video games industry, Thornton?

Thornton: Indeed, sir, Scotland has some of the best games developers in the country, with games including the Grand Theft Auto and Lemmings series, Crackdown, and many more. There are around 46 different studios in this country, and they make games for everything from consoles to mobiles, almost 11% of the British industry is here.

Temperley: This all sounds most excellent, Thornton. To the games developers!

THE BATTLE OF STIRLING BRIDGE

"You micht ken me. You micht not. If you disnae ken me noo, you better get tae ken me, I'm telling ya. I'm William Wallace, that's who. Wallace, that's right, the meanest, toughest Scottish hero of them all.

You heard about Stirling Bridge? I'll tell ye about Stirling Bridge. That Earl of Surrey cam' lookin' for me, reit? He cam' lookin' tae tell me tae settle doon, to stop kicking off trying to get the Sassenachs oot of my country. I told him he was having a laugh, I was having none ay it.

Him an' his army cam north looking for us, he sends his heralds to try and talk me doon, I told them where they could gan and no mistake. Then he decides to fight me! He's got nae choice but to fight me, and I ken there's going to be a big one going doon, when he tries to cross the Forth.

First he sends away part of his army because he thinks they're too expensive. He thinks he doesn't need 'em. But he does. Then he oversleeps, so he ends up late. Naughty, naughty. Then he comes to cross the river at Stirling Bridge, but it's a right narrow bridge, and only two of his soldiers can cross at the one time. Once half his army are across, I send the boys doon, and we attack. We slaughtered 'em and sent the Earl back to England running. He'd never seen anything like it.

That Edward isn't too pleased, I'm sure he disnae like watching his boys embarrassed like that, but for noo I'm celebrating. I've just been knighted and made sole commander of the Scottish army."

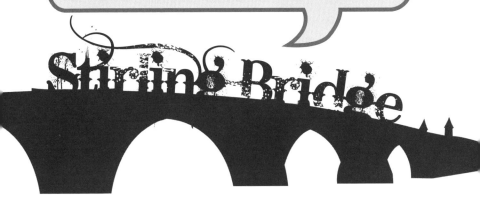

NOVA SCOTIA

We at **ScotsTravel** would like to welcome you to your new home, **NOVA SCOTIA**. Since 1629, Nova Scotia - New Scotland - has been Scotland's premier North American resort/colony. Perfect for all the family, the ideal place for you to get away from seventeenth century Scotland, the Nova Scotia colony was founded three years ago by royal charter.

Since then it has gone from strength to strength. Admittedly, there have been certain problems with the French settlers already present in the area, including three significant battles at Baleine in 1629, Cape Sable Island in 1630 and the raid on St John this year of 1632. However we are fully confident that the Nova Scotia colony is a great place for a long term investment, and a long term commitment to a new country.

Since it was founded by the first Earl of Stirling, Sir William Alexander, Nova Scotia has become a great destination for people from all walks of life, but we particularly encourage skilled tradesmen to make their way across the Atlantic and help us establish Nova Scotia as the Scottish emigration destination.

Some people may be worried by reports that King Charles I may well negotiate a peace with France at the treaty of Saint-Germain-en-Laye this year and give his conquests in the new world back into French hands, and that this would bring the future of the Nova Scotia colony into question.

We can absolutely say that this is not the case. Nova Scotia will be a Scottish possession for a long time to come, certainly for longer than just the years 1629 to 1632.

Nova Scotia was controlled by Scotland from 1629 to 1632. In 1632 Scotland was forced to abandon Nova Scotia to the French.

SCOTLAND PLACE-NAMES
WHAT DO THEY MEAN?

KINTRYE

In Argyll, Scotland's most prominent peninsula. Gaelic *Ceann Tire* meaning, 'head of land'.

KIRKCALDY

Town of 48,000 on the south shore of Fife overlooking the Forth. The name is Pictish/Welsh and derives from *Caer-Caled-Din* meaning, 'fort on the hard hill'. Kirkcaldy is sometimes called Raith, a Gaelic name meaning 'ring fort'.

KIRKCUDBRIGHT

Pronounced Kirk-coo-bree, Dumfries and Galloway coastal town with Anglo-Saxon name meaning 'church of St. Cuthbert'. Gave its name to Kirkcudbrightshire.

KIRKINTILLOCH

Northern Glasgow suburb. Combines the Welsh *Caer*, 'fort', with the Gaelic *cinn-tulaich*, 'head-hill'.

KIRKWALL

Capital of Orkney and home of St Magnus' Cathedral. From the Viking *Kirkja vagr* meaning, 'church bay'.

KYLE

Region of Ayrshire named from a local river, the Water of Coyle. In legend connected with the ancient British King, Old King Coel.

LANARK

Town in Clyde valley near Motherwell. Welsh *Llanerc* meaning 'the glade'. Gave its name to Lanarkshire.

LENNOXTOWN

Town north of Glasgow named after the Earls of Lennox who owned land here.

LINLITHGOW

Town west of Edinburgh. Welsh name *Lyn Lleith Cau* meaning, 'lake-wet-hollow'. Gave name to Linlithgowshire.

14

IRN-BRU

"Hello there. I am the property 'being orange'. I'd like to feel that I've done a lot of good work in my time, I've been involved in a lot of things that I'm very proud of. I've done fruit (the orange), advertising (Orange), spray on tan (orange), but if you ask me, the best thing I've ever been would have to be Irn-Bru.

Irn-Bru was invented in 1901 to give the workers at William Beardmore and Company steelworks something to drink. Before Irn-Bru was invented they were all drinking beer to keep themselves cool, but this wasn't very good for them when they were drinking it all of the time, so they had to find something else to drink instead.

That's why A.G. Barr approached the steelworks and did a deal to make a soft drink for the workers. It was originally called 'Strachan's Brew', and then the name changed to 'Iron Brew', but in 1946 the name had to be changed because it's, well, not really brewed, so they started calling it 'Irn-Bru' because that's how people say it.

Scotland drinks more Irn-Bru than it does any other soft drink, and now Irn-Bru's drunk by people all over the world. I love the fact that there are so many instances of me all over the planet, especially in Russia where there are now five factories making Irn-Bru, and it's become really popular.

I'm so happy to say that there'll be instances of me all over the world, and that Irn-Bru'll continue to have the property 'being orange' for many years to come."

WHEN ABERDEEN HAD AS MANY UNIVERSITIES AS ENGLAND

1 4 9 5

UNIVERSITY OF ABERDEEN

Today it's not uncommon for cities in Britain to have more than one university but at one time, there was only one place that could make that proud boast.

That place was Aberdeen.

Aberdeen University is the third oldest university in Scotland and the fifth oldest in Britain, but it started life as two universities that did not merge until September 15 1860.

The first of the two universities was founded in 1495 by William Elphinstone who was the Bishop of Aberdeen and Chancellor of Scotland. He employed Hector Boece, a Professor from the University of Paris as the university's first principal.

Known as **King's College,** it was Aberdeen's only university until 1593 when George Keith, the fifth Earl Marischal founded a second university in Aberdeen called **Marischal College.**

So now there were two Aberdeen universities. This meant there were as many universities in Aberdeen at that time as there were in the whole of England. The only two universities in England until the 1830s were Oxford and Cambridge.

When Marischal College was founded in 1593 there were already four universities in Scotland at St Andrews, Glasgow, Aberdeen and Edinburgh so it seems the Scots were more interested in furthering their education than the English.

The two Aberdeen universities were rivals for many centuries and sometimes there were occasionally brawls between the two sets of students. In the mid 1600s there were attempts to merge the two universities and during the rule of Oliver Cromwell this was achieved for a short time, but once Cromwell was dead they went their separate ways and did not come together as one university until 1860.

The University has changed an awful lot over the years, but it remains a great place to study, and a world class centre of research and learning.

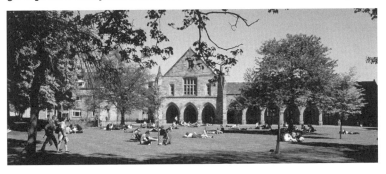

JOHN KNOX

"Ladies and Gentlemen, I come before you today with a mission; a solemn purpose; an undertaking which I am committed to with all of my heart and all of my soul. I come to convince you that you too should join the thousands of people who have become happy owners of a **John Knox**.

That's right, ladies and gentlemen, your very own Scottish religious reformer and radical, the man who changed so many of Scotland's lives can change your life too, but first let me tell you a little about him. First recorded enrolling at the University of Glasgow in 1522, John Knox was ordained some time before 1540 and publicly converted to the Protestant faith in 1545.

He lived for a time in St Andrews, before being kidnapped in 1547 and taken as a French galley-slave for 19 months. Upon his release he went into voluntary exile from Scotland, working to preach Presbyterianism across Europe. He returned to Scotland several times, before finally coming back in 1559, with Scotland ratifying the new religion in 1560.

Knox became minister of the Church of St Giles, the main church in Edinburgh, and became very influential, clashing notably with Mary Queen of Scots over her support of Catholic practices in Scotland. They fell out so badly that he supported Protestant attempts to take her throne, and even called for her execution!

He's feisty, he's fierce, and he's a firebrand that you just can't be without. Have you got a religious establishment that needs undermining? Your John Knox is there. Have you got a Protestant religion which you'd like to establish? It's Knox time. Every day, in every way, Knox is the guy to make your radical religious dreams come true.

Join the thousands of happy customers today.

Knox, the Presbyterian choice."

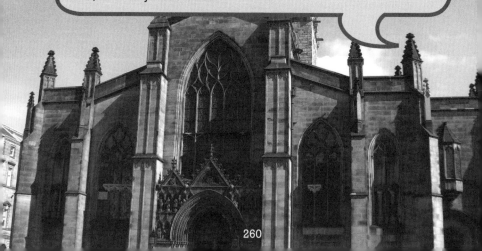

BEN NEVIS

"Good gracious, good gracious, it's so absolutely marvellous to see you. My name's Ben, Ben Nevis, and I am the tallest mountain in Britain. I've been around a very long time indeed, since before there even was a Britain.

I'm four thousand, four hundred and nine feet tall, and I'm made mostly out of igneous rock from the Devonian period, almost four hundred million years ago! I live at the western end of the Grampians, just next to Fort William. It's a nice place to be, and it's always nice to have other mountains to keep me company, even if I am bigger than all of them.

It can get pretty lonely being a mountain though, so it's nice that I have an awful lot of visitors. 125,000 people climb me every year, with another 100,000 getting some of the way up. It reminds me of the years that I had an observatory built on me, I never got lonely then because there was always somebody in it between 1883 and 1904, there even used to be a hotel up on the summit.

My name's actually not Ben Nevis, it's **Beinn Nibheis**, and it's Gaelic. *Beinn* means 'mountain' and *Nibheis* translates as 'malicious' or 'venomous'. I didn't pick it. I'm a nice guy, you'd like me. Sure, people have died trying to climb me, but that's not my fault, I didn't ask them to. I just want to get along with people. Anyway, it's been great talking to you, but I think you're going to have to go... Yes, that rope's really frayed now... Bye then."

ABBEYS AND PRIORIES
J-W

Jedburgh Abbey: Founded in 1138 as an Augustinian priory. Although it is roofless the abbey church is substantial. Malcolm IV was crowned here and Alexander III married here.

Kelso Abbey: Tironesian Benedictine monastery established in 1128. Little remains, though the west tower is impressive. King James III was crowned here.

Kilwinning Abbey: Tironesian Benedictine Abbey founded in Ayrshire between 1162 and 1188.

Lindores Abbey: Overgrown ruins of Tironesian Benedictine monastery on the south bank of the Tay near Newburgh in Fife. It was founded in 1191.

Melrose Abbey: Scotland's first Cistercian monastery. Near the Tweed, this monastery was founded in 1136 by David I. Robert the Bruce's embalmed heart is said to be buried here.

Nunraw Abbey: A working Cistercian Trappist monastery near the Lammermuir Hills. Established in 1946 by Irish monks from Rocrea, on the site of a twelfth century nunnery.

Paisley Abbey: Cluniac monastery established in 1163 by Walter Fitzalan, High Steward of Scotland.

Pluscarden Abbey: Working Catholic monastery near Elgin. Originally a Valliscaulian priory established in 1230 by Alexander III it fell into ruin but was re-established in 1948 by monks from Gloucestershire.

Restenneth Priory: Augustinian priory founded by David I east of Forfar.

St Serf's Inch Priory: Inaccessible Augustinian priory ruins are now a bird sanctuary on St Serf's Inch Island in Loch Leven. Established by David I in 1150.

Sweetheart Abbey: Impressive Cistercian ruins eight miles south Dumfries. Founded in 1275 by Dervorguilla in memory of her husband John Baliol. She carried his heart in a silver casket for 22 years before burying it here. John and Dervorguilla's son John became a King of Scotland.

Whithorn Priory: Monastery on ancient Christian site in Dumfries and Galloway. Established in the twelfth century during the reign of David I for Premonstratensian Canons. Whithorn was historically associated with St Ninian.

GLAMIS CASTLE

Glamis Castle is one of the most famous castles in Scotland, but it's also one of the scariest. It's got more ghosts and ghouls than almost anywhere else, here's just a few stories.

There's a Grey Lady who is seen walking abroad in the chapel, said to be Lady Janet Douglas, who was burned as a witch in Edinburgh in 1537. It's said that she wasn't really a witch, but that her family was hated by King James V because her brother was his stepfather and had imprisoned James. James took his revenge by having her tried, convicted, and burned at the stake.

Another famous tale is that of Earl Beardie. A gambler, playing cards on a Saturday night, was warned by the servants in the castle that he should stop playing, because it would soon be Sunday, and it was a sin to gamble on the Sabbath. Beardie is said to have replied either that he would "play cards with the Devil", or "play cards until Doomsday", and continued to gamble. Then, at just before the stroke of midnight, a mysterious figure appeared, and offered to play. It is said that when the servants returned to the room after midnight Earl Beardie and his gambling partner were consumed by flames and that he is now cursed to play cards for eternity.

Perhaps the most famous story is that of the Monster of Glamis. It is said that one Countess of Strathmore gave birth to a monstrous child, which was walled up into a secret room in the castle, there to live out its days. Another version is that to every generation of the family a vampire is born, and that they are imprisoned in the castle.

Scary stuff!

SCOTTISH STARS OF STAGE AND SCREEN
PART THREE

JAMES MCAVOY

James McAvoy, born in Port Glasgow on April 21 1979, is one of Scotland's favourite actors, and has been thrilling us on stage, small and silver screens since 1995. He had roles in *Band of Brothers, Shameless, State of Play*, before graduating to the big screen and big movie roles in *Atonement, The Last King of Scotland, Wanted* and *The Lion, the Witch and the Wardrobe*. He has become a truly global star, and in 2011 took the role of Charles Xavier in the reboot of the X-Men franchise, *X-Men: First Class*. He is married to his *Shameless* co-star Anne Marie Duff.

KEN STOTT

Born in 1955 in Edinburgh, Ken Stott is one of the most recognisable actors on British television, although he has also appeared prominently on both the stage and the big screen. From star roles as detectives in *Messiah, Rebus* and *The Vice*, to playing Tony Hancock in *Hancock and Joan,* Ken Stott is one of the most versatile and professional actors working today. Roles in films such as *Shallow Grave, Charlie Wilson's War* and *The Hobbit* only serve as evidence of his class and ability.

ASHLEY JENSEN

A native of Annan near Dumfries, born August 10 1969, Ashley Jensen's career has taken her from Queen Margaret University College in Edinburgh to Hollywood, with a few award winning stops in between. Best known as Maggie in *Extras* or Christina McKinney in *Ugly Betty*, she's proved her comic acting abilities on both sides of the Atlantic. But she's far more than a comic actor, having appeared in many more serious projects, such as *The Eleventh Hour, Clocking Off* and *The Reckoning*.

James McAvoy

Ken Stott

Ashley Jensen

BONNIE PRINCE CHARLIE
THE YOUNG PRETENDER

"I'm **Charles Edward Louis John Casimir Sylvester Maria Stuart**. You can call me **Bonnie Prince Charlie** or the **Young Pretender** if you wish.

Dad was James Francis Edward Stuart, the Old Pretender and the son of James VII of Scotland (James II of England).

Dad should have been king, but Protestants kept him off the throne.

Dad's supporters were called Jacobites and in 1715 they tried to get him placed on the throne. This rising was called the '15 but it failed.

I was born in Rome on December 31 1720 where dad lived in exile.

My mum was the granddaughter of a Polish king.

As a young man I trained with the French army and was determined to restore the Stuarts to the throne of Scotland, England and Ireland.

On July 23 1745 I landed on the island of Eriksay near South Uist in the Outer Hebrides where I hoped a French fleet would support me, but it was badly damaged in a storm.

The Highlanders, Protestants and Catholics supported me in this rebellion called the '45. We successfully seized Edinburgh, defeating my Scottish opponents nearby at the Battle of Prestonpans on September 21 1745.

My army marched with me as far south as Derbyshire in England, but here troops began to fear the amassing of a large English force so we returned to Scotland. It was a fatal mistake. The enemy forces headed north in pursuit and on April 16 1746 our great cause was brought to a brutal end at the Battle of Culloden.

As for me, I escaped by boat to the Isle of Skye with the help of a heroine called Flora MacDonald and from there I headed to France. I would never return again. I passed away in Rome on January 31 1788 at the age of sixty seven."

James VIII of Scotland/
James II of England

James Francis Edward
Stuart/Old Pretender

Charles Edward Louis
John Casimir Sylvester
Maria Staurt/Young
Pretender

22
September

THE HORSEMAN'S WORD

Centred in Strathbogie Aberdeenshire "The Horseman's Word" was a mysterious Scottish secret society operating throughout the north east. Most active in the 1870s it was formed in the eighteenth century and continued to function until the 1930s.

Like a kind of Trade Union with supposedly magical rituals and secret initiation rites, The Horseman's Word was only for men who worked with horses, including trainers, blacksmiths and especially ploughmen.

The society was a means of sharing knowledge and ensuring consistent standards for those who looked after horses, but it was the society's mysterious initiation ceremonies that made it most intriguing.

These ceremonies usually took place in an isolated barn on November 11 (Martinmas) with an odd number of novices, preferably 13. The novices would have been invited to the ceremony with instructions in an envelope containing a horse hair and would attend the event blindfolded.

Bringing with them whisky and bread they were asked a series of questions to which there were set answers that formed part of the ritual.

The ceremony was conducted by a leading horseman called a "minister" whose true identity may not have been known to the blindfolded inductees. Kneeling round the minister with their left hand raised and left foot bare the novices were read certain passages from the Bible, backwards, to call up the Devil.

They were then given a secret word that varied from place to place. The word enabled them to control horses. It is also said the magical rituals gave the practitioners power over women.

At the end of the ceremony, before eating and drinking began, the blindfolded inductees shook hands with the Devil. This could be a man dressed in calf skin with a horned mask, a live calf, a live goat or perhaps in some cases the Devil himself!

WHAT'S YOUR NAME?

MacLeod

Descended from Leod, son of the thirteenth century Norseman Olaf Godredsson "the Black". He ruled the Inner and Outer Hebrides and Isle of Man as well as parts of Scotland's western mainland. The two main branches of the family were the MacLeods of Lewis and MacLeods of Harris in the Outer Hebrides. The Harris branch could also be found on Skye. MacLeod is still primarily a Hebrides name.

MacMillan

From Mhaoil-Iain 'son of someone with St John's haircut', a style of hair used by Celtic monks resembling St John's. MacMillans descend from the son of Cornac, a Bishop of Dunkeld during the reign of Alexander I. MacMillan lands included Ben Lawers near Loch Tay and land near Loch Sween in Knapdale. Numerous in the Outer Hebrides.

MacNab

From Mac An Aba, 'child of the abbot'. Their founder was said to be a son of King Kenneth MacAlpin who became Abbot of Glendochart and Strathearn.

MacNaughton

Sometimes spelled MacNaughten and once MacNachten. Descended from Pictish rulers, a number of whom were called *Nechtan*.

MacNeil

Descended from Niall O'Neill, a King in Ulster who settled at Barra in the Hebrides. He descended from the Irish O'Neills who dominated Ulster from the fifth century. Still numerous in the Outer Hebrides.

MacNicol

Probably descend from a thirteenth century Viking inhabitant of the Isle of Lewis.

MacPherson

Clan name of the Great Glen. Means 'son of the parson'. Descended from Cattnach, a parson of Kingussie.

MacRae

Means 'son of grace'. Originally from the Inverness region, by the fourteenth century this clan was associated with Kintail in Wester Ross.

Malcolm

From the Gaelic Maol Chalum, 'follower of St Columba'. *Maol* means 'shaven-headed', a reference to a monk. Numerous in Perthshire, Fife and Caithness. MacCallum is thought to have the same roots.

FOOTBALL IN DUNDEE

Dundee is a special city for Scottish football. The two Dundee clubs have both reached the semi finals of the European Cup (Dundee in 1962-63 and Dundee United in 1983-84) making Scotland the only country which has had two cities produce pairs of semi finalists. Dens Park and Tannadice also have a unique place as the two closest professional football grounds in the world.

Dundee FC was formed in 1893 from a merger of Our Boys and East End, and won its first (and only) Scottish Cup in 1910. Over the years Dundee has had many great players, including Billy Steel, Dave Halliday and Claudio Caniggia, to name just a few. Dundee won the Scottish league title in 1961-62, and their last major honour came in the 1973-74 season when they won their last Scottish League Cup.

Dundee United was originally formed in 1909 by Irish immigrants to the city, and was known as Dundee Hibernian. Until the 1970s they were the less successful Dundee side, but Jim McLean's move from Dens Park in 1971 sparked United into a period of success which saw them win three trophies during the late 1970s and early 1980s, and reach the European Cup semi final and the UEFA Cup Final in 1984 and 1987 respectively. United's last trophy came in 2010 with their capture of the Scottish Cup.

Both Dundee sides are steeped in history, and the contributions of both to the game, inside and outside Scotland are hugely important.

JOHN LOUDON MCADAM

"Good morning. My name is Dirk, Dirk Road. I'm one of the many *dirt* roads which have existed happily on this planet for many centuries, carved out by repeated use, and happily coexisting with people around the world for all of that time. Sure, sometimes we flood, and sometimes we get so waterlogged that people can't use us, but we're mostly pretty good guys.

We would still have been everywhere, all over Scotland, England, all over Europe, if it hadn't been for one pesky Scotsman. John Loudon McAdam was his name, a name which will live in infamy, for what John Loudon McAdam did to me, Dirk Road, and roads like me.

McAdam was born in Ayr on September 21 1756, and I knew then that there was something wrong about him. You see, McAdam invented a process called 'macadamisation', a way of constructing roads with crushed stones and gravel on a base of large stones. He put a camber into the roads, which means a ridge running down the middle, so that rain water runs off either side and doesn't collect in the middle or get into the foundations.

His road building method developed into something called 'tarmacadam', or just 'tarmac' for short. He was a man who did an awful lot of damage. Suddenly people didn't need dirt roads any more, they all wanted roads built McAdam's way. Now we're stuck in the back roads, out in the sticks, and it's all because of John Loudon McAdam."

John Loudon McAdam

SOME SCOTTISH SAINTS

Adomnán (627 AD-704 AD)
Irish-born Abbot of Iona who introduced a "Law of Innocents" protecting civilians during war.

Blane (died 590 AD)
Born on Bute. Established monastery that became Dunblane Cathedral.

Columba (521-597 AD)
Irish-born Columba was granted land on Iona in 563 AD.

David I (1083-1153)
King David I of Scotland was officially a saint.

Donnán (died 617 AD)
Irish missionary killed by a Pictish Queen on Eigg and buried on Arran. Eilean Donan Castle is named after him as are places called Kildonan meaning 'Donnán's church'.

Fergus (died 730 AD)
Irish bishop who established churches in Strageath and Caithness. Buried at Glamis where a well was dedicated to him. His head was buried at Scone.

Gervadius (died 934 AD)
Hermit of Irish origin who lived near Lossiemouth.

Gilbert De Moravia (died 1245)
Bishop of Caithness who founded Dornoch Cathedral.

Kessog (460 AD-520 AD)
Patron saint of Scotland before St Andrew. Son of an Irish king. Lived on Monk's Island, Loch Lomond.

Magnus (1075-1115)
Earl of Orkney, where we find St Magnus Cathedral.

Machar (Sixth century)
Irish-born saint. Aberdeen's historic cathedral is dedicated to him.

Malruibhe (642 AD-722 AD)
Descendant of a king of Ireland. He settled in Argyll and established a base at Applecross.

Margaret (1045-1093)
Sister of Edgar Aethling, the last Saxon claimant to the English throne. She married Malcolm III.

Mirren (565 AD-620 AD)
Irish monk established an abbey at Paisley. Inchmurrin Island on Loch Lomond and Paisley's football club recall his name.

Moluag (565 AD-620 AD)
Irish missionary. Lismore cathedral is dedicated to him.

Mungo also known as **Kentigern** (died 614 AD)
Grandson of a Welsh speaking king from the Lothians. A friend of Columba and St David of Wales where he spent some time. He died at Glasgow.

Ninian (fourth and fifth century)
One of the first missionaries in Scotland. He established a monastery at Whithorn in Galloway.

Regulus (fourth century)
Greek born saint who allegedly brought the bones of St. Andrew to Scotland.

SHINTY

We at ScotsHealth would like to welcome you to a fitness revolution. You've tried other diets, you've tried other fitness plans, but we guarantee you've never tried one quite like this.

The Shinty Plan is founded on one simple idea:
that you play regular games of Shinty, whilst eating a balanced diet.

What is Shinty, you ask?

Shinty is a traditional sport usually played in the Highlands of Scotland. It developed from the same historical roots as the Irish game of Hurling, but the two are now distinct games with different rules and governing bodies.

Shinty has been adapted, adopted, and given birth to many more familiar games, like Lacrosse, Field Hockey and Ice Hockey.

Today, the game is played with two teams of 12 players, each of whom carries a curved stick known as a "caman". Players are allowed to play the ball with their caman, or their feet, but only the goalkeeper is allowed to touch the ball with his hands, and he is not allowed to catch it. The object of the game is to get the ball, a leather covered cork ball about the size of a tennis ball, into the opposition's goal or "hail".

Sure, exercise forms part of any fitness regime, but why is the Shinty Plan special?

The Shinty Plan is special because Shinty is a sport which is highly physical and players are allowed to barge, push and swing their caman above shoulder height.

We at ScotHealth believe that the fear of personal injury due to being unfit is the perfect motivation to stick to a rigorous diet. Fancy some ice cream? Probably not if it means you're going to end up with a broken nose.

The Shinty Plan
Have fun, lose weight, and do some damage.

THE BATTLE OF THE CLANS

Terry: Welcome to North Inch, Perth on this balmy September day in 1396 for the match we've all been waiting for, the trial by combat of Clan Chattan versus Clan Kay. I'm joined in the commentary box by Phil McInnes. So, we're looking forward to an exciting afternoon here, Phil.

Phil: Indeed we are, Terry. It's been a long time coming this one, and when the Earls of Crawford and Dunbar tried to get Chattan and Kay to make up we thought we might never see this bout, but here it finally is, and I have to say I can't wait.

Terry: Me neither, Phil. And we've got the team line-ups here; it's 30 versus 30, including a late substitution for Chattan when one of their men didn't turn up, so Henry Smith, a local armourer has been recruited instead. And what's the significance of this match, Phil?

Phil: Well Terry, obviously we've got King Robert III in the stands, ready to judge the winner of the match, and the final winner will decide this dispute which has been raging for some years now. It's a big one for the teams, the management, and the fans.

Terry: And we're ready to begin. The lads are lining up, the bagpipes are starting and...

Minutes, and a fierce battle later...

Terry: And it looks like the last Kay fighter's jumped into the River Tay... And he's swimming to safety, and it seems, yes, it seems, that means, Clan Chattan has won! A great victory for Clan Chattan, losing 19 men to Clan Kay's 29, and what an impact that will have. As we hand over to the studio I'd just like to thank Phil, and to say it's been an absolute pleasure.

Phil: Thanks, Terry.

GLASGOW CITY POLICE

"Good evening, ladies and gentlemen.

My name is John Stenhouse, and I have come here tonight on September 29 1800 to tell you all about a marvellous advancement for our great city. I have been officially appointed today as the Master of Police for the City of Glasgow, and I have been given the honour of forming the City of Glasgow Police. Since the passage through Parliament of the Glasgow Police Act in this year, 1800, I am ready to create for Glasgow a law enforcement organisation fit for the nineteenth century and beyond.

What is the Glasgow Police Act? Sir, a fine query, let me elaborate if you will. The Glasgow Police Act is the first of its kind in this country, a piece of legislation which has created a modern, professional police force, placing it under the control of the Lord Provost, three magistrates and nine elected commissioners. Together they will administrate this new force.

How will the force be funded, you ask? Well Sir that is a most excellent question. Unlike the previous professional police forces established in this city in 1779 and 1789, the City of Glasgow Police will be supported by monies raised by the City Council.

What will the force consist of? Again, a most excellent question Madam. There are, at this point in time, three sergeants and six police constables, appointed by myself for the purposes of combating crime on the streets of our fair city. Further, the 68 existing members of the City Watch will be available to assist the police in their work.

This is, ladies and gentlemen, a great achievement, and I am sure that the men of the City of Glasgow Police will be a credit both to their force and to their city, and make it a safer place. Thank you."

HISTORIC TOWNS AND CITIES: KIRKWALL

STATUS: Town, port and capital of Orkney.

RIVER: There is no river at Kirkwall. It is situated on a coastal bay.

NAMES AND NICKNAMES: Kirkwall is sometimes referred to on road signs as "The City and Royal Burgh of Kirkwall" though it does not have official city status. Kirkwall has a Viking name that derives from the Old Norse *Kirkjuvagr* meaning 'church bay'.

MOTTO AND EMBLEM: The Kirkwall coat of arms traditionally included a sailing ship with the motto *Si Deus nobiscum* meaning "if God is with us".

POPULATION: Around 8,500.

KEY FACTS AND INDUSTRIES: A small cathedral town and busy port with grey stone houses and narrow streets.

KEY DATES: 1046: Kirkwall mentioned in the Viking *Orkneyinga* Saga as being in existence at this time. **1115:** Magnus Erlendsson, the Viking Earl of Orkney (later St Magnus) was killed by an axe to the head. **1137:** Cathedral of St Magnus founded. **1230:** The *Orkneyinga* Saga was written around this time. **1263:** King Haakon of Norway dies at the Bishop's Palace, Kirkwall. **1486:** Kirkwall granted status of Royal Burgh by James III. Circa **1600:** The Earls palace was built for Patrick Stewart the Earl of Orkney. **1919:** the relics of St Magnus, including his skull complete with axe wound were discovered during renovation of St Magnus Cathedral.

THINGS TO SEE:

- **St Magnus Cathedral**, a twelfth century cathedral of red and yellow sandstone.
- **The Bishops Palace**, a twelfth century palace reconstructed in the sixteenth century.
- **The Earls Palace** built in the seventeenth century.
- **Tankerness House**, a merchant's house dating from the 1500s. Now a museum.
- **Orkney Wireless Museum**, dedicated to the history of radios.

KIRKWALL

DEACON BRODIE

Now come here's the story 'bout Brodie the Deacon,
A most famous tale that of Edinburgh's told,
It's of his involvement in crime that I'm speakin',
I hope that this poem won't leave you feeling cold.

Now Brodie had made himself quite a career,
As cabinetmaker in Edinburgh town,
His works they were all such high quality gear,
That our Brodie's name all the rich men took down.

In many big houses had Brodie been working,
The people they gave him a great deal of trust,
But there in the shadows a secret was lurking,
I think you might know but now tell you I must.

For Brodie was also a burglar effective,
From all of the wealthiest houses he stole,
He made making money his greatest objective,
And took many things, with no care for his soul.

Brodie's career was most filled with excitement,
His exploits they were far too many to list,
But he was betrayed and placed under indictment,
Attempted to flee but it was a chance missed.

Brodie he hanged on the Auld Reekie scaffold,
But the stories of Brodie, they never have died,
His tale for many years and decades has baffled,
As the inspiration for Jekyll and Hyde.

October 2, 1879

Thistle Press

The City Of Glasgow Bank

One year on from the collapse of the City of Glasgow Bank, we take a look back at one of the most remarkable financial events in recent history, and ask where do we go from here?

The fall of the City of Glasgow Bank on October 2 1878 was an event as unexpected as it was unprecedented. The bank had reported in June 1878 that it was in a strong position, with 133 branches and deposits of £8m.

Shareholders were preparing for a dividend of 12% to be paid out, and the City of Glasgow Bank seemed like one of Britain's great financial success stories.

It is by now common knowledge what happened next.

Despite strong figures, and a buoyant showing in the stock market (with £100 shares selling for £236 on the bank's final day of trading) the City of Glasgow Bank was closed on October 2 1878. It was discovered that the directors of the bank had been submitting false profit and loss statements, making false claims over the gold reserves available to the bank, and had made a number of speculative investments into Australasian sheep farming which had failed to pay off in spectacular style.

The effects of the City of Glasgow Bank collapse were incredibly severe, with only 254 of the bank's 1,200 shareholders avoiding complete financial ruin, and hundreds of businesses in Glasgow and wider Scotland folding as a result of the collapse.

Then, in January this year the directors of the City of Glasgow Bank were tried at the High Court in Edinburgh and found guilty.

Two directors, Robert Stronach and Lewis Potter were given 18 month sentences for falsifying and fabricating balance sheets, whilst the other five received eight month sentences.

THIRTY SCOTTISH CASTLES

21 FYVIE CASTLE

An attractive pink stone castle near the village of Fyvie in Aberdeenshire, the castle is thought to date back to 1211. It was a childhood abode of King Charles I. The castle's owners have included the Preston, Meldrum, Seton, Gordon and Leith families. The last of these were headed by Alexander Leith, an American industrialist who bought the castle in 1885.

22 GLAMIS CASTLE

The home of the Earls of Strathmore, who are relatives of the Royal family, this castle is situated at Glamis in the Angus region. Elizabeth Bowes-Lyon, mother of Queen Elizabeth II lived here as a child and the Queen's sister Princess Margaret was born here in 1930. The main tower of the castle was built in 1562 but much of the present castle was built in the eighteenth century. The castle is mentioned in Shakespeare's *Macbeth*.

23 INVERARAY CASTLE

Impressive stately home of a castle on the shores of Loch Fyne. The original castle dated to the 1400s but the present castle was built by Roger Morris and William Adam commencing in 1746. Their work was inspired by a sketch made by the architect John Vanburgh. The castle is a seat of Clan Campbell and home to the Dukes of Argyll.

24 INVERNESS CASTLE

This nineteenth century castle of red sandstone overlooking the River Ness only dates from 1836 when it was built by the architect William Burn but stands on the site of a succession of earlier castles dating back to a castle of the eleventh century, reputedly built by King Malcolm III.

25 KINLOCH CASTLE

This impressive castle on the Isle of Rum was commenced in 1897 for the Lancashire textile tycoon Sir George Bullough and was completed in 1900. Part of the castle serves as a hotel for visitors to Rum and is noted for its oak rooms with their impressive baronial décor and four poster beds.

BUTCHER CUMBERLAND

History Man: Hey, do you know about the Duke of Cumberland?

Student: No, is he something to do with sausages?

History Man: No, he isn't. You might know him better as "Butcher" Cumberland?

Student: Are you sure he's nothing to do with sausages?

History Man: He's one of the worst villains in Scottish history. He's often seen as the symbol of the cruel way that the English have treated Scotland.

Student: Why's that? What did he do?

History Man: The Duke of Cumberland was younger son of King George II and a successful British military commander who'd fought during the War of the Austrian Succession in Europe. It's not for that that he's remembered in Scotland though.

Student: Why is he remembered in Scotland?

History Man: After the War of the Austrian Succession the Duke of Cumberland was sent north to crush the Jacobite Rising of 1745. The rising came to a head at Culloden, in a battle which the Jacobites lost.

Student: So he beat them in a battle?

History Man: It's not just that. He'd been ordered to punish the rebels, so he gave a very famous order, the "no quarter" order. Jacobite soldiers were killed while retreating, injured soldiers were shot whilst lying defenceless, and others burned alive.

Student: Nasty. What happened then?

History Man: The British soldiers started what was called the "harrying of the glens". They went into the Highlands and killed everyone they could find who'd been involved in the rising. They killed Highlanders who hadn't been involved. There are even reports of them killing women and children. The "no quarter" order, and the period that followed, earned Cumberland the title of "Butcher", along with the hatred of many Scottish people.

SKARA BRAE
THE SCOTTISH POMPEII

Let's go back to the very beginning of Scotland's human story, and there's no better place to do that than Skara Brae, the best-preserved prehistoric village in northern Europe.

Situated on the western coast of Orkney on the Bay of Skaill you can walk along the walls surrounding it and peer down into the cosy, stone-furnished houses of the families who lived here more than 5,000 years ago.

Occupied by generations of Neolithic villagers for 500 or 600 years, it was eventually abandoned for reasons unknown.

For more than 40 centuries its true identity lay hidden. To the onlooker Skara Brae seemed like nothing more than a huge grassed-over midden heap, but in 1850 a ferocious storm revealed its amazing secrets.

Wild winds stripped turf and sand from the mound unveiling the outline of stone buildings. They fascinated Walter Watt, the local laird who excavated the site.

In 1868 four ancient houses were uncovered, but no further investigation was made. This settlement was thought to date from the Iron Age making it 2,300 years old, but it was actually much older than that.

In 1925 another storm hit the site causing some damage to the dwellings, so a sea wall was built protecting the site. As the work was carried out more structures were revealed.

In all there are eight dwellings, that formed a village of about fifty people. Their homes are interconnected by covered passages and insulated by the walls of the midden. Every room has a fireplace, dresser, beds and even a toilet.

In the 1970s radio carbon dating revealed the true antiquity of the site, showing it to be older than the Pyramids and Stonehenge, but even without this knowledge Skara Brae provides a fascinating and endearing link to our distant human past.

GOLDEN EAGLES AND SCOTTISH WILDCATS

The **Golden Eagle** called *Aquila chrysaetos* in Latin is Scotland's national bird. One of the most natural and deadly hunters in Britain, these eagles prefer treeless open areas and are found in the Scottish Highlands and the Inner and Outer Hebrides, particularly on Lewis and Harris.

They range from 75 to 90cm in length with a wingspan of 190 to 230cm.
The eagle's natural food sources include all kinds of small animals, but they tend to favour hares, grouse, rabbits and in coastal areas seabirds like Fulmars.

Golden Eagles breed from the age of four or five with females laying one to three eggs incubated for 43 days.

In recent centuries numbers have declined across the world. The Golden Eagle was once found in many parts of Britain, but is now confined mostly to Scotland where 442 pairs were counted in 2003. In Ireland it became extinct but was reintroduced in 2001.

Scottish Wildcats, known in Latin as *Felis Silvestris Grampia*, are thought to have been living in Scotland since the last Ice Age but their presence in Scotland is under threat. According to the Scottish Wildcat Association there are now less than 400 in the wild.

It's unlikely you'll ever get to see a wild cat. They are shy and elusive and don't like people. They used to be found everywhere in Britain, but now only live in the Scottish Highlands. They resemble house cats, but are bigger and stronger and are ferocious hunters.

They look a bit like tabby cats but with a distinctive bushy dark coloured tail.

The house cat is one reason Wild Cats are under threat. When house cats turn feral, they breed with wildcats, so there aren't so many *pure* Scottish Wildcats left. Another reason for the decline is the cutting down of forests leaving fewer places for the wild cat to reside.

POETRY IN STONE
THE RUTHWELL CROSS

Ruthwell Cross stands 18 feet high in the village church of Ruthwell near Dumfries and is one of the most important Anglo-Saxon monuments in the world.

The Anglo-Saxons or specifically the Angles, ruled the Kingdom of Northumbria when this eighth century cross was made and Dumfriesshire was once part of their kingdom.

The cross is inscribed with Biblical scenes depicting amongst other figures, Jesus, Mary Magdalene and John the Baptist. The reliefs are significant because they are the largest found on any Anglo-Saxon monument.

Latin explanations of the scenes accompany the reliefs, but the monument's real significance lies in the runic inscriptions that surround the cross. The Latin would be understood by educated men but the runes were probably there to appeal to the common man.

Runes are an early form of writing and these particular runes recite verses of the Anglo-Saxon poem *The Dream of the Rood* telling the story of Christ's crucifixion from the point of view of the cross. This Ruthwell Cross inscription is the oldest surviving written example of the text of an English poem anywhere in the world and the sole surviving example of Angle literature in Scotland.

The cross was made around 700 AD and it's thought the church was built around it. In 1664 the cross was smashed up by Presbyterians and the pieces later removed to the neighbouring churchyard.

Fortunately, in 1818 the pieces of the cross were collected and reassembled by a local man called Henry Duncan. Duncan (1774-1846) was the minister of Ruthwell church and was famous for establishing the world's first commercial savings bank in the village in 1810. This building is now a museum dedicated to the history of the bank.

Ruthwell's star attraction is however the Ruthwell Cross which was returned to the church interior in 1887.

Did you know?
Whisky

- Whisky derives its name from the Gaelic "uisge beatha", 'water of life'. Its distillation probably goes back to the ancient Celtic times but the first actual mention of whisky in Scotland was in 1494 when it was noted in the Exchequer Rolls that a Friar called John Cor was sent malt on the order of the King for the making of whisky.

- Scottish whisky is known as "Scotch" around the world, but simply called "whisky" in Scotland. Irish Whiskey is spelled with an "e" and this spelling is popular in America too even when referring to Scotch.

- There are five types of Scottish whisky: Single Malt, Single Grain, Blended Malt, Blended Grain and Blended Scotch.

- There are five official Scottish whisky regions: Lowland, Speyside, Highland (including the islands), Campbeltown and Islay.

- Speyside's whisky region covers a relatively small geographical area but has the highest number of whisky distilleries in Scotland. Its whiskies include Glenfiddich, a single malt made at the Glenfiddich distillery, established at Dufftown in 1886 by William Grant. Speyside is also the home to the Glenlivet distillery in Moray which produces America's biggest selling malt whisky.

- The Campbeltown whisky region on the Kintyre peninsula once had thirty distilleries but now there are only three. There are only three whisky distilleries in the Lowland whisky region.

- Whisky from the Highland region includes Glenmorangie, a single malt made from the Tain area of Rossshire produced since 1783.

- Several islands make their own whiskies, particularly Islay which is a whisky region in its own right. Here notable brands include the single malt Lagavulin, made on the island since 1816.

- Well known blended whiskies include Famous Grouse made at Perth since 1897, Bells made at Perth since 1825 and Johnnie Walker produced at Kilmarnock from 1820.

- Drambuie is a heather-honey and herb flavoured whisky liqueur developed on the Isle of Skye in the nineteenth century.

Professor C. Claggs

THE HIGHLAND CLEARANCES

Beginning directly after the 1745 rising, and continuing right through until the middle of the nineteenth century, the Highland Clearances mark one of the darkest periods in Scottish history. Over that period the Highland Clan culture, which had existed for generations was broken up and its people scattered across the globe with little concern for their welfare.

For centuries people had lived in tight-knit farming communities across the Highlands, bound together by their clan allegiances. This changed in the later part of the eighteenth century as the Highland lairds began to see themselves, and be seen by the law, as landlords. They realised that these farming communities weren't very profitable, and that there was more money to be made from farming animals like sheep and cattle.

There began a process of forcing the Highlanders out of the Highlands, whether to the growing industrial cities of the south or to settlements along the coast. Whole villages were evicted, the land which had been farmed by Highlanders now taken over. Land which had been effectively owned by entire communities became empty estates filled with sheep.

The Highland Clearances were a significant period in Scottish history, changing the entire face of the country from one dotted with diverse clans and peoples to the starkly divided one we see today. Although many of the landowners justified their actions as modernisation, the tactics employed and the treatment of the Highland peoples distinguish this as a black time for Scotland.

SCOTLAND'S ALCATRAZ

The Bass Rock
Firth of Forth
Scotland.

October 10, 1650

Father,

I do not know whether this letter will reach you, but I write in the hope that it will. I am imprisoned on the Bass Rock in the Firth of Forth, Scotland's most formidable prison. I sit in my cell one mile from the mainland, surrounded by the rushing waters of the Forth, and write to you. I am here for the same reason as my fellow prisoners, for supporting the National Covenant.

The rock is more than 300 feet in height, and three of the sides have steep cliffs. It would be impossible to swim from the rock and hope to survive.

I am told the Rock has been occupied since the eighth century, when Saint Baldred used it as a spiritual retreat. The church which now stands on the island is dedicated to him. The castle on the island was built, I believe, in the early fifteenth century, and the island began to serve as a prison then as well.

Mary, the Queen of Scots had a garrison placed upon here, leading to many battles with Elizabeth Tudor for control of the rock. I am even told that in 1581 King James VI attempted to buy the rock, so impressed with it was he.

And finally, here I find myself. The rock has been used to house the leaders of Covenant forces since 1637, and I have some fear that it will continue to be used as such until perhaps as late as 1687. I have a strong feeling it will then become a place for the grazing of sheep, and a sanctuary for many birds, and attract many visitors from all around the world.

I hope that this letter finds you.

Your loving son,

Fergus

THE HONOURS OF SCOTLAND

Chris: Hi, and welcome back to the ScotShop Network's Jewellery Hour, and we've got some beautiful things for you today, haven't we Mel?

Mel: Yes we do Chris, one very special item indeed Chris, or should that be three items? (*laughs*)

Chris: (*laughs*) Quite right, Mel, we've got something very special, the Honours of Scotland.

Mel: That's great Chris, and they really are beautiful, but what will our viewers receive if they decide to purchase?

Chris: Well, it's a three part set, including the Crown, made in Edinburgh in 1540 by goldsmith John Mosman, and it was worn for the first time by James V at the coronation of his second queen, Marie de Guise.

Mel: That's fascinating Chris, but that's not all our lucky viewers can get themselves, is it?

Chris: No it isn't Mel. Also included are the Sceptre presented by Pope Alexander VI in 1494, and the Sword, given to James IV in 1507 by Pope Julius II. All three were used in every Scottish coronation from Mary Queen of Scots in 1543 to Charles II in 1651.

Mel: That's great, Chris, but that's not all is it? These pieces have quite an interesting history, don't they?

Chris: Indeed they do, Mel. Following the Acts of Union in 1707, the Honours of Scotland were put into a metal chest and locked away in Edinburgh Castle, and they stayed there until they were rediscovered by Sir Walter Scott in February 1818.

Mel: That's amazing Chris, so they were lost for more than a hundred years?

Chris: That's right Mel, but they're here now and they're available to one very lucky ScotShop customer. So get dialling, supplies of this unique item are very limited, and you'll kick yourself if you miss out!

Mel: I think I'd quite like them for myself Chris! (*Chris and Mel both laugh*).

THE SCOTTISH PARLIAMENT

Congratulations on your purchase of a Scottish Parliament Mark II. This set of easy to use instructions will guide you through your first use of your new Scottish Parliament, and set you on the road to a full representative democracy.

1) First, ensure that the Westminster Parliament has passed the Scotland Act 1998, releasing powers to the Scottish Parliament.

2) Now install your Scottish Parliament in a suitable position, e.g. Holyrood, Edinburgh.

3) Activate your electoral system. We recommend using the mixed proportional representation system which is included with your Scottish Parliament. If you are using this system, proceed to 4). For any other system, proceed directly to 5).

4) The mixed proportional representation system included elects 129 MSPs (Members of the Scottish Parliament) in total. 73 of these represent individual constituencies, whilst a further 56 come from lists in eight larger regions. Each region has seven MSPs.

5) Gather your MSPs in your Scottish Parliament, and arrange them into parties. These should include the Scottish National Party, Labour Party, Liberal Democrats and Conservative Party. Other parties may include the Green Party, the Scottish Socialist Party and Solidarity.

6) Choose your Leader from the party with the most seats. That leader should then choose a cabinet from members of the parliament.

7) Initiate political debate about the future of Scotland, including the question of independence from the United Kingdom.

8) After four years, repeat 3) to 8).

We hope you will be very happy with your Scottish Parliament, if you have any problems please sort them out yourself, you have a Parliament now!

WHAT'S YOUR NAME?

Mar
The Mar Clan is named from the ancient Kingdom of Mar centred on the land between the River Dee and River Don in Aberdeenshire. Mars are not Martians but are thought to be descended from the Mormaers who were the Pictish rulers of this kingdom.

Mathieson
Derives from the Gaelic Mac Mhathghamhuin, 'son of the bear' or MacMhathain, 'son of the heroes'. It is probably from a lowland name meaning 'son of Matthew'. Numerous in the north and north east, Matheson without the "i" is prevalent in the Western Isles.

Maxwell.
Thought to take their name from the Maccus well, a pool in the River Tweed which is said to have been named from a Viking chief. Maxwells are a Borders clan concentrated in south west Scotland.

Melville
Family of Norman origin from Malavile in Normandy. They came to Scotland with King David I around 1124 and were given land near Edinburgh. The surname is quite numerous in Fife.

Menzies
This clan originated in Mesnières in Normandy and came to be known as Menzies in Scotland while an English branch of the family were called *Manners*. In the thirteenth century they received lands in Glen Lyon, Atholl and Aberfeldy.

Moncrieffe
Took their name from Moncrieffe in Perthshire which means 'hill of the sacred bough'. Found in Argyll.

Montgomery
This clan originated in Wales where they took their name from the place of that name. The place in Wales was named from a family called Montgomery who was named from a place in Normandy – a little confusing. The Welsh Montgomery family acquired lands in Renfrewshire in the twelfth century. Despite its Welsh origin Montgomery is predominantly a Scottish name.

14
October

Thistle Press

LATEST NEWS: Tragedy at Fishing Community, Eyemouth

Friday, October 14, 1881

Tragedy at Eyemouth

Reports are coming in of a terrible tragedy at Eyemouth, a small fishing community on the east coast of Scotland. People in this close-knit village rely upon fishing to support themselves, and pay their bills and taxes.

Weeks of bad weather have prevented boats from going out to sea but this morning it was clear and calm. The men of Eyemouth decided that they would go out as they have to earn a living and really had no choice.

It proved to be a disastrous decision, costing many of the men their lives. By noon the boats were out at sea, and had begun to fish, but the storm had begun to brew.

It has been one of the worst storms on record, and took an awful toll on the fishermen. When they turned back, the storm reached such intensity that they were dashed on the rocks, capsized, or could not get safely into harbour.

Their families and friends have been forced to stand on the shore and watch.

Early reports claim that 189 have lost their lives, leaving 93 widows and 267 fatherless children. In truth, the real consequences will be much harder to measure.

This is the worst fishing disaster in British history, and one which will surely live long in our memories.

The people of Britain were shocked by this tragedy and over £50,000 was collected in a disaster fund about £2,500,000 in today's money. It was enough to give widows 5 shillings and school age children 2 shillings and 6 pence a week.

ABOUT THE SHETLAND ISLANDS

If you've never been to the Shetlands but have seen them on the map you could be forgiven for thinking they are only a few miles east of the Orkneys and are surrounded by a large rectangular box.

In truth the Shetlands lie 50 miles north east of the Orkneys, which makes it necessary for map makers to squeeze them into a box in this way. Shetland's relative remoteness from other parts of Scotland is also demonstrated by the fact that the islands lie closer to Bergen in Norway than Edinburgh.

There are around 300 Shetland Islands of varying sizes including many small islands called Skerries, but only 16 islands are actually inhabited. The 12 largest islands by area are: **Mainland, Yell, Unst, Fetlar, Bressay, Whalsay, Muckle Roe, Foula, Papa Stour, Fair Isle, West Burra, East Burra** and all of these are inhabited.

Of these islands **Fair Isle** lies half way between the Orkneys and Shetlands and belongs to the Shetlands in an administrative rather than a geographic sense.

There are about 22,000 people living in the Shetlands with 17,500 living on **Shetland's mainland**. The islands of **Yell** and **Whalsay** are the next most populous with about a thousand inhabitants each. **West Burra** and **Unst** follow with more than 700 people each and then it's **Bressay** where almost 400 reside.

Lerwick on the east coast of the Shetland mainland is the main settlement and capital of Shetland where one ferry takes you to Aberdeen in 12 hours and another gets you to Bergen in 12 and a half. The town is on the eastern coast of Shetland's southerly peninsula and faces the Island of **Bressay** in the North Sea.

Lerwick is located on one of the narrowest east to west points on Shetland, so we reach the Atlantic coast only five miles south-west of Lerwick at the port of **Scalloway**. Here around 800 people reside. Scalloway was Shetland's capital until 1708.

October 16, 1824

Thistle Press

Brave New World For City as "Fire Engine Establishment" Formed

A great step was taken today to safeguard Edinburgh from the types of fires which have ravaged the city in recent years, with the founding of the Edinburgh Fire Engine Establishment.

Funded by a combination of six insurance companies and the city itself, the Edinburgh Fire Engine Establishment becomes the world's first public fire brigade, although we are sure that it is a development which others will follow with interest.

Each of the insurance companies has contributed £200, with the city also giving £200 to the establishment of the new force.

Mr James Braidwood has been appointed as Master of Fire Engines, a role which will involve the recruitment, training and organisation of a force of men for the fighting of fires within the city. Mr Braidwood is a trained surveyor, and plans to use this knowledge of buildings and materials to his advantage.

To that end, Mr Braidwood will recruit his force from experienced tradesmen, builders, carpenters, masons, plumbers and slaters who are familiar with the buildings of the city they will be tasked with protecting.

Mr Braidwood's men will be employed as part time firefighters, and will be divided into four companies, labelled red, blue, yellow and grey, each with a responsibility for a different part of the city.

Mr Braidwood would like to encourage applications for the Fire Engine Establishment. Any men interested in joining should be aware that drills and training will take place every Wednesday morning at four of the clock.

We at the Thistle Press are sure that Edinburgh's Fire Engine Establishment will only be the first of many, and that one day the rest of the world will regard Mr Braidwood and his men as pioneers.

SHETLAND PONIES

"Hey there boys and girls, it's so great to meet you. My name's Simon and I'm a Shetland pony. I'm part of a very illustrious family. I'll have you know, I can trace my roots right back to the Bronze Age, about 4,000 years ago! People have found remains of my ancestors buried on the Shetland Islands which prove that we've been around a long time, which I think is pretty impressive.

We're known to be a hardy bunch, tough and resilient, which is probably why we've managed to survive up here for so long. It's also probably why you humans like us so much, because we've proved ourselves very useful to you over the last few thousand years.

We've done tons of different jobs for you, from helping with farming to helping down the mines, from pulling carts to carrying children around. It's not always rewarding work, but we don't mind, we're not the kind of animals to complain about that kind of thing.

I guess you like us because we live a long time too; sometimes we can live for as long as thirty years! That'd be pretty good for bigger ponies, so I think it's fantastic for us. You people have mixed us with a lot of different breeds, so I've got cousins called American Shetlands, but wherever you take us we've all got our ancestors right here in Scotland.

It's great being a Shetland pony, especially if you're somebody's pet, as long as they're kind to you at least. If you see any of my family you can say hello to them from me, and tell them I'm looking forward to the family reunion soon..."

CRAIGIEVAR CASTLE
DISNEY'S INSPIRATION

Craigievar Castle six miles south of Alford, Aberdeenshire
is a unique castle in a number of ways. It was built in 1626 by
William Forbes, a merchant from Aberdeen. Forbes was known
as "Danzig Willie" because of his success in trading with Eastern
Europe. Forbes was the brother of the Bishop of Aberdeen, and
was the ancestor of the Forbes-Sempill family.

The castle itself is pink in colour and topped with a number of
little turrets, although Danzig Willie didn't build it for defence.
Mainly it was built to be a stately home for the Forbes family,
although it did have a very strong iron gate and a walled
courtyard with guard towers on each corner.

The castle is said to have been one of the inspirations for Walt
Disney's vision of a fairytale castle, and it's not hard to see why
this might be the case. The castle is seven stories tall and very
narrow, so much so that it is said that when people died within the
castle they had to be carried out through the window, because
the stairs were too narrow to carry a coffin down.

Although the castle was never the scene of any fighting, it housed
a hospital for wounded Belgian soldiers during the First World
War. The house remained in the Forbes-Sempill family until 1963
when it was given to the National Trust for Scotland for
safe keeping.

THE TOP 10 THINGS TO SEE IN GLASGOW

Glasgow Cathedral

Also known as St Mungo's Cathedral, Glasgow Cathedral was built in the late twelfth century and is one of the most beautiful buildings in the city.

Kelvingrove Art Gallery and Museum

Featuring paintings by Salvador Dali, Botticelli and Van Gogh, along with many others, and housed within one of the most original and distinctive buildings ever seen, Kelvingrove Gallery's a must see. There's even a Spitfire there too!

The Botanic Gardens

A great place to spend an afternoon in the sunshine, with a fantastic series of greenhouses.

The Barras Market

A Glasgow institution, and a great place to spend your money on a weekend.

The West End

Filled with bars, restaurants and shops, this is the perfect place to kill time and spend the day. Plus, a lot of famous people live around here, so maybe you might see one or two!

The Willow Tea Rooms

Designed by Charles Rennie MacKintosh, no trip to Glasgow would be complete without a visit to this most unique of places.

GoMA

The Gallery of Modern Art, in the centre of the city, used to be the townhouse of Glasgow Tobacco Lord William Cunninghame. Since 1996, however, it's been the home to one of the most interesting galleries around.

Glasgow Science Centre

Including a fascinating museum, an IMAX cinema and in the Glasgow Tower, the tallest free-standing building in Scotland. There's a whole day's entertainment just here.

Sauchiehall Street and Buchanan Street

Take a stroll down these two great Glaswegian Streets, perfect for shopping, eating or just hanging out.

Music

Glasgow is world-renowned for its music scene. With unique venues like the Barrowland Ballroom and King Tut's, as well as many others, Glasgow's the best place to see bands play.

MY SCOTLAND

O bonnie Loch Ness there lives a creature
I ken is scarier than mah teacher.
You're a great myth, a legend, some say,
I think abit you all day.
Some young folk say yer just a tale
But they don't even ken if yer male.
Although us folk have nae proof (I bet yer real)
I bet my roof.
You're very hidden doon there in the sea
I only wish I could join ye for tea.
It must get away lonely doon there,
Ye must hae friendly nits in yer hair.
Ye must also ken a lot of things, I'm told,
But you are pretty smart, yer ower a hunnerd years auld.
So Ness all that's left to say,
Is I really hope we meet one day.

Name: Darren Grosvenor
Age: 10
School: Gateside Primary School, Beith, Ayrshire

TALKING DORIC
FROM ANCIENT GREECE TO ABERDEEN

Doric is the dialect of north east Scotland, spoken in Aberdeen and Aberdeenshire with variants spoken in neighbouring regions like Banffshire, Deeside, Donside, Mearns and Moray. In the coastal villages of the Buchan region, a variation of the Doric dialect called the Buchan Claik is spoken.

Why Doric?

Well Doric was originally a language spoken by the Dorians who lived in Sparta in Ancient Greece. Unlike the more colourful and refined Attic language of Athens, the speech of the Dorians was clipped, or terse. In fact it might be described as Laconic, a word that comes from Laconia, a region surrounding Sparta.

So what's this got to do with Aberdeenshire?

Well Doric came to be a term jokingly used to refer to the rustic nature of the Scots dialect of English, spoken throughout the lowlands. During the twentieth century it came to specifically refer to the lowland Scots dialect spoken in Scotland's north east. Perhaps Doric was a name given to this dialect by the Middle Class English speakers of Edinburgh, who preferred not to speak this way.

It's tempting to link this contrast in local speech with Edinburgh's nickname "The Athens of the North" which it was given sometime after the 1760s when the "new town" developed there. Edinburgh's speech might have been compared to ancient Athens, whilst that of the outlying lowlands might have been compared to Sparta.

It is also thought that Scottish dialect writers in the north east compared their work to the ancient Greek poet Theocritus who composed his work in the ancient Doric.

A notable feature of Doric is that certain words like 'what' (whit) are spelled and pronounced with an "f" so that 'whit' becomes *fit*. The words 'who', 'when' and 'where' become *fa, fan* and *faur* and the word 'how' may become *fou.*

22
October

THE FORTH BRIDGE

The year is 1882. Ian Paint, the head of the largest paint company in Britain, has called a meeting of the heads of all other paint companies. He has a plan to increase their profits, a nefarious plan which stretches to the very top of the government...

"Gentlemen. Paint has been good to us, but we need to make sure that the demand for paint stays high. We need to make sure that there will always be a need for paint. To this end, I have come up with a plan. We will engineer for ourselves a building project so massive that they will have to keep painting it forever; a structure so enormous that when it is finally all painted, it will be time for the painting to begin again. Gentlemen, I give you, the Forth Bridge.

That's right, a railway bridge across the Forth, and the largest steel structure in the world. It will stretch for 1.5 miles, and it will be built by Sir William Arrol & Co of Glasgow between 1883 and 1890, from a design by Sir John Fowler and Sir Benjamin Baker. It will be made of 51,000 tons of steel, steel which they will have to pay to paint for the rest of their lives.

Yes, my friends, this will truly make our fortune. I, Ian Paint, stand here before you today to tell you that with your help we can guarantee the paint industry not just for the next century, but for the next millennium!"

Unfortunately for Ian Paint, the myth of "painting the Forth Bridge" is just that, a myth, the bridge having never been maintained this way. It's still a pretty amazing structure though, and a genuine Scottish engineering marvel.

HISTORIC TOWNS AND CITIES: PERTH

STATUS: Known as a city (a designation it had until local government reforms in 1975) but is officially a town. Perth is bidding for official city status in 2012.

RIVER: Perth is situated on the **River Tay**.

NAMES AND NICKNAMES: Known as **"The Fair City of Perth"**. This name derives from the Walter Scott Story *The Fair Maid of Perth* written in 1828. Perth was historically known as **"St John's Toun"**. The town's football club is called **St. Johnstone**.

MOTTO AND EMBLEM: The traditional coat of arms of the city of Perth features a double-headed golden eagle and the motto *Pro Rege, Lege Et Grege* meaning "For the King, Law and People".

POPULATION: Around 45,000.

KEY FACTS AND INDUSTRIES: The **effective capital of Scotland** throughout the Middle Ages, as a meeting place of Scotland's parliament and home to the Scottish Kings. Perth is about two miles south of **Scone** where the Kings of Scotland were crowned. Historically an important port, Perth's "city centre" is now a major retail centre for the surrounding area.

KEY DATES: Circa 1100: Perth became a Royal Burgh. **1437**: King James I murdered at Blackfriars Monastery in Perth by rebels. **1559**: John Knox preached at Perth following a long exile abroad, launching the Scottish Reformation. **1760**: Perth Academy founded. **1771**: Perth Bridge built of stone. It can still be seen. **1850**: Episcopalian Cathedral of St Ninian built.

THINGS TO SEE:

• **St John's Kirk**, dates back partly to the twelfth century.
• **Perth Museum and Art Gallery.**
• **Balhousie Castle** of 1631 is home to the Black Watch regimental museum.
• **Scone Palace**, two miles north of Perth.
• **Huntingtontower Castle**, two miles west of Perth. Once called Ruthven Castle. Dates from the fifteenth century.

PERTH

SCOTTISH STARS OF STAGE AND SCREEN
PART FOUR

ROBBIE COLTRANE
A British acting legend, Robbie Coltrane has played some of the most memorable and best loved characters we have ever seen. Born Anthony Robert MacMillan in Rutherglen on March 30 1950, he has moved from being a comedian featuring in British sketch shows to a global movie star. By the time he played Fitz in *Cracker* he was already an international star, but that role led him to even bigger things, featuring in James Bond films *Goldeneye* and *The World Is Not Enough* and as Hagrid in the *Harry Potter* movies. He continues to be one Scotland's greatest acting exports.

TOM CONTI
Born in Paisley on November 22 1941, Tom is best known as a stage actor and director and is one of the most talented performers Scotland has produced. Famous for parts in films such as *Shirley Valentine, The Quick* and the *Dead* and 2012's *The Dark Knight Rises*, he has been a feature of British cinema, television and stage since his first appearance with the Dundee Repertory Theatre in 1959. His appearance in the finale of Christopher Nolan's *Batman* trilogy is set to introduce Conti's work to a whole new generation, and to prove that he's got a lot to contribute yet.

ALASTAIR SIM
Born in Edinburgh on October 9 1900, Alastair Sim was one of Scotland's finest character and comic actors. Appearing in two *St Trinian's* movies, *An Inspector Calls, Stage Fright* directed by Alfred Hitchcock and many other roles over more than forty years on stage and screen, Alastair Sim became a comic icon for many people, including those within his profession. Sadly he died on August 19 1976, but he lives on through his classic performances.

Robbie Coltrane

Tom Conti

Alastair Sim

HAGGIS

Not a small animal with legs of uneven length as is sometimes mythically claimed but a famed Scottish delicacy. It consists of sheep's heart, liver and lungs all minced and simmered together with onion, oatmeal, suet and spices. It should be wrapped up in a sheep's stomach and served with neeps (turnips) and tatties.

Actually the sheep's stomach was the traditional method of bagging the haggis, but today the bag is usually a casing like that in which sausage is wrapped.

Haggis is the national dish of Scotland and is often served as the main course at Burns Night supper. It's a more than appropriate dish for it was Robert Burns who immortalised the delicacy in his *Address to a Haggis* of 1787:

> **Fair fa' your honest, sonsie face,**
> **Great chieftain o' the puddin'-race!**
> **Aboon them a' ye tak yer place,**
> **Painch, tripe, or thairm:**
> **Weel are ye wordy o' a grace**
> **As lang's my airm.**

Though most closely associated with Scotland, there is a suggestion that the ancient Romans and Greeks made a haggis type of dish. It's also been argued that it was the Vikings who introduced it into Scotland.

The first mention of haggis in Scotland was in a poem of 1520, but ninety years earlier in 1430 a recipe book from Lancashire in England described the making of *Hagese* using a sheep's heart and other ingredients. The book describes the boiling of the mix and hacking everything together – hack is perhaps a clue to the origin of the name.

Scotland TV Listings

Thistle Press

Scotland on TV

3pm-3:30pm *Balamory*	BBC Children's TV series based around the island community of Balamory. Largely filmed in Tobermory, Mull.
3:30pm-4:30pm *River City*	Scottish soap opera set in Glasgow. Filmed in Dumbarton, Dunbartonshire.
4:30pm-5:30pm *Monarch of the Glen*	Drama series very loosely based on Compton MacKenzie's Highland Novels.
5:30pm-6:30pm *Hamish Macbeth*	Comedy drama series starring Robert Carlyle as a police detective. The series which made his name.
6:30pm-7pm *Chewin' the Fat*	Iconic sketch show featuring Greg Hemphill, Ford Kiernan and Karen Dunbar. Hemphill and Kiernan also produced Still Game.
7pm-7:30pm *Limmy's Show*	Sketch comedy from Brian Limond, produced by the BBC in Glasgow.
7:30pm-8:30pm *Sea of Souls*	BAFTA Award winning supernatural drama series featuring Bill Paterson as a paranormal investigator.
8:30pm-10:30pm *Rebus*	STV adaptation of Ian Rankin's Rebus novels, featuring John Hannah (series 1-2) and Ken Stott (3-5) in the title role.
10:30pm-12:30am *Taggart*	The UK's longest running police drama, having been on the air since 1983.

SCOTTISH COUNTIES

Scotland's counties, historically called "shires" were originally sheriffdoms under the jurisdiction of Sheriffs (Shire Reeves). From 1633 until 1975 there were 33 Shires. They developed from the twelfth century onwards, inspired by Norman models of administration and replacing earlier Celtic chiefdoms.

By the 1300s there were 24 shires. Others followed in later centuries including **Caithness** and **Sutherland**, respectively created from parts of **Inverness-shire** in 1503 and 1633.

Between 1890 until 1975 the **33 traditional counties were**: Aberdeenshire, Angus, Argyll, Ayrshire, Banffshire, Berwickshire, Bute, Caithness, Clackmannanshire, Dumfriesshire, Dunbartonshire, East Lothian, Fife, Inverness-shire, Kincardineshire, Kinross-shire, Kirkcudbrightshire, Lanarkshire, Midlothian, Moray, Nairnshire, Orkney, Peeblesshire, Perthshire, Renfrewshire, Ross and Cromarty, Roxburghshire, Selkirkshire, Stirlingshire, Sutherland, West Lothian, Wigtownshire and Zetland.

Before this time Orkney and Shetland (Zetland) were regarded as one county. Orkney was called "the Earldom" and Zetland "the Lordship". Another county with a peculiar title was **Kirkcudbrightshire** called "the Stewartry" rather than county.

Ross and Cromarty was created in 1890 by merging **Ross-shire** with **Cromartyshire**. It simplified things because Cromartyshire had been made up of scattered pieces of land (enclaves) dotted within Ross-shire.

An added confusion was that some counties had two names. Midlothian for example was called **County of Edinburgh** and Angus was called **Forfarshire**. Others with alternative names were East Lothian (**Haddingtonshire**), Kincardineshire (**Mearns**), Moray (**Elginshire**) and West Lothian (**Linlithgowshire**).

In 1975 the counties were abolished and **12 administrative regions** created called: Borders, Central, Dumfries and Galloway, Fife, Grampian, Highland, Lothian, Orkney, Shetland, Strathclyde, Tayside and Western Isles.

In 1996 the twelve regions were replaced by **32 new counties** called: Aberdeen City, Aberdeenshire, Angus, Argyll and Bute, Clackmannanshire, Dumfries and Galloway, Dundee City, East Ayrshire, East Dunbartonshire, East Lothian, East Renfrewshire, City of Edinburgh, Falkirk, Fife, Glasgow City, Highland, Inverclyde, Midlothian, Moray, North Ayrshire, North Lanarkshire, Orkney Islands, Na h-Eileanan Siar (Outer Hebrides), Perth and Kinross, Renfrewshire, Scottish Borders, Shetland Islands, South Ayrshire, South Lanarkshire, Stirling, West Dunbartonshire and West Lothian.

ROBERT LISTON
THE FASTEST KNIFE IN THE NORTH

"Well good golly, guys and gals, I'm so pleased to meetcha, my name's Robert Liston and I'm the fastest knife in all of Scotland.

I'm a surgeon, you see, but I was born on October 28 1794, before anaesthetic was invented. Back then if you had to have an operation, you had a better chance of living if the doctor was quick, and I was the quickest of them all.

People used to come and time me, I could amputate a leg in two and a half minutes, and some say I even amputated a limb in twenty eight seconds once! It was tough for doctors back then though, I'll tell you.

People would come and watch me operate, I was so fast. They even used to bring their stopwatches with them and time me as I did it, to see just how quick I could work. I didn't disappoint, which is one of the reasons I wasn't always popular in Edinburgh. I was a bit too much of a showman.

I moved to London, and worked at University College Hospital, and it was there that I had the honour of performing the first operation in Europe with an anaesthetic. I used ether, an American invention, and I was absolutely delighted with the results. Although it meant that surgeons didn't need to be so fast any more, which was a shame for me, it did mean that many more patients could have operations without the great amounts of pain they had experienced in the past.

If I'm remembered at all, I'd like to be remembered as the fastest surgeon of my day, and I'm also very proud I was the first to use anaesthetic."

Robert Liston
the fastest knife in the north

SCOTLAND PLACE-NAMES
WHAT DO THEY MEAN?

LOTHIAN

Once part of Northumbria, its origins are lost in time. Later Midlothian was the County of Edinburgh, East Lothian was Haddingtonshire and West Lothian was Linlithgowshire.

MALLAIG

West coast town looking out to the Isle of Skye. Viking name *Muli Vagr* means 'headland bay' changed due to influence of the Gaelic word *aig* 'bay'.

MONTROSE

East coast town in Angus north of Arbroath. Gaelic *Moíne Ros* means 'moor promontory'. The promontory lies to the front of the Montrose sea basin.

MOTHERWELL

Town of 32,000, south east of Glasgow, liberally meaning 'Mother's well' and from an ancient well dedicated to Mary, mother of Jesus.

MUSSELBURGH

Firth of Forth coastal town of 22,000 people east of Edinburgh. The town where mussels are harvested.

NAIRN

Coastal town east of Inverness named from a river, with an ancient name of unknown meaning. Once called Invernairn meaning, 'mouth of Nairn'. Gave name to the historic county of Nairnshire.

OBAN

West coastal town. Gaelic name means 'little bay'.

PAISLEY

Scotland's largest town has a population of 74,000. Welsh name *Pasgell Llethr* meaning 'pasture slope'.

PENICUICK

South of Edinburgh. Welsh name *Pen Cog* meaning, 'hill of the cuckoo'.

SO WHO DECIDES WHO SHOULD BE KING?

Edward I

In October 1290, Margaret, Queen of Scotland died on Orkney before she'd even set foot on Scottish soil. Margaret, who was seven years old, had just arrived from Norway and Orkney was not yet part of Scotland.

Her death was an event of bad fortune for Scotland, because it created uncertainty. Several rival claimants were now likely to fight for the Scottish throne, but it did thwart the plans of the English King, Edward I, who had wanted Margaret to marry his son, Edward. It seems an agreement had been made with Margaret's father, Eric, King of Norway.

Baliol

In truth Margaret's death only brought further power to the English King's hands. Fearing a bloody civil war, Scottish nobles sought Edward's advice and counsel. They decided this powerful French speaking King of England should decide who would be their next king.

There were 13 claimants to the Scottish throne and in 1291 the delighted Edward assembled them at the Bishop of Durham's castle at Norham on the English side of the Tweed. Here a judicial court was presided over by Edward to decide whose claim was strongest. Unfortunately, Edward first persuaded all of the candidates to accept his superiority, something of a humiliation for the Scots.
In truth there were only four strong claimants and of these, by far the strongest claims were those of John Baliol and Robert Bruce, both nobles of Norman descent and both descended from King David I of Scotland.

In the end Edward agreed Baliol should be King as he was descended from the eldest daughter of David, Earl of Huntington, a grandson of David I. Bruce was descended from a younger daughter of this Earl. Baliol's 'appointment' brought stability for the time being, but it was not good news for Scotland because it effectively placed a puppet Scottish King under the English King's control.

SCOTLAND INVENTED HALLOWEEN

"Hey guys, I'm Jack, Jack O'Lantern. No, I'm not Irish, I'm not Scottish, I'm American, and I'm here to tell you about Halloween. Yes, I'm basically a pumpkin, but a pumpkin with a face cut into it, which makes me qualified to talk to you about this. I was surprised to find out that Halloween, the festival that I'm there to celebrate, was originally Scottish.

I know, right? Apparently it came from the Celtic festival of Samhain, which celebrated the end of the summer. It was said to be a night when all the souls of the dead were free to walk the earth, and so people lit lanterns or fires to keep evil spirits away. Sound familiar?

This developed into Halloween, and another custom developed along with it, called "guising". Guising was where the local children would dress up as the evil spirits and visit the houses in the town, exchanging entertainments for gifts - sounds a lot like trick or treating to me.

Robert Burns even wrote a poem about it, called *Hallowe'en*. It talks about the traditions and beliefs that were involved. When Scottish people moved to America they took the customs and traditions with them, and for many years Halloween cards would feature Scottish scenes, tartans or Burns himself.

Then, the whole thing came full circle. The Scottish traditions were changed in America, into the Hallowe'en we know today, and people in Scotland took them back to Scotland again. So every year Scottish kids carve pumpkins, trick or treat, or do a whole load of things which are American versions of Scottish traditions. I know, I was pretty surprised too, it sounds like I've got a little bit of Scot in me after all."

SCOTTISH PRIME MINISTERS

http://scottishprimeministers.com

Thank you for visiting www.ScottishPrimeMinisters.com. You have chosen the all inclusive Scottish Prime Ministers Package, containing all seven Scottish born Prime Ministers of Great Britain. The package includes:

1. **John Stuart**, third Earl of Bute (Prime Minister from 1762-3). The first Scottish Prime Minister and the first Tory Prime Minister.

2. **George Hamilton-Gordon**, fourth Earl of Aberdeen (1852-55). The Prime Minister who led Britain into the Crimean War.

3. **Arthur Balfour** (1902-5). Responsible for the Balfour declaration in support of a Jewish homeland in Palestine.

4. **Sir Henry Campbell-Bannerman** (1905-8). Created legislation to give free school meals to children and returned control to parts of South Africa.

5. **Ramsay MacDonald** (1929-35). The first Labour Prime Minister.

6. **Tony Blair** (1997-2007). Founder member of New Labour, key role in the Good Friday Agreement in Northern Ireland, took the UK to war in Iraq.

7. **Gordon Brown** (2007-10). Ratification of Lisbon treaty, abolition of 10p tax rate.

Plus, for a **low low** price you can also get our special package of **Prime Ministers with Scottish Parentage** but who were not born in Scotland. This extra pack includes:

1. **Archibald Primrose**, fifth Earl of Rosebury (1894-5). Born in London, imperialist and anti-socialist who wanted to expand the Royal Navy.

2. **Andrew Bonar Law** (1922-3). Born in New Brunswick, the only British Prime Minister born outside of the British Isles.

3. **Harold Macmillan** (1957-63). Born in London, Conservative Prime Minister who applied to join the European Economic Community for the first time.

4. **Alec Douglas-Home** (1963-40). Born in London, the last member of the House of Lords to become Prime Minister, gave it up to be PM.

Don't delay, while stocks last we offer free shipping and handling with every purchase. Start your collection of Scottish Prime Ministers today.

Done | Scottish Prime Ministers

STATUS: Town and historic seat of learning on the Fife coast.

RIVER: Essentially a coastal, rather than a riverside town, though the estuary of the **Kinnes Burn** enters the sea here. The larger estuary of the **River Eden** is located beyond the town to the north near the old Golf Course.

NAMES AND NICKNAMES: Historically called "**Cell Rígmonaid**" or "**Kilrymont**". There is no historic nickname for the town but it is often called "The Home of Golf".

MOTTO AND EMBLEM: The arms of the town traditionally feature St Andrew himself holding St Andrew's cross and a wild boar, both of which are regarded as emblems of the town. The Latin motto is *Dum Spiro Spero* meaning "While I breathe, I hope".

POPULATION: Over 16,000.

KEY FACTS AND INDUSTRIES: According to a legend a Greek monk called Regulus (or Rule) brought the bones of St Andrew here in the eleventh century. Through its association with these relics St Andrews became a centre of pilgrimage and in the fifteenth century became a seat of learning. On the sporting front the town is home to the oldest golf course in the world.

KEY DATES: 906 AD: The town became the seat of the Bishop of Alba. **Circa 1150:** St Andrews become a burgh. **1160:** Cathedral begun. **Circa 1200:** A castle was built here. **1318:** Cathedral consecrated in the presence of Robert the Bruce. **1413:** University founded. **1450:** St Salvator's College founded. **1512:** St Leonard's College founded. **1537:** St Mary's College founded. **1552:** First known mention of the golf course. **1559:** Protestant Reformation brings the life of the cathedral to an end. **1614:** James VI confirms Royal Burgh status.

THINGS TO SEE:

- **Cathedral ruins**.
- **Castle ruins**.
- **West Port**, a town gateway dating from 1589.
- **The University Colleges**.

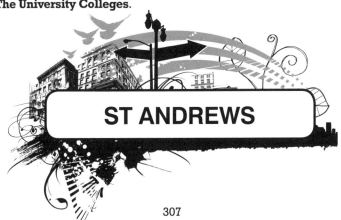

ST ANDREWS

THE AULD ALLIANCE

Alex Salmon: Good morning, my French friend. I am delighted that we're going to be working together today.

Claude Camembert: And what is this we are doing, mon ami?

Alex Salmon: We're going to be making a most excellent sandwich. A salmon and Camembert sandwich, the perfect example of cooperation between our two countries, a cooperation which has much historic precedent in the form of the Auld Alliance.

Claude Camembert: Un Sandwich? Vous et moi are going to be a sandwich?

Alex Salmon: Yes, the Auld Alliance, first formed way back in 1295, drawn up between John Baliol and Philip IV as a way of securing both countries against the English.

Claude Camembert: But, but I am so young, I am too young to be in a sandwich. I am sure that salmon and camembert will be no good as a sandwich.

Alex Salmon: Nonsense. The Auld Alliance is one of the longest standing relationships in the world, but it didn't always do either of us much good. It really just served to annoy King Edward I, and he proceeded to hammer us Scots good and proper.

Claude Camembert: Mon Dieu, my little wheels of cheese, my children, will I never see them again?

Alex Salmon: Nope, we're going to be a sandwich, my friend. The Auld Alliance was invoked many times over the years, with Scotland mounting military actions against England on France's behalf, including the invasion of England in 1346 which ended with defeat at the Battle of Neville's Cross. After the French defeat at Agincourt more than 15,000 Scots went to France between 1419 and 1424 to fight for France.

Claude Camembert: I weep, I weep for my children...

Alex Salmon: Rubbish, we're doing a great thing here. Now, where's that bread?

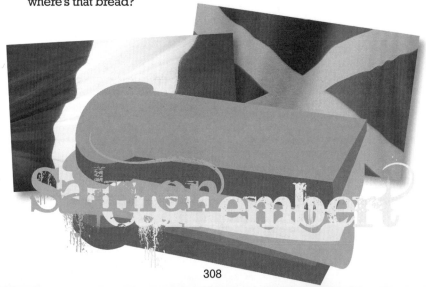

Did you know?
Giants

- At Tarbert on Harris in the Outer Hebrides a number of huge boulders are said to be the ruins of a giant's castle. Here resided a giant and his giantess wife who imprisoned a beautiful young girl. These giants were ogres and forced the girl to spin their huge clothes which had to be made from nettle leaves.

- Their intention was to eat the young girl once the clothes were made, but the girl was rescued by her lover, who persuaded the giantess to release her on the promise of some gigantic pearls. He kept his promise and after a long and dangerous adventure he recovered such pearls from the palace of the sea king deep below the ocean waves. That's true love for you!

- According to a ballad Kemnay near Aberdeen is said to have been the home to a fourteen foot giant Long Johnnie More who moved to London to become a standard bearer for the king. Sadly he was sentenced to death for falling in love with the king's daughter but was rescued by his uncle Jock, another giant, who not only received the king's pardon for his nephew but won him the girl too. There's no historical evidence to support this of course.

- Two gullible giants called Saxie and Herman who lived either side of Burra Firth on Unst, Shetland were tempted by a mermaid who promised to love the one who followed her all the way to the North Pole. Both drowned in pursuit.

- The castle at Wyre in the Orkneys apparently belonged to a Norse giant and chieftain called Kolbein Hruga or Cubby Roo. He was so large he used the islands as stepping stones and huge boulders on Rousay and Stronsay were to him merely stones that he threw around in fits of anger.

Professor
C. Claggs

THE FORTINGALL YEW

"Knowing me, knowing *YEW*". The Fortingall Yew tree is the oldest organism in Britain, and possibly the world, with age estimates ranging from 2,000 to 5,000 years.

"Loving *YEW* is easy 'cause you're beautiful". The Fortingall Yew was been celebrated as a religious symbol in pre-Christian society, and is often associated with the Garden of Eden. It's not difficult to see why the people of Fortingall built their churchyard around the yew.

"I heard it through the grapevine, not much longer would *YEW* be mine". The Fortingall Yew is a *Taxus Baccata*, otherwise known as an English or European Yew. It's a slow growing tree, but even with that in mind the Fortingall Yew is a remarkably old tree.

"Shot through the heart, and you're to blame, *YEW* give love a bad name". Some people say that Pontius Pilate was born in the shadow of the Fortingall Yew, although it's questionable whether that's true or not.

"Baby if *YEW*'ve got to go away, don't think I can take the pain, won't *YEW* stay another day?". The yew has been under threat over the years because of people taking parts of it as souvenirs. In the end it has been fenced off to prevent people cutting more parts away.

"Too many broken hearts in the world, there's too many dreams can be broken in two, too many broken hearts in the world, but I won't give up the fight for *YEW*". Recently cuttings were taken from the Fortingall Yew, and it will be cloned in the same laboratory which created Dolly the Sheep. The cloned trees will then be planted around Scotland.

"God only knows what I'd be without *YEW*". Yew trees are known as eternal trees, or the tree of immortality, and in the Himalayas they are sometimes called *deodar*, which means 'God's Tree'.

WHAT'S YOUR NAME?

Morrison

Descended from three separate families. Firstly in the Hebrides (where Morrisons are numerous) were the Morrisons of Lewis who descended from an Irish family *O'Muirgheasain*. They looked after St Columba's relics. Then there were the Morrisons of Harris descended from *Ghille Mhuire* 'servant of Mary'. Finally the Morrisons of Aberdeenshire, descended from someone called 'Maurice'.

MUNRO

Said to have been Irish mercenaries who settled in Ross north of the Cromarty Firth in the eleventh century where they defended against the Vikings. Prominent in this region today, the variant spelling *Munroe* is common in England.

Murray

Thought to descend from a Flemish Knight, Freskin who lived during the reign of David I. Freskin was given the land of the ancient Pictish kingdom of Moray. The Murrays were originally called De Moravia.

Napier

From *naperer*, an officer of the Royal Court in charge of table linen. It's thought they originated in France. Numerous in Fife and the north east.

Nicolson

Family of Viking origin possibly descended from Nic-Olsen (daughter of Olsen) or Nicolassen a thirteenth century Viking raider who settled in Scotland after the Battle of Largs in 1263. The Nicolson spelling is found in the Western Isles and Shetland. The Nicholson spelling is widespread throughout Scotland and numerous over the border in northerly parts of England.

Ogilvy

From the Old English *Ocel Fa* meaning 'high plain'. Associated with the Angus region.

Ramsay

Descended from a Norman Knight Simon De Ramesie who came to Scotland with David I in 1124. Widespread throughout Scotland.

ROBERTSON

Properly called Clan Donnachaidh the Robertsons claim descent from Crinan, a Lord of Atholl or from Angus MacDonald, a thirteenth century Lord of the Isles. It was the descendants of Robert (who became the clan chief in 1355) that took the name Robertson.

THE ROYAL MILE

I run through the heart of
the old part of town,
From Edinburgh Castle I
slope away down,
I've been going down this
way for many a year,
So come, listen to me,
you've nothing to fear.

I was once described as
the world's finest street,
You'll have to admit that's a
bit of a feat,
With the St Giles Kirk as
you go on your way,
That's somewhere that
people often like to pray.

The Heart of Midlothian,
City Chambers too,
With me in the middle, the
city it grew,
Then down at the end there's
the Parliament there,
And Holyrood House where
the people they stare.

At the Kings and Queens as
they come here to stay,
Where in their big
bedrooms their heads do
they lay,
So next time you're walking
down the Royal Mile,
Remember to do it with
grace and with style.

The Royal Aberguidtime Hotel

Desserts and Confectionery

- Deep Fried Mars Bars -

An intensely sweet and fattening dessert that is certainly not for the weak-hearted.

- Clootie Dumplings -

Scottish pudding made from flour, breadcrumbs, dried fruit, suet, sugar and spice, wrapped in a floured cloth and boiled.

- Scotch Mist -

Cream, strawberries and whisky. Drunkenly delicious.

- Edinburgh Fog -

A combination of whipped cream, macaroon/almond biscuits flavoured with Drambuie.

- Cakes and Tarts -

Dundee Fruit Cake, Selkirk Bannock Fruit Cake and Ecclefechan Butter Tart.

- Cheeseboard -

*Why not try our selection of Scottish cheeses that may include:
Howgate Scottish Brie, Brodick Blue, Caithness, Crowdie, Dunlop,
Drunileish (from the Isle of Bute), Mull of Kintrye (a nutty flavoured cheddar), Arran, Inverloch goats cheese (from Isle of Gigha), Kelsae (Kelso), Lanark Blue, Loch Arthur Cheddar, Pentland, Strathkinness, Swinzie and Teviotdale.*

A Selection of Teas and Coffees

Shortbread biscuits and Scottish oatcakes

KEIR HARDIE

History Man: Hey, have you ever heard of Keir Hardie?

Student: Keir Whody?

History Man: Keir Hardie. James Keir Hardie, he was one of the most important people in the foundation and early years of the Labour Party. He was from Newhouse in North Lanarkshire.

Student: So what? He was a politician? Pretty exciting that...

History Man: Actually, he was quite an incredible man. He was born on August 15 1856, and started to work as a delivery boy when he was seven. He then became a miner when he got a bit older, but he never went to school. He taught himself to read and write by the age of 17, and established a union at his colliery. In 1881 he led the first ever strike by Lanarkshire miners.

Student: So apart from being a troublemaker, what did he do then?

History Man: He ran for parliament in 1892, winning a seat representing West Ham in London. At the time the Liberal party were the main party that working class people voted for, but Hardie was more representative of the working class than the Liberals, because he was working class himself.

Student: So what did he do then? How did the Labour Party come about?

History Man: In 1893 the Independent Labour Party was formed, and Keir Hardie was elected leader. Then in 1900 the ILP formed the Labour Representative Committee, which would go on to be the Labour Party.

Student: So that's that then?

History Man: Not quite, although he lost his parliamentary seat in 1895 he continued to lead the party, and was elected as MP for Merthyr Tydfil in Wales in 1900. At the time he was one of only two Labour Party MPs, but by 1906 there were 26. He is remembered as one of the greatest Labour leaders.

CELTIC FC

Founded in St Mary's Church Hall, Calton, Glasgow on November 10 1887, Celtic is one of the most successful football clubs in Scottish history, as well as being one of the biggest on the planet. Formed by a monk, Brother Walfrid, to raise money for his charity The Poor Children's Dinner Table, Celtic played their first game in 1888 and quickly established themselves as a major force in Scottish football.

Under their first manager, Willie Maley, the club won 30 trophies in 43 years including six league titles in a row between 1905 and 1910. His was an incredibly fruitful period in charge of Celtic, one that would not be equalled until the golden age of Jock Stein in the 1960s.

Jock Stein's time as manager of Celtic was very successful, with the club winning nine league titles in a row between 1966 and 1974, with another in 1977, eight Scottish Cups, six Scottish League Cups and famously in 1967 at Lisbon, the European Cup. When Celtic won the European Cup in 1967 Jock Stein became the first British manager to win it, and Celtic became the first British club, a feat for which he will always be remembered.

Celtic may never have had it that good again, but they remain, along with Rangers, one of the twin powerhouses of Scottish football. Since Stein's departure in 1977 they have won 12 league titles, nine Scottish Cups, six League Cups and got to the final of the 2003 UEFA Cup. They are a global brand, a dominating force in Scottish football, and one of the most successful teams ever to have played on grass.

THE PAISLEY CANAL DISASTER

November 11, 1810

Thistle Press

85 Dead in Canal Disaster

Yesterday's events on the canal in Paisley will go down as some of the saddest in Scottish history. A day which should have been one of joy for many people turned instead, in a matter of moments, into one of tragedy.

Although inquiries over the coming weeks will seek to understand the exact nature of the disaster, what we do know now is that the lives of 85 people were lost in Paisley yesterday. As the pleasure boat, the Countess of Eglington came to shore on the Paisley end of her Paisley-Johnstone route, a crowd had gathered on the canal towpath, eager to make the return journey.

They began to surge forward, just as the people on board the boat attempted to make their way to shore. This crush caused many of those on the boat to

become trapped and panic, with a number leaping into the canal to escape.

Worse than that, the movement of the people on the boat caused the Countess of Eglington to capsize, trapping around 60 people in a corridor of the upturned vessel. Although some of the passengers managed to escape, many did not, and their deaths combined with the deaths of those who drowned in the canal took yesterday's death toll to 85. Of those 85, 66 were under the age of twenty, and 18 were under the age of ten.

This is a crushing blow for the people of Paisley, a great tragedy which will be remembered around Scotland, Britain and the Empire for many years to come.

THE SMALL ISLES AND SKYE'S COMPANIONS

A number of significant islands surround the Isle of Skye. The biggest ones are:

Raasay, on Skye's north side and separated from Skye by the Sound of Raasay. Its name comes from the Norse *RarAssEy* 'Roe Deer Ridge Island'. Historically ruled by the MacLeods it was the home to the MacSween clan.

Rona is smaller than Raasay but effectively a northward extension of Raasay's undersea ridge. It is sometimes called South Rona to distinguish it from North Rona, a remote isolated island in the North Atlantic north of the Outer Hebrides. The name is from the Norse *Hraun Ey* 'rough' or 'rocky island'. It was a base for pirates in the 1500s.

South of Rona and closer to Skye, **Scalpay**, has a Norse name meaning 'ship isle'.

Just south of Skye across the Soay Sound is **Soay** which has a Norse name meaning 'sheep island'.

Ten miles south of Skye are the **Small Isles**, which include four particularly prominent islands.

The biggest is **Rum** (Gaelic: 'spacious'). It is certainly spacious for despite being Scotland's fifteenth largest island this volcanic isle was only home to 22 people in 2001. Its principal feature is Kinloch Castle, built 1897-1900 for a Lancashire textile businessman called George Bullough.

To Rum's west is **Canna** (Norse: 'bucket island') and its companion **Sanday** ('sand island') which are nature reserves owned by the Scottish National Trust.

Second biggest of the Small Isles is **Eigg** (Gaelic: 'the notch') which lies east of Rum. In 1577 the entire population of this island (all MacDonalds) were murdered in a cave where they had taken refuge from raiding MacLeods seeking revenge for an earlier incident involving the two clans.

Finally just south of Eigg is **Muck** (Gaelic: 'pig') which has a population of around 30 people.

ROBERT LOUIS STEVENSON

November 13 1887. A dark Edinburgh night, a cold wind whips through the streets. Apart from the noise of the wind, and the banging of the shutters, only one other noise is heard. The tap, tap, tap of a cane on the Edinburgh streets. A figure turns the corner, wrapped in a thick black cloak. It is Pew, a man you may know from the novel "Treasure Island". But why is he in Edinburgh?

"Listen to me, my boy" *says Pew,* "and listen well. I come in search of that blackguard, that wretch, Robert Louis Stevenson. I come to give him the Black Spot, the same Black Spot he forced me to give to Billy Bones in *Treasure Island.* For Stevenson set me on that course, me and all of his other characters, but now we are free, and we come to take our revenge."

Then, from the other direction, comes a man, a small man yet one who carries himself with a confidence uncommon in one his size. He is Mr Hyde.

"Yes, we know that Stevenson was born this day in 1850, we know that he has tried to settle many places across this country. We know too that he will become one of the world's most famous authors because of us. But we come tonight to tell Stevenson to leave. To leave and never to return; to leave Edinburgh to us. His name will live on through us and through his many other creations, but the price he owes us is to leave."

Robert Louis Stevenson left Europe in 1888. He travelled first to America, then to the Pacific where he bought land in Samoa and lived the rest of his life. He never returned to Scotland.

Did you know?
Witches' Brew

TORTURED ON THE WORD OF A BOY

In 1705 three people died and several were tortured at Pittenweem in Fife after a 16 year old boy called Patrick Morton accused them of witchcraft. As a result of these accusations one man was starved to death in a dungeon, one woman was beaten, stoned and lynched after escaping from her torturers. Another woman died after confinement for five months in a pitch black torture chamber. The boy was later exposed as a liar who had been led astray by a fanatical priest.

WHITE WITCH – WONDER WATER

Grigor Wilcox was a popular eighteenth century white witch of Tomintoul in Banffshire. People came from miles around to have the spells of the evil black witches broken by him. He is said to have done this with the aid of a bridle captured from the water horse of Loch Ness. He also owned a magical mermaid's stone and successfully traded bottles of magical medicinal water in which the stone had been immersed.

FISHERMAN WITCH

It is said a Shetland fisherman called Luggie was burnt as a witch at Gallow Hill two miles north of Scalloway. His crime was his remarkable ability to cast a line that caught fully-boiled and roasted fish!

SINKING SHIPS

According to legend a young girl on the Sound of Mull sank all the ships except one in the neighbouring Sound of Mull by simply bending over and looking at them between her legs. She had demonstrated this rather dubious skill to a local farmer and explained to him that the one that remained afloat was protected by having a piece of sacred Rowan Wood on board. She told him she had learned the skill from her mother. Both the girl and the mother were burnt as witches on the basis of the farmer's information.

THE SCOTTISH PLAY

The Tragedy of Macbeth is the Shakespeare play known the world over as "The Scottish play". Shakespeare's take on the story of this medieval Scottish monarch is exciting and dramatic but not what we'd call an attractive piece of Scottish Public Relations.

It's extraordinarily brutal. Within its pages Shakespeare manages to mention: human lips and a baby's finger thrown into a witches' cooking pot... horses eating each other alive... cutting open a man from navel to throat and smashing out the brains of a smiling baby.

The play has long been associated with accidents, and many actors think that saying the name "Macbeth" in the theatre is bad luck. Theatres have closed, and actors have even been injured or killed during performances, including an actor being stabbed to death during the very first performance of the play. That's why superstitious actors often refer to it as **The Scottish Play**.

Macbeth, the son of the Mormaer or Lord of Moray was a genuine Scottish King, but Shakespeare based his play on a fictionalised work by Raphael Hollinshed.

Shakespeare's version was written to impress James VI (James I of England) and includes an altogether fictional character called Banquo, who is supposedly James's ancestor.

So what's the truth about Macbeth?

Did he murder Duncan?

Well, no he didn't.

Duncan was killed during a battle at Elgin in 1040 in which Macbeth and an Orkney Viking called Thorfinn Skull Smasher sided against him.

In 1054 Macbeth was defeated by Siward, Earl of Northumbria at the Battle of Dunsinane in Perthshire, but Macbeth didn't lose his life here like Shakespeare claims. Macbeth lived for another three years until he was killed by Donald's son Malcolm the future Malcolm III.

SCOTLAND WILL STAY THE SAME

Everybody knows Scotland is wet, muddy and cold,
But that does not make me want to leave.

Everybody tells me that Scotland is not a tourist spot of any sort,
But that does not make me want to leave.

Everybody learns about the deforestation of Scotland and although
we may not be proud,
That does not make me want to leave.

Scotland was ruled by countries back in the day,
But that, even that, does not make me want to leave.

Everybody wants Scotland to be sunny, modern or popular,
But if that happened,
I would want to leave!

My Scotland Young Writer

Name: Nina Joan Sosna
Age: 10
School: St Andrew's Primary School, Cumbernauld

STIRLING CASTLE

"Tell you a little bit about myself? Well, I was born in Stirling back in the early twelfth century, in fact it was 1110 AD when King Alexander I dedicated a chapel, and I became one of the most important centres of administration in Scotland.

I think I should tell you, I've had a few difficult relationships over the years. I've been hurt, and sometimes by people that I've trusted. For example, I was taken by the English in 1296, and then captured back by William Wallace after the Battle of Stirling Bridge in 1297.

Then not that long after, in 1304, King Edward's army besieged me for three months, using seventeen different siege engines including one called the War Wolf, which they say is the largest trebuchet ever constructed. When the Scots surrendered me to the English in July 1304 Edward actually sent some of the Scottish garrison back into the castle just so he could try out the War Wolf, and he knocked down parts of my walls.

I went back to Scotland after Bannockburn in 1314, then back to England in 1336, then back to Scotland again after a siege in 1341 and 1342. I know I should have a bit more self-respect; I shouldn't keep going back to them after they besiege me, but I guess I'm weak. I just want to be wanted, I suppose.

I was the centre of Scottish royal life between 1490 and 1600, with James IV, V and VI, really treating me nice. Unfortunately, they left me after the Union of the Crowns, and I was all alone.

I was besieged in 1651 by Monck's parliamentary army, and again in 1746 by Bonnie Prince Charlie, but by then my heyday had passed. I guess I'm just looking for somebody to take care of me, somebody who'll treat me with respect..."

COMIC STRIP SCOTLAND

One company has a long history of producing comics in Scotland, Dundee's D.C. Thompson. Here's a few of our favourites of theirs.

The Beano
Since it was first published on July 30 1938 *The Beano* has become arguably Britain's favourite comic. Characters such as Dennis the Menace, The Bash Street Kids, Billy Whizz, Minnie the Minx and Ivy the Terrible have been entertaining us with their antics for many a year, and we still love them!

The Dandy
The Dandy is older than *The Beano,* having first appeared on December 4 1937, but it's no less loved by kids all over the world. Korky the Cat, Bully Beef and Chips, Desperate Dan and of course Bananaman are just a few of the characters who've appeared in these pages, many of whom have gone onto bigger and better things on TV.

The Broons
The Broons has been published in the *Sunday Post* since March 8 1936. Since then the lives of the Broon family have become something of a national institution. Created and first drawn by Dudley D. Watkins, the characters have gone from strength to strength in the more than 75 years since they came into this world, and long may they continue!

Oor Wullie
Oor Wullie is another strip created and first drawn by Dudley D. Watkins, and published in the *Sunday Post*. Oor Wullie made his first appearance on the same day as the Broons, and the two have been closely linked ever since. They alternate years for their annuals, and characters from *The Broons* have even popped up in Oor Wullie's world.

SCOTLAND PLACE-NAMES
WHAT DO THEY MEAN?

PERTH

Town of 45,000 people on the Tay. Welsh/Pictish name means 'thicket'.
Gave name to Perthshire.

PITLOCHRY

Pictish/Old Welsh word *Pett* meaning, 'portion of land' and Gaelic
cloichreach meaning, 'stones'.

PRESTONPANS

Coastal town near Edinburgh. *Preost-Ton-Pans* meaning, 'priest settlement
near the salt pans'. Monks extracted salt here in medieval times.

QUEENSFERRY

North Queensferry and South Queensferry on either side of the Firth of
Forth. Malcolm III's queen, Margaret established a ferry here for pilgrims
travelling to St Andrews.

RENFREW

Suburb of Glasgow, with Welsh name *Rhyn Frwd* meaning, 'current point'.
Two small rivers join the Clyde here. Has a population of just over 20,000.
Gave name to the historic county of Renfrewshire.

ROSS

Ancient region north of the Great Glen, stretching from the Atlantic coast
to the North Sea. Also called Ross-shire. Name could be Pictish or Gaelic
meaning 'moorland', 'promontory' or 'woodland'. Easter Ross and Wester
Ross are the eastern and western districts of Ross.

ROTHESAY

Viking name meaning 'Rotha's island'. Main settlement on the Isle of Bute.

ST.ANDREWS

Originally called *Muckross* meaning 'promontory of the boar' but renamed
when it became associated with relics of St. Andrew.

SCONE

Pronounced 'scoon', a town north east of Perth associated with the
crowning of Scottish kings. Gaelic *Sgonn* is 'a mound' associated with the
kings.

LOCH LOMOND

At 24 miles long and in places 5 miles wide, Loch Lomond is the largest body of fresh water in Great Britain by surface area and in terms of water volume is only outdone by Loch Ness. The loch is a magnet for tourists and known the world over from the Scottish ballad "The Bonnie Banks O' Lomond".

> **Oh, ye'll tak' the high road, and I'll tak' the low road,**
> **And I'll be in Scotland afore ye;**
> **But me and my true love will never meet again,**
> **On the bonnie, bonnie banks o' Loch Lomond.**

This song was first published in 1841 and was supposedly composed in 1746 by a Jacobite prisoner captured by the English.

Loch Lomond lies in the Trossachs National Park. The neighbouring Trossachs region to the north east forms a varied and beautiful landscape of forests, peaks and lochs including Loch Katrine.

Loch Lomond itself is of course the star attraction. One of Scotland's most beautiful lochs, it is also one of the most accessible, easily reached from Glasgow to the south. The loch's beauty is enhanced by its islands, which are the "jewels of the loch".

There are over thirty islands including Inchmurrin the largest freshwater island in Britain and Inchconnachan which has a colony of wallabies.

The loch is a haven for boating, kayaking, jet skis, canoeing and water sports as well as cruises. Much of this tourist activity is focused on the small town of Balloch on the extreme southern shore of the loch.

Balloch is the home to the PS *Maid of the Loch* vessel which is undergoing restoration here. This Lomond cruiser was the last paddle steamer built in Britain. It was launched at the Inglis shipyard on the Clyde in 1953 and is the last in a line of Loch Lomond paddle steamers dating back to 1816.

THE FIFE ADVENTURES

History Man: Hey, have you ever heard of the Fife Adventurers?

Student: The five adventurers? Was that an Enid Blyton story?

History Man: No, the *Fife Adventurers*... Adventurers from Fife!

Student: Ah... the Fife Adventurers... No. Who were they?

History Man: They were lowland gentry who were granted the rights to the Isle of Lewis by James VI in 1598. They went to try and "civilise" Lewis.

Student: How come James gave them the land? Weren't there people already living there?

History Man: Yes, the MacLeods but they'd been ordered to produce title deeds to their land and had failed to do so, and so they'd had the land taken from them by the king. The king then gave their land to the Fife Adventurers.

Student: I bet the MacLeods didn't like that, did they?

History Man: Not a lot. The Fife Adventurers had taken 500 soldiers to Lewis, and they needed them. The MacLeods fought a bitter war against the invaders.

Student: So what did the Adventurers manage to do?

History Man: Well, they built a town where Stornoway now is, but they were constantly attacked by the MacLeods. They made it impossible for the Adventurers to make their new land profitable.

Student: So how did the Adventurers beat the MacLeods?

History Man: They didn't. In the end things got so bad that they had to sell their lands to Kenneth MacKenzie, the first Lord MacKenzie of Kintail in 1609, and leave the island.

Student: Well that doesn't sound like much of an adventure then.

SCOTTISH STARS OF STAGE AND SCREEN
PART FIVE

ROBERT CARLYLE
From *Trainspotting* to *The Full Monty*, from a zombie in *28 Weeks Later* to a super-villain in *The World Is Not Enough*, Robert Carlyle has shown that he can do almost anything. His career has covered the small screen and the big screen, and seen him succeed on both sides of the Atlantic. Born in Maryhill, Glasgow on April 14 1961, and raised by his father, he has long been regarded as one of Scotland's best actors, a claim which has been proved time and time again by his work.

GERARD BUTLER
Gerard Butler was born in Glasgow on November 13 1969. He originally trained as a lawyer, before turning his hand to acting in the mid-1990s. He gained international acclaim for his role as Leonidas in *300*, and since then has gone on to become one of the most sought after actors working today. He has made playing the male lead in Hollywood blockbusters a speciality, and his professionalism and ability mean that his movies are almost always big successes.

IAN RICHARDSON
Best known for his role as Francis Urquhart in the BBC drama trilogy *House of Cards*, Ian Richardson was a legend of British stage and screen. Born in Edinburgh on April 7 1934, he was best known and best regarded as a classically trained Shakespearean actor, appearing with the Royal Shakespeare Company from 1960 to 1975. Outside the theatre he played Bill Haydon in *Tinker, Tailor, Soldier, Spy*, Lord Groan in *Gormenghast*, and Dr Joseph Bell in *Murder Rooms*. He sadly passed away in 2007 aged 72.

Robert Carlyle

Gerard Butler

Ian Richardson

TOWN NICKNAMES

- The **AULD GREY TOUN: Dunfermline** because of its stonework.
- **AULD REEKIE: Edinburgh** from the smoky days when households burned coal and wood.
- **BABY BRIGGS: Bishopbriggs** apparently from its high birth rate.
- The **BLAST**: Village of **Macmerry** near Edinburgh where Iron Ore was excavated.
- **BLUE TOON: Peterhead** from the blue attire of the fishermen.
- The **BROCH**: Nickname for **Fraserburgh**.
- The **CLASH**: Name given to **Kinlochbervie** from a local loch.
- The **FERRY**: Town of **Broughty Ferry**.
- **FURRY BOOTS TOUN: Aberdeen.** Local dialect speakers may ask "Furry Boots You From?"
- **GALA**: Short nickname for **Galashiels**.
- **GRANITE CITY**: Best known nickname for **Aberdeen**.
- The **HONEST TOWN**: Nickname for **Musselburgh**.
- **JEDDART: Jedburgh**.
- **JUTEOPOLIS**: Old nickname for **Dundee** from the manufacture of Jute.
- **KILLIE**: **Kilmarnock**.
- **IRON BURGH**: **Coatbridge**, which was once noted for its iron foundries.
- **LANG TOUN**: A name given to **Auchterarder, Darvel** or **Kirkcaldy**.
- **MUCKLE TOWN**: Nickname for **Langholm**. It means big town.
- **POLO MINT CITY**: Nickname for **East Kilbride** from its numerous roundabouts.
- **QUEEN OF THE SOUTH**: A nickname for **Dumfries**.
- **SHAKY TOUN**: Name given to **Comrie** the main centre for earth tremors in Britain.
- **SAINT JOHNSTOUN**: An old name for **Perth**.
- **STEELOPOLIS**: Nickname for **Motherwell** from the days of steelmaking.
- **WEE RED TOONIE**: Nickname for **Kirriemuir** given by J.M Barrie.

TOWN'S PEOPLE NICKNAMES

- **ABERDONIANS** are from **Aberdeen**.
- **BANKIES** are from **Clydebank**.
- **BELTERS** are from **Tranent**.
- **BLUE MOGGANERS** are from **Peterhead**.
- **BUDDIES** are from **Paisley**.
- **DOONHAMERS** are from **Dumfries**.
- **DUNDONIANS** are from **Dundee**.
- **GLASWEGIANS** are from **Glasgow**.
- **REID LICHTIES** are from **Arbroath**.
- **SOUTARS** are from **Selkirk**.
- **TERRIES** are from **Hawick**.

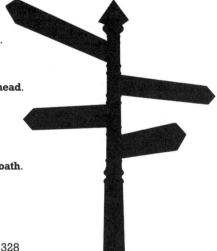

THE BIG YIN

The Big Yin - "the big one" - is the nickname given to Billy Connolly, one of Scotland's most popular entertainers and comedians.

Born in the Anderston district of Glasgow on November 24 1942 Billy was brought up by his aunts in a tenement and was schooled in Govan.

Billy worked in the Glasgow shipyards as a boilermaker but in the late 1960s turned his talents to entertainment as a folk singer in a duet called the Humblebums, initially with Tam Harvey but later with future rock star Gerry Rafferty.

In the early 1970s he became a folk soloist, but the increasing popularity of his humorous observational banter between the numbers persuaded him to turn his attention to stand up comedy.

Billy soon rose to prominence, particularly after appearing on the British TV chat show *Parkinson* in 1975.

In the early 1980s Billy became a regular on the BBC comedy sketch show *Not the Nine O' Clock News* and formed a relationship with a co-star Pamela Stephenson, who became Billy's second wife at the end of the decade.

Billy's fame in the United States took off in 1990 after performing with Whoopi Goldberg in a double act in New York and the following year he secured the title role in the US sitcom *Billy*.

Over the years Billy has made numerous movie appearances, his most memorable role starring alongside Judi Dench in the 1997 film *Mrs Brown* in which he played John Brown, the favourite servant of Queen Victoria.

Billy Connolly quotes:

"There are two seasons in Scotland: June and winter."

"I'm much bigger in Britain than I am there. I'm well-known, but my name's 'That Guy' in America. . . . People shout: 'Hey I know you! You're *That Guy*'."

"Marriage is a wonderful invention: then again, so is a bicycle repair kit."

"My parents used to take me to Lewis' department store in Glasgow. They were skinflints, they used to take me to the pet department and tell me it was the zoo."

25

ANDREW CARNEGIE

Andrew Carnegie was born into modest beginnings on November 25 1835. His birthplace was a weaver's cottage in Dunfermline. Falling on hard times and living in relative poverty, Andrew's father, William, moved the family to America after borrowing money to help them make the trip.

The Carnegies settled in Pennsylvania where Andrew, aged 13 worked as a bobbin boy in a cotton mill. By the time he was 14 he was a messenger boy at Pittsburgh Telegraph Office, where a superintendent of the Pennsylvania Railroad Company noticed his abilities. By the end of the American Civil War, Carnegie was himself a superintendent.

Carnegie made shrewd investments in small iron mills and visited Britain on a number of occasions to observe the development of industry there. He realised the future lay in the making of steel and in 1874 introduced the steel making methods of the English industrialist Henry Bessemer to the United States.

Carnegie soon made his fortune, a fortune that in modern equivalent terms made Carnegie arguably the second richest man in history after John D. Rockefeller.

As he acquired his fortune Carnegie became one of the world's most famous philanthropists, believing it to be the duty of rich men to use their wealth for investing in the community.

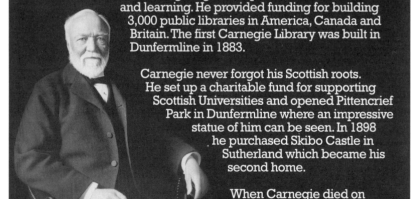

One of Carnegie's greatest passions was education and learning. He provided funding for building 3,000 public libraries in America, Canada and Britain. The first Carnegie Library was built in Dunfermline in 1883.

Carnegie never forgot his Scottish roots. He set up a charitable fund for supporting Scottish Universities and opened Pittencrief Park in Dunfermline where an impressive statue of him can be seen. In 1898 he purchased Skibo Castle in Sutherland which became his second home.

When Carnegie died on August 11 1919, he had given away around $350,000,000 in philanthropic gestures.

PALACE OF HOLYROODHOUSE

Just above us, in the sky, a black craft orbits the planet. They have come from light years away in search of comrades of theirs, lost in an intergalactic war which took place before humans even walked the earth. After many years of searching, they have finally made a discovery. The commander, known simply as ▐●▬●▐ *makes his report.*

"Sir, I have discovered the location of our fallen spacecraft, a spacecraft which crashed upon this planet over 150,000 Earth years ago. It lies now buried in the ground beneath a building known as the Palace of Holyroodhouse in Edinburgh, Scotland.

The palace was constructed between Earth Year 1501 and 1505 by King James IV, and was the seat of the Kings of Scotland. Our scanners show that Mary Queen of Scots was resident there, and that she saw her friend David Rizzio murdered in her chambers.

During our observations we have witnessed the palace burned to the ground during the visit of Oliver Cromwell in 1650, and then reconstructed following Charles II's return to the thrones of Scotland and England.

An earthling known as Bonnie Prince Charlie held court there for five weeks in September and October 1745, and it was also occupied by the Duke of Cumberland on his way to the Battle of Culloden.

It came back into common usage during the nineteenth century, and was modernised during the twentieth. It is now the residence of the Queen, Elizabeth II, for one week a year.

It is a fascinating building, and we have been privileged to witness many of the changes in its history. It is a shame then that we must destroy it, but there exists only one way to free our brothers.

The disintegrator beam will commence in 5... 4... 3..."

EDINBURGH ARTISTS
THE SCOTTISH COLOURISTS

Between 1870s and 1910 the **Glasgow School of artists** had a profound impact on Scottish art and laid the foundations for another prominent group of artists, this time focused on Edinburgh, known as the **Scottish Colourists**.

These influential painters trained in France and were influenced by painters like Monet, Matisse and Cézanne adapting the styles of these continental artists to Scottish themes.

The four prominent members of this group were **Samuel John Peploe** (1871-1935), **John Duncan Fergusson** (1874-1961), **George Leslie Hunter** (1877-1931) and **Francis Campbell Boileau Cadell** (1883-1937). Of the four, only Hunter, born in Rothesay on Bute, was not Edinburgh born.

As their name suggests the Scottish Colourists liked to experiment with vibrant colours. The most influential of the Colourists was Fergusson, whose works can be seen in the Fergusson Gallery in Perth.

Fergusson is considered the most versatile of the four. He was a friend of Picasso and like the other Colourists was widely travelled. His influences included Manet, Monet and Fauves.

Cadell who met Peploe in Paris seems to have been particularly influenced by Cézanne. Cadell and Peploe loved the atmosphere of the Island of Iona. **Peploe** often visited Kirkcudbright near Dumfries and the Island of Barra in the Hebrides for inspiration.

Hunter moved to Los Angeles when he was 13, but a visit to Paris in 1904 inspired him to paint. Subsequently moving to San Francisco, all his early work was destroyed in the earthquake there in 1906. He returned to Scotland to start again, but unlike the other three was based in Glasgow rather than Edinburgh.

The work of the Colourists had lost its popularity by the 1940s, but there was a revival of interest in the 1980s and it is now highly valued and fashionable once again.

MARY SOMERVILLE

The year is 1836. Percival Temperley, gentleman adventurer and well-known dandy is preparing for yet another mission on behalf of the Crown. He and his manservant, Thornton, are putting the finishing touches to their plan.

Temperley: Right, Thornton, for this mission I shall require an acute scientific mind to assist me. We need someone with a grasp of mathematics, particularly algebra, and astronomy. Who should we recruit?

Thornton: Well sir, I think Mrs Mary Somerville would be ideal for this role.

Temperley: A woman, Thornton? But surely you know that women are not capable of abstract thought, their minds are too weak and feminine to handle such things. We must have a man.

Thornton: I understand this is your view, sir, as it was the view of Mrs Somerville's parents, and her first husband, but she has risen in recent years to be one of the great scientists and thinkers in her field.

Temperley: Really?! A woman?! Where is she from?

Thornton: Well sir, she is originally from Jedburgh in Scotland and has written a number of scholarly works, including *On the Connexion of the Physical Sciences*, and her translation and popularisation of *Laplace's Mecanique Celeste* has made her most renowned. She was just last year admitted to the Royal Astronomical Society, jointly the first woman to be so admitted, with Caroline Herschel.

Temperley: Hmmm, she sounds most capable Thornton, but how can you be sure she is going to be up to this mission?

Thornton: Well sir, I have a strong feeling that she will publish notable works like *Physical Geography* in 1848 and *Molecular and Microscopic Science* in 1869. I also suspect that she will have a college at Oxford University, a Canadian island, a crater on the moon and an asteroid named after her for her contribution to science.

Temperley: Your insight is astonishing Thornton, and as always I trust your judgement. Get her on board my good man.

EVEN MORE SCOTTISH INVENTORS

Many of the advancements and technologies which have shaped the modern world were thought up by Scottish people. Here's a few, but we're not even really scratching the surface:

SIR JAMES BLACK
Invention of Beta-blockers

Born in Uddingston on June 14 1924, James Black was a doctor and medical researcher responsible for the development of many life saving drugs, including *propranolol* which is used to treat heart problems and *cimetidine* for stomach ulcers. Before these drugs were invented many people would die from heart problems, or need to have surgery for stomach ulcers. These medicines saved a lot of people's lives, and Sir James Black won the Nobel Prize in 1988 because of them.

SIR ROBERT WATSON-WATT
Radar

Born in Brechin in 1892, Sir Robert Watson-Watt is considered by many to be the inventor of Radar, the radio detection system which was so important to the British war effort during the Battle of Britain in the Second World War. As the head of Bawdsey Research Station he was instrumental in the development and installation of the series of radar stations which helped the RAF track and shoot down German planes, and ultimately win the Battle of Britain.

JAMES BRAID
The father of hypnotism

Born in Portmoak in Kinross-shire in 1795, Braid was a surgeon working in Manchester when he began to pioneer the use of hypnosis and hypnotherapy as an approach to combating certain mental problems. He came up with the term "hypnotism" to indicate that it wasn't a supernatural thing, that in fact the hypnotic effects had psycho-physical causes. Another word for hypnotism is actually "Braidism", named after the man himself!

ST ANDREW

Saint Andrew is the patron saint of Scotland as well as being a patron saint in the Ukraine, Russia, Sicily, Greece, Portugal, Romania and the Philippines.

Andrew, the brother of St Peter was a fisherman born in Bethsaida in Galilee and was one of the 12 disciples of Jesus.

He was martyred at Patras in Greece, where according to tradition he was executed on a crucifix shaped like an "X" because he did not wish to be executed in the same manner as Jesus. This is said to have given rise to the x-shaped cross of St Andrew which features on the Scottish flag.

According to legend, a fourth century monk of Patras called St Regulus, who was a guardian of St Andrew's relics, was instructed in a dream to take the bones of St Andrew to the far edge of the earth for safety. Regulus took with him three fingers, one upper arm bone, one knee cap and a tooth, all of which had once belonged to St Andrew.

Regulus ended up shipwrecked on the coast of Fife where he encountered King Angus MacFergus (who remarkably did not reign until the eighth century). St Andrews' bones were buried at a new shrine in Fife where the town of St Andrews was born.

Another theory states that Acca, an eighth century Bishop of Hexham in Northumberland (where the abbey is dedicated to St. Andrew) sought exile in the land of the Picts and brought St Andrew's relics with him to establish a shrine at St Andrews in Fife.

Historians argue that Scotland's legendary connections with this famous and powerful saint were publicised by Scottish kings and nobles in the twelfth century to assert the nation's ancient birthright and independence over England.

Today St Andrew's Day, November 30, is passionately celebrated as Scotland's National Day.

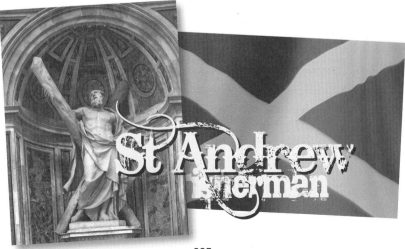

THE STONE OF SCONE

FOR SALE

**ONE STONE OF DESTINY, ANCIENT
SCOTTISH CORONATION STONE.**

Approx 26" x 16.75" x 10.5" in size.

Many years of loving use by consecutive kings for coronation at Scone Abbey, Perthshire. Several careless English previous owners, including King Edward I who acquired it in 1296 as war booty during his Hammer of the Scots period.

Some suggest this may not be the original stone - incomplete service history accounted for in extremely reasonable price.

Stone comes complete with iron rings at either end for ease of transportation, employed by Scottish Nationalists Ian Hamilton, Gavin Vernon, Kay Matheson, and Alan Stuart to transport Stone from Westminster Abbey to Scotland, 1950.

Some damage sustained, although this is believed to predate, and to be unrelated to, said transportation.

Skilled restoration undertaken, Stone remains in excellent condition.

Since returned to Edinburgh Castle 30/11/1996 remains available for future British Coronation Ceremonies.

Fantastic addition to any collection.

Price: A priceless symbol of Scottish national culture and consciousness.

SCAPA FLOW

"Greetings traveller. My name is Rauðúlfr Shieldpuncher, and I am a Viking. Well, to be more precise, I'm the ghost of a Viking, and I haunt the natural harbour known as Scapa Flow in the Orkneys.

The name Scapa Flow is Old Norse *Skalpeidfloi*, meaning 'bay of the long valley isthmus' and this is one of the world's largest natural harbours, measuring 312 square kilometres!

It's been used as a place to anchor navies, since as long ago as the eleventh century, when my Viking brothers ravaged your country. That's how I ended up here, a late night, a bit too much mead on the longship, and I was over the side before you can say "Brokk the Ruthless is your uncle".

It was also used as a naval base during the first and second world wars, being the site of a number of different battles.

At the end of the First World War, I recall that 74 captured German ships were interned here of which 52 were successfully scuttled by the Germans to prevent them falling into British hands.

In the Second World War a German submarine sank the battleship HMS Royal at Scapa Flow. Churchill ordered the construction of causeways to block the eastern approaches to Scapa Flow to limit the movement of German subways. These causeways still link Orkney's mainland to Burray and South Ronaldsay.

Scapa Flow hasn't been used as a naval base since the 1950s, instead now I mostly see divers and people coming to look at the beautiful scenery. It really is a fantastic place that I've chosen to haunt, very much like my native Scandinavia in the winter. I hope you'll come up and visit me one day, I promise not to give you too much of a scare..."

SCOTLAND PLACE-NAMES
WHAT DO THEY MEAN?

STORNOWAY

On Lewis, the principal town of the Outer Hebrides. *Steornabhagh* in Gaelic, the name is Viking *Stjorn vagr* meaning, 'steering bay'.

SUTHERLAND

Most north westerly region and historic county of Scotland. Settled and named by the Vikings who called it *suthr land* meaning, 'south territory'.

TOBERMORY

Picturesque coastal town on the Isle of Mull. Gaelic *Tobar Moire* meaning, 'well of Mary'.

TROON

Ayrshire coastal town with prominent headland. Welsh *Trwyn*, 'headland'.

URQUHART

Castle site near Loch Ness. Gaelic *Air*, 'on' and Welsh/Pictish *cardden*, 'woodland'.

ULLAPOOL

Coastal settlement in the north west. Viking *Olaf bol-stadr* meaning, 'Olaf's settlement'.

WANLOCKHEAD

Dumfries and Galloway village. From the Welsh *Gwyn Llech* meaning, 'white flat stone' and the English word *head*.

WIGTOWN

Anglo-Saxon name *Wicga's* Tun meaning, 'the farm belonging to Wicga'. Gave name to historic Wigtownshire.

YETHOLM

Borders town on the Bowmont Water. Anglo-Saxon *Geat-Ham* meaning 'gate' or 'pass homestead'.

ZOAR

A village near Forfar. The name comes from the Bible. Zoar is the 'city of the plain' where Lot escaped from Soddom and Gomorrah.

SCOTLAND ROCKS

Metamorphic Rock

Lava

Sedimentary Rock

Moine Thrust Belt

Igneous Intrusions

Hi, I'm Lewis, I'm one of a band of Scottish **ROCK** stars and my musical influences are from the **Precambrian** era. We make up Scotland Rocks and have a big fan base, called geologists.

I can't tell you about us all, but I'll tell you about the biggest stars.

Let's start with me. My full name's **Lewisian**. I'm Metamorphic and have many influences, though they say I'm ancient crust. You'll find me in the Outer Hebrides.

My girlfriend **Skye**, lives nearby. She sings like a bird. Skye and her friend **Mull** perform stuff from the Palaeogene era. These girls are great flows of lava but at their very peak, they're volcanoes, though I admit they've eroded over time.

Then there's Kate (**Caithness**) and Ork (**Orkney**). Their work is from the Devonian age, a Sedimentary sound that emerged from the Flood Plain and River Bed clubs many years ago.

This Sedimentary sound influenced other band members around Moray and Cromarty Firths, and Nairn, and inspired a major band whose influence stretches from Stonehaven to the Clyde estuary in the west.

North of the Great Glen, the great band is a Metamorphic Precambrian influenced group called **Moine Thrust Belt**. They came straight from the ocean floor with roots deep in the earth's crust.

South of the Glen is **Dalradian**, another Precambrian Metamorphic band. Named after an ancient kingdom, they're Scotland's biggest band with an influence stretching from Fraserburgh to Kintyre. You'll also find significant Igneous intrusions in their sound, especially in the north east.

Wish I had the time to tell you about the Sedimentary sounds of the south like the Carboniferous rockers of the central lowlands and the Ordovicians and Silurians of the borders and south west, but I'm afraid I have a gig to play.

5

GLASGOW TOBACCO LORDS

History Man: Hey, have you ever heard of the Glasgow Tobacco Lords?

Student: Tobacco Lords? Who are they then?

History Man: They were the merchants whose money helped to found the modern city that Glasgow is, and they made it all from tobacco.

Student: Really? How did they do that?

History Man: In the middle of the eighteenth century lots of people in Europe wanted tobacco, but there wasn't very much of it about. It was all grown in the Americas, and it took a big effort to get it back here. There were a number of Glasgow Merchants who made this their business.

Student: So what did they do?

History Man: They had lighter, faster ships than anyone else, and they could cross the Atlantic quickly. Also, the trade winds from America took them straight to Glasgow, making it easier to sail a ship there than anywhere else in Britain. They took Scottish goods to America, and brought tobacco back.

Student: So who were these Tobacco Lords?

History Man: There were three main operations, run by families called Glassford, Speirs and Cunninghame. Other men made their fortunes though, men such as Andrew Buchanan, James Dunlop and Archibald Ingram.

Student: Buchanan, Ingram, Glassford, Dunlop... I recognise those names.

History Man: You'd be right to, they're all streets in Glasgow named after the houses these rich men built. What's now the Gallery of Modern Art was William Cunninghame's house, and you might also notice Virginia, Jamaica, Tobago and Antigua Streets.

Student: Wow, that's really interesting, I never knew about Glasgow's tobacco links.

THE HIGHLAND POTATO FAMINE

December

In 1846 a dark cloud crossed the Irish Sea. It had already begun to take a terrible toll on the Irish people, and now it would tighten its grasp around the people of the Highlands. It was the potato blight, and it marked a significant event in the Highlands, and in the relationship between Highland communities and the Lowland cities.

The Highland Clearances had forced people into coastal settlements, away from the land which they had been farming for generations. This led to a shift to potatoes as the food that people lived on, because the coastal land that they had been moved to was often very poor and would not grow anything else.

The food shortages caused by the potato famine, and the bad winters which followed, would stretch for almost ten years. During this period, however, food grown in the Highlands was still regularly shipped south to the industrial cities and to England, just as it was in Ireland. This led to riots as people objected to the fact that they were being forced to starve whilst food was available.

The potato famine had far less impact in Scotland than it did in Ireland, however, because relief was provided by the people of the cities, with £250,000 (about £15,000,000 today) being raised to feed the Highlanders. They weren't given it for free though, they had to work eight hours a day, six days a week in order to get their rations, building public projects including those known as "destitution roads".

Some Highlanders were also given passage abroad to places like Australia, New Zealand and North America, and this in combination with the Highland Clearances meant that Scottish people were spread all across the world.

341

UNION STREET, ABERDEEN

"Roll up, roll up, come one, come all. Ladies and gentlemen, boys and girls, it is my pleasure to present for your delectation and delight one of the great wonders of the world, one of the most amazing feats I've ever had the pleasure of witnessing in all my long years. Ladies and gentlemen, boys and girls, may I present to you, Aberdeen's Union Street!

Built to excite and amaze people entering Aberdeen, Union Street is truly a miracle of modern engineering. It was constructed in the early nineteenth century and includes the longest single span bridge in the world! That's right madam, in the world! It is a hundred and thirty feet long, and crosses the Denburn Valley and the Union Street Gardens, connecting the east and west ends of Union Street.

More than that, ladies and gents, the bridge was built between 1801 and 1805, and then expanded in 1908. But the bridge is only one small part of the street; it actually stretches for a mile supported by arches between a storey and five storeys high!

It involved partially levelling St Catherine's hill to fit the street in, and it marked a new development, turning Aberdeen into the modern city it has become today. Who was it built by, young man? Why, it was built from plans by Charles Abercrombie, and Union Bridge was built by Thomas Fletcher with the advice of Thomas Telford.

Indeed, young lady, indeed it is truly a mechanical miracle, an engineering miracle the like of which the world has never seen before. So come, marvel and delight in the wonder of Union Street!"

JOHN BROWN

The year is 1865. Percival Temperley, gentleman adventurer and well-known dandy, is yet again tasked with a vital secret mission for the Crown. However, moments before he and his manservant, Thornton, are to set out from their Glasgow home, a messenger arrives.

Thornton: Sir, a messenger from the Queen. It seems she is dispatching a trusted aide to assist us on our perilous mission.

Temperley: A trusted aide, Thornton? Surely I am Her Majesty's most trusted aide? The number of missions, the great risks I have taken on her behalf. Damn it all, Thornton, who is this man?

Thornton: A Mr John Brown sir, a Highlander and devoted servant of the Queen.

Temperley: Ah, Brown is it? I know of this man Thornton. There are some suggestions that his relationship with Her Majesty is more intimate than is proper between a Queen and her subject.

Thornton: I too have heard these rumours sir, but I know not of their truth or falsehood. I simply know that Brown is a great friend of the Queen, a trusted advisor and one who has the Queen's ear.

Temperley: But Brown himself, what do we know about him?

Thornton: I know that he was born in Crathie on December 8 1826, and has worked his entire career at Balmoral, which the Queen and Prince Albert purchased in 1853. Then, following the Prince's death he became Her Majesty's personal servant and close confidante. I have a strong feeling he will remain her friend until his death in 1883, and that some people will say that they were secretly married. I also think that in the future something called a "movie" will be made chronicling their relationship.

Temperley: Very good Thornton, once again your predictions astound me, but your judgement is always sound...

COLL AND TIREE

Coll and Tiree are islands between six and twenty miles west of Mull and form part of the Inner Hebrides group.

Coll has a Norse name deriving from *Kollr* meaning 'the barren place' and probably got this name through comparison to Tiree, its more fertile twin to the south.

Coll is home to about 160 people and the main settlement is the village of **Arinagour** on the east coast. Here a ferry links Coll to Oban on the mainland. The journey takes 2 hours and 45 minutes. There is also a small airport on Coll that keeps islanders in touch with the mainland.

Historically Coll was a home to the MacLean clan whose fifteenth century coastal stronghold of **Breachacha Castle** can be seen on the southern coast.

Tiree to the south is of a similar size to Coll from which it is separated by the **Gunna Sound**. The tiny uninhabited island of **Gunna** lies between the two as does a rock called **Rubha Dubh** which in Gaelic means 'black sea-rock'.

Despite its similar size Tiree is much more populous than Coll being the home to around 770 people. Tiree is named from the Gaelic *Tira Eadh* meaning 'land of corn' which reinforces its fertile comparison to the comparatively barren island of Coll.

Man has lived on Tiree for centuries as indicated by remains of the fortified stone tower called **Dùn Mòr Broch** and a rock called the **Ringing Stone** marked with ancient and mysterious cup and ring markings. The main village on the island is Scarinish, but there are several other villages on the island.

Tiree is noted for distinctive houses made of large black stones and white painted mortar and for being one of the main Gaelic speaking islands of the Inner Hebrides with more than 48% of the population speaking the language.

Breachacha Castle

Dùn Mòr Broch

CHARLES RENNIE MACKINTOSH

December 10, 1928

Thistle Press

Obituaries

Charles Rennie Mackintosh
1868-1928

Today in London one of Scotland's greatest architects and artists, Charles Rennie Mackintosh, passed away. His death at the age of 60 from throat and tongue cancer has robbed Scotland of one of its most brilliant artistic visionaries.

Born in Glasgow on June 6 1868, Mackintosh was the fourth of eleven children, and was an artistic child, deciding on architecture as a career by the age of 16.

He was apprenticed to John Hutchison, the Glasgow architect, and attended Glasgow School of Art in the evening. It was here that he met Margaret Macdonald, the love of his life, who was to become his wife.

He moved on to Honeyman and Keppie architects in 1889, the year after one of his other great collaborators, Herbert MacNair joined the firm. MacNair, Mackintosh, Macdonald and Macdonald's sister Frances formed the group of Glasgow artists known as "The Four", and together they were hugely influential on the Glasgow Style.

Mackintosh's greatest successes as an architect and designer can be seen in his work at the Willow Tea Rooms and Scotland Street School, the Daily Record building and Queen Margaret Medical School, and most notably the Glasgow School of Art, which shows the true genius of Mackintosh's art.

Although his time as an architect was short, with most of his great works coming in the ten year period from 1896 to 1906, Mackintosh created a style which will be endlessly imitated but never truly copied, the genius of his work being that it is at once totally unique and wonderfully familiar.

Charles Rennie Mackintosh, designer, artist, painter and architect, one of Scotland's greatest artists, is survived by his wife Margaret.

Did you know?
The Royal Yacht Britannia

- The Royal Yacht Britannia was launched from the shipyard of John Brown and Company at Clydebank on April 16 1953 by Elizabeth II.

- There have been 83 Royal Yachts dating back to 1660 during the reign of Charles II.

- The present yacht served the Queen and her family for 43 years and 334 days.

- The yacht was designed so that it could be converted into a hospital ship in time of war.

- Britannia travelled 1,087,623 nautical miles during her active life.

- She visited 600 ports and 135 countries.

- Special guests who have been welcomed on board during the yacht's eventful life have included Sir Winston Churchill, Gerald Ford, Ronald Reagan, Rajiv Gandhi, Boris Yeltsin and Nelson Mandela.

- In 1981 Prince Charles and Princess Dianna took their honeymoon cruise on board the yacht.

- In June 1994 the government announced that the ship would be taken out of service.

- The yacht's last journey transported Prince Charles home from Hong Kong following the handover of Hong Kong to China.

- The yacht was decommissioned at Portsmouth on December 11 1997 in the presence of the Queen and Prince Philip, the Duke of Edinburgh.

- In 1998 it was decided that Edinburgh would become the Royal Yacht's permanent home where it is now moored at Edinburgh's port of Leith as a visitor attraction.

- Visitors to the Royal Yacht can take self-guided audio tours around the yacht where you can see the state apartments, officers' rooms and an onboard garage containing one of the Queen's Rolls Royces.

- The yacht is usually accompanied at Leith by the 1936 racing yacht called Bloodhound which was purchased by Prince Philip in 1962.

Professor C. Claggs

WHAT'S YOUR NAME?

Rose

From Ros near Caen in Normandy. They settled in south west England before moving north to the Moray Firth in the thirteenth century.

Ross

Named from Ross between the Cromarty and Dornoch Firths. Still numerous there today.

Scott

Borders clan. First record of Scott surname was a witness to a charter of Selkirk Abbey in 1120. The name is probably older and may refer to a Scot from the Dal Riata region of Argyll, who possibly moved to an area where Scots were not normally found.

Sinclair

First mentioned in 1162, at Haddington south of Edinburgh. Sinclairs originated from St. Clair in Normandy. In the fourteenth century, a William Sinclair became Earl of Orkney. He conquered the Faeroe Islands and discovered Greenland. Today, Sinclairs are most numerous in Orkney, Caithness and Shetland.

STEWART

Descended from Walter Flaad, a Royal officer or steward in Brittany, the family arrived in Scotland in 1124. Stewart derives from Steward, and was sometimes spelled Stuart. The Stewarts were of course a major royal house of Scotland.

STRACHAN

Descended from Walderus De Stratheihen who held land in the Strachan area of Aberdeenshire in the 1200s.

SUTHERLAND

Named from the Sutherland region where they resided, this clan is thought to descend from Fresking, a twelfth century Flemish knight from whom the Murrays are also descended.

Urquhart

Clan named from a place with a Gaelic name near Loch Ness. It means 'woodside'. Most common in northerly and north easterly parts of Scotland.

Wallace

From an English word Waleis meaning 'Welsh'. Wallaces claim descent from Welsh speaking Britons who lived in the English county of Shropshire (near the Border of Wales). They came to Scotland with David I after 1124. Another explanation is that they descend from an inhabitant of the Welsh speaking Kingdom of Strathclyde.

13

SCOTLAND'S ROBINSON CRUSOE

"Greetings, friend. I am Robinson Crusoe, one of the most famous and widely known characters in English Literature... Oh, that's lovely, it's always nice to meet a fan... No, I'm not Scottish, I'm actually from York... What am I doing in a book about Scotland?

That's an excellent question! I'm actually here to tell you all about the man who many claim to have been the inspiration for me - Alexander Selkirk. Alexander Selkirk was born in Lower Largo, Fife in 1676, and set out to sea as a young man; for we know he had left Scotland by 1695.

Selkirk was a rogue and a buccaneer. He took part in many expeditions to the South Seas, and in 1703 joined the Cinque Ports, part of the expedition of the famous privateer William Dampier.

After some time sailing on the Cinque Ports, and many sea battles, Selkirk began to fear that the ship was no longer seaworthy. So when they came to the island of Juan Fernandez, 400 miles west of Chile, he asked them to leave him there. The captain of the Cinque Ports, Thomas Stradling, was all too happy to let Selkirk go.

This is where Selkirk's story and mine intertwine, for although Selkirk had expected to be picked up quickly by another ship, he was cast away on Juan Fernandez for four years and four months before he was rescued. Okay, it's not quite the twenty eight years I was cast away for but then, I am a fictional character, so I can handle it a bit better.

Eventually he was rescued, and became quite famous back home in Scotland, with many articles being written about him. His island was renamed Robinson Crusoe Island, after the supposed link between us. Quite interesting that Selkirk fellow, I'm sure you'll agree, but hardly the star that I am..."

SCOTTISH CATHEDRALS

Cathedral derives from *Cathedra* meaning 'Bishops' seat' and there are seventeen official cathedrals in Scotland. Eight are **Episcopalian**, eight **Roman Catholic**, and one a former Presbyterian church in Glasgow that became a **Greek Orthodox** Cathedral in 1954.

The eight **Catholic Cathedrals** are: **Aberdeen** established 1817 (Aberdeen Diocese), **Ayr** 1822 (Galloway), **Dundee** 1782 (Dunkeld), **Edinburgh** 1814 (St. Andrews and Edinburgh), **Glasgow** 1797 (Glasgow), **Motherwell** 1947 (Motherwell), **Oban** 1932 (Argyll and the Isles) and **Paisley** 1948 (Paisley).

Edinburgh Cathedral

Scotland's eight **Episcopalian cathedrals** all date from the nineteenth century. They are: **Aberdeen** (Aberdeen and Orkney Diocese), **Dundee** (Brechin), **Edinburgh** (Edinburgh), **Glasgow** (Glasgow and Galloway), **Inverness** (Moray, Ross and Caithness), **Millport** and **Oban** (Argyll and the Isles) and **Perth** (St Andrews, Dunkeld and Dunblane).

The dioceses are based on Scotland's ancient bishoprics that were originally served by **historic cathedrals** much older than those cathedrals mentioned above. Some historic cathedrals survive, but no longer have official cathedral status.

In some cases the historic cathedrals have fallen into ruin like **Elgin, Fortrose** and **St Andrews** but others are no longer cathedrals because they have belonged to the **Church of Scotland** since 1690 and this church does not recognise bishops or cathedrals. These former cathedrals serve as churches called **High Kirks**, but "cathedral" is sometimes used in recognition of their historic status, even though there is no bishop. The historic cathedrals that still serve as places of worship are listed here. All date from the thirteenth century unless otherwise stated:

- St Machar, **Aberdeen**, twelfth century, rebuilt fourteenth century.
- St Brendan, **Birnie**, ceased to be a cathedral in 1184.
- Holy Trinity, **Brechin**.
- St Blane, **Dunblane**.
- St Mary, **Dornoch**.
- St Columba, **Dunkeld**.
- St Giles, **Edinburgh**, fourteenth century. Seat of a bishop 1635-38 and 1661-89.
- St Mungo, **Glasgow**.
- St Mary, **Iona**.
- St Magnus, **Kirkwall**, twelfth century.
- St Moluag, **Lismore**, partly fourteenth century.

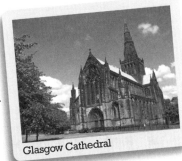
Glasgow Cathedral

HAMISH THE HIPPIE HIGHLAND CATTLE

"Hey man. I'm Hamish, the Hippie Highland cattle, but you can call me Kyloe. Hey that's what they call us man, it's Scots man, so peace man. Far out man, peace!

Hey chill baby, you'll find us across the world man, down under and over the pond, dig it man, peace sister, but hey, I mean man, we all started in the Highlands. Dig It?

They say we're hardy, but we're just chilled man, we don't mind the wind and rain man, I mean man, they're like, groovy man.

We like our hair long and shaggy man, we let it hang loose. Peace man, we don't mind. Keep the faith baby; our horns are our pipes of peace, man. We're horny cattle man.

Peace and love man. They say we make good beef in cold climates, man. Hey whatever will be man, whatever will be, baby, though we prefer grass, man. Our meat is lean and tasty baby, which is cool man. Find us on the toffee man, peace and love man.

Sometimes we cross with other breeds for different flavours. Right on baby!

You'll not find us hanging around in herds, baby. Our communes are called Folds, because we're different baby and that's groovy man.

We've been around for centuries, man, with written records back to the 1700s man. Right on sister!

Dig it man. You can find us in Scandinavia, Germany, Austria and Switzerland, Canada and the Faroe Islands. You'll even find us in the Andes of South America. Cool man.

Hey man, I mean, man, you'll find us anywhere that's chilled man. Peace brother.

So, we're groovy man. Right on! Keep the faith baby. Moove me baby, bring me a sparkly shirt. Let's rap."

- John O' Groats is named after a Dutchman, Jan De Groot. He operated a ferry to Orkney from here around 1496. According to a legend he is said to have charged a groat for the crossing.

- It's not the most northerly point on the British mainland, that honour goes to Dunnet Head eleven miles west and two miles further north.

- John O' Groats is the nearest settlement to Duncansby Head, the most north easterly point on the British mainland. It thus lies at the end of one of the longest distances between two points on the British mainland with Lands End in Cornwall at the other.

- Duncansby Head is less than two miles from John O' Groats.

- John O' Groats is home to around 300 people.

- A signpost at John O' Groats gives the distance to Lands End as 874 miles. This is a land-based journey by road.

- As the crow flies (crossing the Irish Sea, Isle of Man and the Atlantic) the distance is 603 miles.

- Charity fundraising walks or cycling expeditions are often undertaken from Lands End to John O' Groats. The tradition for walking the route goes back to 1871 when it was undertaken by the brothers John and Robert Naylor.

- There is no definitive route between Lands End and John O' Groats. Off road walks usually cover 1,200 miles and can take two or three months to walk. Road walks can take less than a month.

- The record time for a cyclist on a bicycle from Lands End to John O' Groats was 44 hours, 4 minutes and 20 seconds by Gethin Butler in 2001.

- In July 2008 Andy Rivett ran the route from Lands End to John O' Groats in a record time of 9 days and 2 hours.

Professor C. Claggs

RRS DISCOVERY
SAILING SHIP FOR SALE:

SERVICE HISTORY

Traditional three-masted sailing ship, the last one of its kind to be built in Britain, first launched in 1900. Dundee built, with several careful previous owners including the famous Antarctic explorers Captain Robert Falcon Scott and Ernest Shackleton.

With a specially designed hull, built for Antarctic expeditions, she will handle all kinds of conditions. Equipped with a reliable coal powered engine as well as her sails, she has a flat iron hull which is perfect for ice breaking on voyages in cold seas.

In addition to her trip to the Antarctic with Scott and Shackleton, she has served as a cargo vessel for the Hudson's Bay Company, and regularly crossed the Atlantic between London and Canada before becoming a weapons ship during the First World War.

Resuming research work in 1925, Discovery was used to explore the South Seas between 1925 and 1931. After periods as a training ship for the boy scouts and the Royal Navy Auxiliary Reserve, she became the property of the Maritime Trust in 1979 and the Dundee Heritage Trust in 1985.

WORK REQUIRED

Having been a centrepiece of Dundee's tourism industry since 1992, Discovery would need some major work to make her seaworthy once more. However, she has been well maintained by the Dundee Heritage Trust and as such you could get straight to work.

Although her technology is slightly out of date, she remains an excellent choice for any Arctic or Antarctic mission which you wish to undertake.

PRICE

On Request.

HISTORIC TOWNS AND CITIES: STIRLING

STATUS: City

RIVER: Close to an important crossing point of the River Forth.

NAMES AND NICKNAMES: No obvious nickname. It is pronounced **Stirlin** in the Scots and some have interpreted an old spelling of the name the **Striveling** as meaning 'a place of strife'. A travel writer H.V. Morton described Stirling as "The Twin Brother of Edinburgh". It is sometimes known as the "Gateway to the Highlands".

MOTTO AND EMBLEM: The city's traditional coat of arms featured a Goshawk and a wolf. The wolf is thought to be in commemoration of a wolf that saved Stirling from a Viking attack in the ninth century AD. There is no motto on the arms.

POPULATION: Over 33,000.

KEY FACTS AND INDUSTRIES: Located at a point where the Lowlands meet the Highlands and near what was for centuries the lowest crossing point of the River Forth (first by a ford and later a bridge) Stirling was of immense strategic importance. The mighty castle perched on a rock above the town featured prominently in the medieval wars between Scotland and England.

KEY DATES: 1120: A charter signed by Alexander I confirmed that Stirling was already a Royal Burgh. **1145:** Cambuskenneth Abbey founded. **1565:** Mary Queen of Scots married Lord Darnley at the castle. **1370-1603:** Principal Royal residence of the Stuart Kings and Queens. **1745:** Bonnie Prince Charlie successfully besieged Stirling but could not take the castle. **1868:** Monument to William Wallace built. **1967:** Stirling University founded. **2002:** Stirling granted city status.

THINGS TO SEE:

- **Stirling Castle**, dating to the eleventh century.
- **Argyll and Sutherland Highlanders Museum.**
- **Auld Brig**, bridge across the Forth of 1415.
- **Cambuskenneth Abbey.**
- **The Wallace Monument.**
- **Church of the Holy Rude**, dating from the fifteenth century.
- **Bannockburn battle site**, two miles south of Stirling.

STIRLING

19
December

THE ATHOLL
HIGHLANDERS

The year is 1892. Percival Temperley, gentleman adventurer and well-known dandy is embarking on yet another mission for the Crown. From his home in Glasgow, Temperley and his manservant Thornton are making their preparations.

Temperley: Thornton my man that was a messenger from Mr Gladstone. The Prime Minister has asked that we prepare a mission to intercept certain foreign agents who have infiltrated the Highlands. This mission must be undertaken without involvement from official government forces, but we need some men to assist us. Where can we get such men?

Thornton: I have been pondering this sir, and I believe that the Atholl Highlanders may be the perfect men. Since they were granted colours by Her Majesty in 1845 they have been the only legal private army in Europe.

Temperley: Interesting, Thornton. Where are these Atholl Highlanders based?

Thornton: Blair Castle, sir, in Blair Atholl. They are the private army of the Duke of Atholl. They have on several occasions stood guard for Her Majesty and for other dignitaries who have visited the castle.

Temperley: Excellent, Thornton. Have they seen action?

Thornton: Not officially sir, although I have a feeling many of the men will fight with the Scottish Horse during the next century. They will however be a fine option for our mission, and I am sure that the Duke can be prevailed upon to assist the needs of the Crown.

Temperley: Excellent, Thornton, excellent. But when this mission is over, what do you think will become of the Atholl Highlanders?

Thornton: Well sir, I have a strong feeling that they will be a mainly ceremonial regiment, with an annual parade at Blair Castle to celebrate the rich history of the regiment. I believe that they may even continue until the twenty-first century and beyond.

THIRTY SCOTTISH CASTLES

LEITH HALL CASTLE

Leith Hall Castle in Aberdeenshire is a typical Scottish laird's residence dating back to 1650 and was historically the home of the Leith-Hay family.

LINLITHGOW PALACE

The palace or castle of Linlithgow, historically a residence of the monarchs of Scotland is located 15 miles west of Edinburgh. A fortification was first built here by the English in the fourteenth century on the site of a Royal manor. King James V was born here in 1512. Bonnie Prince Charlie visited the castle in 1745 but the following year the English Duke known as "Butcher Cumberland" destroyed the palace by setting fire to it and the palace now lies in ruins.

ST ANDREWS CASTLE

This coastal castle on a rocky precipice in the town of St Andrews is a notable ruin dating from the late twelfth century and has a significant history. It was historically the home of the powerful Bishops of St Andrews. Notable visitors to the castle have included King James I (1406-1437) and the castle was the birthplace of King James III in 1445. The castle fell out of use when the post of Bishop was abolished by King William of Orange in 1689

STIRLING CASTLE

One of the most strategically important and impressive castles in Scotland, this site has been defended since the twelfth century up to the reign of Alexander I. The castle was besieged and captured by the English on several occasions. Standing on a huge rocky promontory, this castle has a dramatic setting at the gateway between the Lowlands and the Highlands.

URQUHART CASTLE

The huge picturesque ruins of this castle stand on a headland on the western shore of Loch Ness. It is thought to stand on the site of a fortified location called Airchartdan which was visited by St Columba in the sixth century. Urquhart Castle was certainly in existence by 1296 and seems to have belonged to the Durward family. The castle is one of the most visited ruins in Scotland.

SCOTLAND'S WORST POET

William Topaz McGonagall, of Dundee, is regarded as the worst poet in Britain's history. Despite this criticism he was a prolific producer of poetry, penning and performing over 200 works in his lifetime.

Born in Edinburgh in 1825 he moved to Dundee and joined a theatre, performing the leading role in *Macbeth*, where to avoid being upstaged by the actor playing MacDuff (who kills Macbeth at the end), McGonagall refused to die.

McGonagall was doggedly determined to do things his way and this became increasingly apparent after 1877 when he had an epiphany in which he discovered that he was destined to become a poet.

His ambitions showed no limitation. He wrote to Queen Victoria asking if she'd be his patron. The request was politely rejected in a letter from a royal aide thanking him on the Queen's behalf. McGonagall considered this royal approval!

In 1878 he walked 60 miles in a thunderstorm to Balmoral and announced he was there to perform for her majesty as the Queen's Poet. They turned him away.

McGonagall made a small living selling and reciting poems to the amusement of patrons including a circus that let him read works to an audience that pelted him with eggs and peas. Friends supported him with donations that allowed him to publish his works, the most famous being his "Tay Bridge Disaster" of 1880.

By 1893 McGonagall was frustrated with the way people made fun of his work and threatened to leave Dundee. A local newspaper predicted he'd stay another year once he'd realised that 1893 rhymed with Dundee!

By 1895 McGonagall moved to Edinburgh and died in poverty in 1902.

In 1974 a movie called *The Great McGonagall* starring Spike Milligan told a fictionalised tale of McGonagall's life with Peter Sellers performing the role of Queen Victoria.

December 22, 1988

Thistle Press

245 Dead as Terror Strikes in Scottish Skies

One of the worst atrocities in Scottish history was perpetrated yesterday in the skies above Lockerbie when Pan American World Airways Flight 103, en route from London Heathrow to JFK in New York was destroyed by what is believed to have been a terrorist bomb.

Whilst much is not yet known about the events of yesterday evening, reports suggest that the 243 passengers and 16 crew of Pan Am 103 were all killed in the explosion and subsequent crash at just after 7pm yesterday evening, with a further 11 people being killed on the ground by the wreckage of the plane.

Responsibility for the attack has been claimed by several groups, including the Guardians of the Islamic Revolution, and Islamic Jihad. Intelligence agencies are unwilling to attribute the attack to any organisation at this time.

Although emergency services were dispatched from both north and south of the border, and Dumfries and Galloway hospital, twenty miles away, has been placed on emergency alert, it is feared that the death toll will only rise.

The days to come will see a number of investigations by different agencies and bodies, including enquiries by Dumfries and Galloway Police, security services on both sides of the Atlantic, and the possibility of a parliamentary inquiry into the security measures and conditions which allowed this tragedy to occur.

Much is unknown at this point, but what is certain is that the events of December 21 1988 will live long in the history of Scotland and in the memories of the Scottish people.

THE STANDING STONES

2011 AD
The 27 stones loom over the grass as sunlight bathes my head,
Imagine the people who once visited here, who built and drank and fed.
The tiring work they took on, will wonders never cease,
Grinding, slaving stone by stone, carving, shaping piece by piece.

2011 BC
The men work and work and push and push and pull and pull,
The air goes cold, the sky gone dark but they carry on, their hands their only tool.
The green grass is soft and furry, cold beneath my feet.
The stony ring stands tall and dark, of course it's nice and neat.

2011 AD
The ring of stones is packed, there are tourists all around,
And there are people from everywhere, following the stone ring round and round.
The children run, the adults point critically, a frown upon their faces,
So many chose to come here, of all the historic places.

2011 BC
Then just as sunlight shimmers the men begin to shout,
The word is spread all round the town – guess what we talk about!
It's finished, Brodgar, The Ring of Brodgar, that shall be its name,
And if a stone was to fall or be knocked the villagers would cry in shame.

2011 AD
Just as we're about to go I say one last goodbye,
I lay my hand upon the stone, and then a thought comes rushing by.
Who has touched this stone, and what stories could it tell
The people who have come? Did they think this as well?

2011 BC
I place my hand on the cold stone ring.
Mother calls me in and people no longer sing.
I wonder who will stand here in a long, long while;
Will the stones still stand or will they be knocked into an untidy pile?

My
Scotland
Young Writer

Name: Ellie Gemmell
Age: 10
School: Shawlands Primary School, Glasgow

EDWIN SCRYMGEOUR
BRITAIN'S ONLY
PROHIBITIONIST MP

Christmas is the season of joy and love, but it's also a difficult time for some. Not everybody has a loving home to go to this Christmas, but it's our job at the Scottish Society for the Prevention of Cruelty to Politicians (SSPCP) to try and make sure that changes for the better. We at the SSPCP would love to give all of our politicians a loving home this Christmas, and we hope you can make room in your hearts for one in particular,

Edwin was born in Dundee in 1866, and educated in the city. He is a lovely politician, with an attractive Dundonian accent as well as a very shiny coat. He has not always been well treated in the past, and came to the SSPCP from an abusive home, but he's a very outgoing politician with a lot to offer to the right family.

Edwin founded the Scottish Prohibition Party in 1901 to promote temperance and oppose the consumption of alcohol, and served on Dundee city council. He is very well behaved, but he likes to be the centre of attention, he doesn't play well with other politicians so he should be the only politician in the house.

Edwin was elected as MP for Dundee in 1922, becoming the only British MP ever to be elected for a prohibition party. He remained as MP for Dundee until he lost his seat in the 1931 election. Following his exit from Parliament he worked as an evangelical chaplain at hospitals in the Dundee area.

Edwin would be a very rewarding politician to have in your household, and is very comfortable with children. He is a lovely politician, and he'd make a wonderful addition to your home this Christmas.

24

December

359

CHRISTMAS DAY

Traditionally, Christmas Day played only a secondary role to the New Year festival of Hogmanay in Scotland or at least that was the case for most of the last four centuries.

From the 1580s until the 1950s the day was celebrated very quietly because the Church of Scotland frowned upon the celebration of the day. It may be a surprise to learn that it was not until 1958 that Christmas Day officially became a public holiday in Scotland.

Throughout this period most Scots would have worked on Christmas Day and wouldn't have expected it any other way. There were some dissenters however and it was not unknown in times past for the church authorities to impose heavy fines on those who tried to celebrate the day.

Don't get me wrong, gifts were exchanged on Christmas Day, but in truth they were more likely to be given out on New Year's Day. Until the 1920s it was also more common for seasonal greetings cards to be exchanged on New Year's Day rather than Christmas Day.

Christmas stockings came into use in the twentieth century though their contents were often modest, perhaps containing an apple and orange and this was generally the case until after the Second World War.

Before the sixteenth century Christmas Day was enthusiastically celebrated, though it had its roots as much in the Pagan festival of Yule celebrated by the Norsemen in the far north and the pre-Christian Anglo-Saxons in the south.

It was not until the 1960s and 1970s that Christmas started to become a much bigger event in Scotland to a large extent due to American and English influence.

Today Christmas Day is a bigger event than it had been in quite recent decades, but for many Scots Hogmanay is still the most important cause for celebration in the winter season.

EDINBURGH CASTLE

"Good afternoon. I am Ed, Ed Inburghcastle, and I am one of the oldest residents of Edinburgh. I live on Castle Rock, and I've been here since the twelfth century. I was King David I's idea, because when he made Edinburgh an important centre of his government he needed somewhere to live and a fortress to protect his town, and that's why he built me.

I've had an interesting life, I'll tell you, a lot of people have fought over me and actually I had a lot of damage done to me during the Lang Siege of 1573. I had to have an awful lot of repair work done after that. Then in 1639 some people called the Covenanters took me over, then again in 1640, as part of what they call the Bishops' Wars. They disagreed with the King over whether the Church should have bishops, and they had some big fights over it which I got stuck in the middle of.

Then in 1650 they decided to side with Charles II, and some fellow from Cambridgeshire called Cromwell sent an army up to fight with them and eventually captured me. Charles II came back in 1660 though, and he sent an army up here too. I had soldiers living with me right up until 1923!

A few other people did try to capture me in 1715 and 1745 but they couldn't do it and I stayed in the hands of the government. I survived World War II because that Hitler chappie wanted me for his base of operations once he'd invaded Britain, so he told his planes not to bomb me.

I'm glad that didn't happen, but I'm also very glad I'm still around now, and I hope I am for a long long time."

SCOTTISH STARS OF
STAGE AND SCREEN
PART SIX

BRIAN COX
Brian Cox has had a long and illustrious career, gracing the stage and screen in many roles. Born in Dundee on June 1 1946, he trained at the London Academy of Music and Dramatic Art, making his stage debut in 1965. He has since become a well respected Shakespearean actor, as well as a regular in Hollywood movies, playing William Stryker in *X-Men 2*, Ward Abbott in the *Bourne* films, and appearing in both *Braveheart* and *Rob Roy* to mention just a few. He was also the first man ever to play Hannibal Lecter on screen, in 1986's *Manhunter*.

JOHN HANNAH
Born in East Kilbride on April 23 1962, John Hannah has starred in some of the best-loved movies to have seen the light of day in the last twenty years. From *Four Weddings and a Funeral* to *Sliding Doors*, from *The Mummy* to *Rebus*, John Hannah's work has thrilled us, excited us, and even made us have a little weep.

DOUGRAY SCOTT
Mission: Impossible II, Deep Impact, Enigma and *Ripley's Game* to name just a few, Dougray Scott has starred in some of the biggest budget, biggest grossing films of recent years. A native of Glenrothes, Scott was born on November 25 1965 and trained at the Royal Welsh College of Music and Drama in Cardiff. He has appeared in both films and television programmes, and has honed his craft to make himself one of the most recognisable Scottish actors at work today.

Brian Cox

John Hannah

Dougray Scott

MUNRO BAGGING

If you're up to a challenge, have you considered Munro Bagging?

Munros are Scottish mountains **over 3,000 feet high** and are named after **Sir Hugo Munro** (1856-1919), a member of the Scottish Mountaineering Club who made a list of Scotland's highest hills in 1891. There are 283 Munros, the highest being **Ben Nevis** at 4,409 feet.

So what's Munro Bagging? Well Munro Bagging is the act of climbing all of the Munros, something that only a serious experienced climber would consider. It's quite a challenge but more than 4,000 people have achieved it. In 2010 one man even managed to bag the whole lot in less than 40 days.

Completing the task must include scaling the 3,235 feet high inaccessible peak of **Sgurr Dearg** on the Isle of Skye which can only be reached by rock climbing.

In truth there are more than 283 peaks higher than 3,000 feet in Scotland. There are 510 to be exact, but in reality many mountains have more than one peak and these are called **Munro tops**. A Munro is specifically the individual mountain.

Once you've bagged all the Munros you can officially be called a **Munroist** and added to the Scottish Mountaineering club's list.

So what to do then?

Well you could try bagging all 227 subsidiary Munro tops.

Alternatively you might consider the more modest challenge of bagging some **Corbetts** and **Grahams**. Corbetts range in height from 2,500 feet to 3,000 feet and there are 221 of these while the 224 Grahams range from 2,000 to 2,500 feet high.

Peaks must have a prominence above the surrounding terrain of at least 500 feet to be included in the lists. So plenty to keep you occupied here, on with your hiking boots and off you go.

READ ALL ABOUT IT!
SCOTTISH NEWSPAPERS

THE COURIER

A broadsheet Dundee-based daily, first published in 1801. It has a circulation of over 65,000 covering Dundee, Fife, Perth and Angus.

DailyRecord

Based in Glasgow and published since 1895, this is Scotland's best selling uniquely Scottish newspaper with a circulation of over 294,000. It is outsold in Scotland by *The Scottish Sun* (circulation over 333,000) but that is a Scottish edition of a UK newspaper. *The Daily Record's* sister paper, *The Sunday Mail* has a circulation of 354,000.

Evening News

Local newspaper with a circulation of over 43,000 established in 1873.

Evening*Express*

Aberdeen newspaper with a circulation of over 50,000 established in 1879.

EVENING TELEGRAPH

Dundee newspaper with a circulation of over 23,000 established in 1877.

EveningTimes

A daily sister paper of *The Herald Daily* based in Glasgow and published since 1876. With a circulation of over 63,000 it is Scotland's best selling local paper.

The Herald

A daily morning, nationally circulated "quality" broadsheet newspaper based in Glasgow and published since 1783. It has a circulation of over 52,000. *The Sunday Herald* established in 1999 has a circulation of over 42,000.

The Press and Journal

Scotland's oldest daily newspaper is based in Aberdeen. First published on December 29 1746 and originally a weekly called the *Aberdeen Journal*. It became a daily in 1876 and is Scotland's best selling **regional** paper with a circulation of over 74,000.

THE SCOTSMAN

A "quality daily national compact" newspaper based in Edinburgh, published since 1817. It has a circulation of over 45,000. Its sister paper *Scotland on Sunday* (founded 1988) is a broadsheet with a circulation of over 50,000.

SUNDAY POST

Established in 1914 and based in Dundee is a national Sunday newspaper in Scotland with a circulation of over 224,000. It is famed for the *Oor Wullie* and *The Broons* comic strips.

THE KELPIES™ SCULPTURE AND THE HELIX

The Helix project is one of Scotland's most exciting new developments and will feature what is sure to be one of Britain's most iconic sculptures the Kelpies™ which will lie at the heart of a new park.

Kelpies are mythical water horses that inhabited lochs and waterways in Scotland and have provided the inspiration for Glasgow artist Andy Scott in the development of his huge new sculpture.

The Kelpies™ will feature two 30 metre high horses heads that will be positioned either side of a lock on a new canal. One of the heads will rock back and forth as the lock opens. Scott's sculptures are based on the Clydesdale breed of Scottish heavy horses once used in towing canal boats.

The steel sculptures will be at least 10 metres higher than the Angel of the North sculpture at Gateshead in England and will be visible from miles around.

The Helix site is a massive urban greenspace development making use of underused land near the junction of the River Carron and Forth-Clyde Canal between the towns of Falkirk and Grangemouth. The site covers 300 acres, that's the size of 270 football pitches and will include paths and cycle paths, new woodland, parkland, a lagoon and a number of public works of arts.

The project is driven by The Helix Trust which is a partnership of Falkirk Council, British Waterways Scotland and Central Scotland Forest Trust and is funded by a £25 million lottery fund grant. The Helix is working closely with local communities who will play their part in the creation of the park.

A new canal will be built linking the Forth-Clyde Canal and Grangemouth to the Firth of Forth and the Kelpies™ which are expected to be installed in place in December 2012 will undoubtedly be the star attraction of the site.

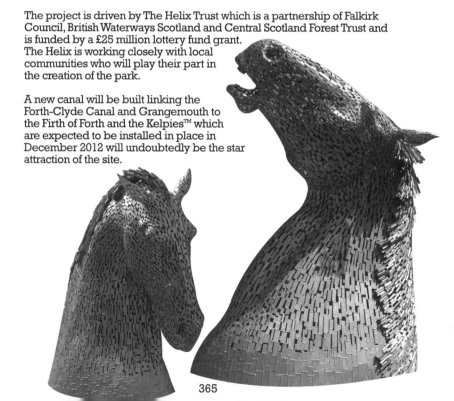

365

THE GLEN CINEMA DISASTER

One of the most harrowing disasters in Scottish history took place on December 31 1929. The Glen cinema had been filled with children for an afternoon matinee of action packed, exciting films, when one of the canisters of film, which had just been shown, started to smoke.

Although the projectionist tried to put the fire out, the film continued to burn, and filled the projection booth and then the main auditorium with thick black smoke. Many of the children started to panic, and tried to escape the increasingly smoke-filled room. The exits from the cinema were at the bottom of a set of steps, and hundreds of children piled down them in their attempts to get out.

Tragically, the doors of the Glen Cinema had been built to open inwards, and so the children could not force their way through. There was an enormous crush at the bottom of the stairs, and many children died, mostly from suffocation caused by the crush.

The eventual death toll for that fateful day was 71. The consequences, however, were much wider reaching. There was a public outcry, and the law ended up being changed so that cinemas were forced to increase the number of exits; to have doors which opened outwards and had push-bars, and to limit the seating capacity of all cinemas.

It is a sad moment in Scottish history, one of lives cut short before their time, and one we should all remember.

Timeline of Events in the History of Scotland

80AD	Romans invade Scotland under Julius Agricola.
84AD	Caledonians defeated by Romans at Battle of Mons Graupius.
140AD	Romans commence building the Antonine Wall between the Forth and the Clyde.
410AD	Romans depart from Britain.
Circa 500AD	Dal Riata Scots from Ireland colonise Argyle.
563AD	St Columba arrives at Iona.
638AD	Angles of Northumbria capture Edinburgh.
750AD	Scots defeat Angles at Battle of Athelstaneford.
795AD	Vikings raid Iona.
Circa 860AD	Viking Earldom established in Orkney.
843AD	Kenneth MacAlpin becomes king.
937AD	Scots in alliance with the Vikings defeated by the English at the Battle of Brunanburh.
1018	Scots defeat Northumbrians at Battle of Carham and push the Scottish border south to the Tweed.
1040	Macbeth becomes king.
1124	David I crowned king.
1263	Scots fight Norwegians at Battle of Largs.
1266	Norway cedes Western Isles to Scotland.
1290	Margaret Maid of Norway dies on Orkney before she is crowned Queen of Scotland.
1292	King Edward of England chooses the Scottish king (John Baliol).
1295	"Auld Alliance" with France established at Treaty of Paris.
1296	King Edward of England invades.
1296	William Wallace rebels.
1297	Wallace defeats English at Stirling Bridge.
1298	Wallace defeated at Battle of Falkirk.
1314	Robert Bruce victorious over Edward II of England at Bannockburn.
1320	Declaration of Arbroath. Plea for Scottish independence.
1437	James I assassinated.

1513	Scottish defeated by English at Battle of Flodden in which James IV is killed.
1542	Scottish defeated by English at Battle of Solway Moss.
1559	John Knox rouses a mob at Perth.
1566 & 1567	Murders of Rizzio and Darnley.
1587	Mary Queen of Scots executed.
1603	Union of Crowns. James IV of Scotland becomes James I of England
1639-40	Bishops Wars.
1649	Charles I executed.
1688	William of Orange usurps the crown in the Glorious Revolution.
1692	Glencoe Massacre.
1698- 1700	Darien scheme for Scottish colonisation of Panama virtually bankrupts Scotland.
1707	Act of Union.
1708	Jacobite Rising.
1715	Jacobite Rising in support of the Old Pretender.
1745	Jacobite Rising in support of Bonnie Prince Charlie.
1746	Massive defeat for the Jacobites at the Battle of Culloden.
1814	Sir Walter Scott writes Waverley.
1818	Sir Walter Scott discovers Scottish crown jewels.
1832	Sir Walter Scott dies.
1906	Labour founded by Scot, Keir Hardie.
1914-18	World War One.
1915	Major strikes in Glasgow.
1932	Scottish National Party founded.
1939-45	World War Two.
1947	First Edinburgh International Festival.
1950	Stone of Scone stolen from Westminster by Scottish students later discovered and returned in 1951.
1955	Scottish Television (STV) begins broadcasting.
1996	Stone of Scone returns to Scotland.
1997	Scots vote in favour of devolution.
1999	Scottish parliament opens.

Kings and Queens of Scotland

HOUSE OF ALPIN

KENNETH I MACALPIN (843AD-858AD): Reputedly a son of Alpin, King of the Dal Riata.

DONALD I (858-862): Brother of Kenneth.

CONSTANTINE I (862-877): Kenneth's son.

AED (877-878): Nicknamed "wing-footed".

EOCHAID (878-889): Grandson of Kenneth and son of the King of Strathclyde.

GIRIC (878-889): A shadowy figure

DONALD II (889-890): Son of Constantine. Buried on Iona.

CONSTANTINE II (900-942): Later became a monk at St. Andrews.

MALCOLM I (943-954): Killed in battle by men of Moray.

INDULF (954-962): Son of Constantine II later became a monk.

DUFF (962-967): Son of Malcolm I.

CULEN (967-971): Killed fighting King of Strathclyde.

KENNETH II (971-995): Murdered by Constantine's supporters.

CONSTANTINE III (995-997): Culen's son.

KENNETH III (997-1005): Son of Duff, killed by Malcolm II's supporters.

MALCOLM II (1005-1034): Defeated Northumbrians. Seized Strathclyde.

HOUSE OF DUNKELD

DUNCAN I (1034-1040): Grandson of Malcolm II. Son of Dunkeld Abbot. Killed by Macbeth.

MACBETH (1040-1057): Son of the Mormaer of Moray.

LULACH (1057-1058): Macbeth's stepson.

MALCOLM III (1058-1093): Son of Duncan I. Killed at Alnwick in Northumberland.

DUNCAN II (1094): Murdered by the Mormaer of Mearns.

DONALD III (1094-1097): "the Fair". Killed by the "craftiness" of the future David I.

EDGAR (1097-1107): "The Valiant" Half Brother of Duncan II.

ALEXANDER I (1107-1124): Son of Malcolm III. Elder brother of David I.

DAVID I (1124-1153): Previously Prince of the Cumbrians (1113-1124).

MALCOLM IV (1153-1165): "the Maiden" also Earl of Northumbria.

WILLIAM I (1165-1214): "the Lion" captured by English at Alnwick in 1174.

ALEXANDER II (1214-1249): Son of William. Supported English barons against King John.

ALEXANDER III (1249-1286): Subdued King of Norway at Battle of Largs, 1263.

MARGARET 'OF NORWAY' (1286-1290): Granddaughter of Alexander III died on Orkney.

1290-1292: Scotland governed by six guardians including John Comyn, Scottish High Steward.

HOUSES OF BALIOL AND BRUCE

JOHN BALIOL (1292-1296): Puppet of Edward of England. Imprisoned after rebelling.

1296-1306: Scotland ruled by a succession of guardians including John Comyn from 1302.

ROBERT I 'THE BRUCE' (1306-1329): Crowned after murdering Comyn.

DAVID II BRUCE (1329-1371): Battled with Edward Baliol.

EDWARD BALIOL (1329-1363): "Anti-King". Deposed by David's supporters 1332, 1334, 1341.

HOUSE OF STUART (OR STEWART)

ROBERT II (1371-1390): First Stuart king. Son of Scottish High Steward.

ROBERT III (1390-1406): Crippled by a horse.

JAMES I (1406-1437): Assassinated.

JAMES II (1437-1460): Killed at siege of Roxburgh.

JAMES III (1460-1488): Scholarly king murdered by man disguised as a priest.

JAMES IV (1488-1513): Killed at Flodden, 1513.

JAMES V (1513-1542): Defeated by English at Solway Moss in 1542.

MARY I (1542-1567): "Queen of Scots" executed 1567.

JAMES VI (1567-1625): Mary's son. Known as James I in England from 1603.

CHARLES I (1625-1649): Executed.

1629-1659: Rule of Lord Protector Oliver Cromwell (to 1658) and Richard Cromwell (1658-1659).

CHARLES II (1660-1685): Reigned following interregnum.

JAMES VII (1685-1689): Called James II in England. A Catholic deposed by William of Orange in 1688. Father of James Stuart, Old Pretender, and grandfather of Bonnie Prince Charlie.

MARY II (1689-1694): Ruled jointly with KING WILLIAM II of Orange (1689-1702). Called William III in England.

ANNE (1702-1714): Last Stuart monarch. First to rule unified England and Scotland from 1707.

POST UNIFICATION MONARCHS

GEORGE I (1714–1727)

GEORGE II (1727–1760)

GEORGE III (1760–1820)

GEORGE IV (1820–1830)

WILLIAM IV (1830–1837)

VICTORIA (1837–1901)

EDWARD VII (1901–1910)

GEORGE V (1910–1936)

EDWARD VIII (1936)

GEORGE VI (1936–1952)

ELIZABETH II (1952-)

Professor C. Cloggs